WHAT WAS LITERATURE?

Class Culture
and Mass Society

LESLIE FIEDLER

SIMON AND SCHUSTER
NEW YORK

8 0 1.9
F452 W
C. 2

10 9 8 7 6 5 4 3 2 1

Library of Congress Cataloging in Publication Data

Fiedler, Leslie A.
  What was literature?

  Includes index.
    1. Criticism—United States—
History.   2. American literature—History and
criticism.   3. Popular literature—United States—
History and criticism.   4. Myth in
literature.   5. Race relations in literature.
I. Title.
PS55.F5 1982   801'.95'0973   82-10394
ISBN 0-671-24983-5

For Sam and Hattie
"gaffer and gammer we're
all their gangsters"
and to SALLY

CONTENTS

CONTENTS ·

PART ONE

SUBVERTING THE STANDARDS

WHO WAS LESLIE A. FIEDLER?

After more than forty years in the classroom talking about books, I find myself asking whether the profession I practice does not help perpetuate an unfortunate distinction, a separation of song and story into High Literature and low, or as some prefer to say, into literature proper and sub- or para-literature. Perhaps "minority literature" and "majority literature" would be more appropriate terms in view of the fact that we are talking about the poetry and fiction prized by a very small audience as opposed to that enjoyed by everybody who reads anything at all, and experienced by an even larger audience through translations into the post-print media. Since the latter is almost invariably turned to on impulse—sometimes in spite of teachers and critics—while the former is not infrequently assigned in English classes, it might be most useful to think of the one as optional and the other as compulsory literature.

It is an odd enough notion, as I have come slowly to realize, to "teach," say, the plays of Shakespeare or the novels of Dickens and Twain, works written to move and titillate the free mass audience: to *require*, in effect, a pleasurable response from a captive student audience. I cannot help feeling that the whole enterprise is a little like giving a course (graded, to be sure, on the curve) in making love or getting drunk. But it is even stranger to insist that while it is proper, indeed incumbent on us, to find such pleasure in Shakespeare, Dickens or Twain, it is shameful or regressive to respond similarly to Zane Grey, Edgar Rice Burroughs or Margaret Mitchell; and strangest of all to try to work out critical "standards" for explaining why.

Yet that is precisely what in my generation literary critics and teachers of English were expected to do; and I have long been both. But how did it happen? Though teaching English is an obvious vocational choice for otherwise inept children gifted in Gutenberg skills, nobody, in America at least, becomes a critic deliberately, whatever his gifts or weaknesses. Certainly I did not—thinking of myself, even after I had first begun to be published, not as a "critic" or even as a "writer," but as a teacher who *also* wrote. The first things I published, however, were not any of the poems and stories which I had been turning out since I was seven years old, but critical pieces, review essays, commentaries on the current literary scene produced on request for editors of periodicals I had vainly bombarded with fiction and verse. I am not sure even now what prompted them to make such requests beyond a vague sense of guilt at having to say no over and over to one so desperately in need of some kind of yes. But in any case, I did not pass up the chance.

Moreover, I proved good enough at what I initially thought of as an uncongenial chore to be asked for more of the same—thus getting and keeping my name in print. What that name was, however, I was not quite certain. During my adventures in radical politics, I had called myself variously "John Simon" and "Dexter Fellows"; the first for the simple nursery-rhyme hero, the second after the PR man for the Barnum and Bailey Circus. But my manuscripts I signed first "A. Lazare," then "Leslie A. Fiedler" and finally just "Leslie Fiedler," though not until I had grown impatient with the pontifical fellow with a pretentious middle initial, who wrote articles with even more pretentious titles like "Archetype and Signature" and "In the Beginning Was the Word: *Logos* or *Mythos.*"

Those essays seem to me at this point unforgivably solemn and heavy-handed, despite the fact that from the start they were intended as a kind of put-on, a joke. As a put-on, however, they worked only too well; getting a couple of pages, for instance, in a history of literary criticism compiled by a pair of righteous "New Critics," who disregarded completely my less solemn but more truly serious work, best exemplified, perhaps, by "Come Back to the Raft Ag'in, Huck Honey." The full implications of that irreverent first-person meditation I did not at first fully understand, any more than I understood that I was a crypto-pop critic destined to subvert rather than sustain the "standards" which my age believed separated "true literature" from mere "junk."

Even more confused than I on this score was Philip Rahv, an editor who first accepted it for publication in the *Partisan Review* only because, he insisted years later, he was convinced that I did not really mean it. And in this opinion the writers of the first fan letters it occasioned concurred, referring to it (troubled elitists turning typically to French) as a *boutade*, a *canard*, a *jeu d'esprit*. But I was, of course, quite in earnest. I am therefore pleased that more than three decades later "Come Back to the Raft . . ." has entered the public domain, becoming in effect itself pop literature.

Quite recently, for instance, I was sent a clipping from a Seattle newspaper which recommended a new dramatic production of *Huckleberry Finn* as "good family entertainment," then added, "Apologies to Leslie Fiedler"; while in another from *The New York Times* a middle-aged commentator recounting his difficulties with his son wrote, "and then he went off on a raft with Nigger Jim or Leslie Fiedler." Both assume a response from many more people than have ever read my article, or perhaps even the novel to which it refers, but have heard at second or third hand that I had dared suggest that Huck and Jim were queer as three-dollar bills. What I actually contended, referring not just to *Huckleberry Finn* but other American classics like *The Leatherstocking Tales* and *Moby Dick*, was that, in a society characterized on the conscious level by fear and distrust of what I called then "homoerotic love" ("male bonding" has since become the fashionable euphemism) and by mutual violence between white and nonwhite Americans, there has appeared over and over in books written by white American authors the same myth of an idyllic anti-marriage: a lifelong love, passionate though chaste, and consummated in the wilderness, on a whaling ship or a raft, anywhere but "home," between a white refugee from "civilization" and a dark-skinned "savage," both of them male.

What is revealed in this archetypal story, I argued, is an

aspect of our psycho-social fantasy life quite different from the nightmare of miscegenation and sexual jealousy which has cued most of our past history, and a cause therefore for modest hope in the future. This hope has seemed justified (however slow the actual changes in the political arena) by the persistence of the myth since 1948, when my essay first appeared, in a score of movies such as *The Defiant Ones*, *The Fortune Cookie* and the belated film version of Ken Kesey's *One Flew Over the Cuckoo's Nest*, as well as in numerous TV shows, ranging from *I Spy* to *Tenspeed and Brown Shoe*, *Chips* and *Hill Street Blues*. And I am especially pleased that as we prepare for our entry into deep space and our first encounter with "aliens," we are taking with us that old American myth, embodied in the relationship of the very white Captain Kirk and his green-blooded Vulcan buddy, Mr. Spock, as portrayed in the cult TV series *Star Trek*—one early review of which was quite properly headed COME BACK TO THE SPACE SHIP AG'IN, SPOCK HONEY!

Encouraged by the early response to that little essay, and eager to make clear that I really meant what I was saying, I fleshed out my original insights in three substantial volumes, *Love and Death in the American Novel* (1960), *Waiting for the End* (1964) and *The Return of the Vanishing American* (1968), then began to gather what I considered illustrative texts in our literature in a multivolume anthology, only the first of which, called *O Brave New World*, ever appeared. In these volumes, I tried to set my exploration of our homegrown myths in the context of the expectation of apocalypse which has always possessed the American imagination: the endless waiting for the end of humanity, whether as a result of total atomic war, overpopulation, desecration of the environment, depletion of organic fuels or—in the pop prophecy of science fiction—an invasion from outer space or the rapid mutation of our species into something no longer quite Man. I had long read futurist fantasy, but only since realizing its connections with our chiliastic view of history have I explored it in depth: compiling an anthology of my favorite stories with a long theoretical introduction under the title *In Dreams Awake* (1976), reflecting on pioneers in the genre like Philip José Farmer and Olaf Stapledon (the latter at book length), and writing such fiction myself, culminating in the most unread of all my work, *The Messengers Will Come No More* (1974).

Imagining the future, however, is for me finally just another way of discovering or inventing a usable past, which, as a vestigial Marxist, I believe is fate; though, to be sure, as a vestigial Freudian, I also believe that character is destiny. In any case, I have never used my criticism as a way of denying history. For me, anti-Jungian Jungian that I am, the archetypes are not eternal but socially determined, changing as our relationship to the environment and each other changes. I have, therefore, traced the peculiarly American myths which concern me from the beginnings of our history to what threatened to be its end: from the moment when ex-Europeans first encountered the nonwhite denizens of the New World wilderness to those fatal years during which we dropped the Bomb on nonwhite Hiroshima and launched our last wilderness war in Vietnam. In the course of doing so, I have felt obliged to qualify the optimism of "Come Back to the Raft Ag'in, Huck Honey" by confronting what is negative and malign in our mythologies of race: especially the bad dream of genocide and the implicit misogyny (specifically the hatred of white women) which complement and contradict the good dream of interethnic male bonding.

These concerns, obsessions some have called them, inform my fiction as well, especially such studies of race and place as the novel *Back to China* (1965) and *The First Spade in the West*, the third novella in a volume called *The Last Jew in America* (1966). And they appear not infrequently in the essays I have chosen to collect, all the way from the first book I ever published, *An End to Innocence* (1955), to *Cross the Border, Close the Gap* (1977). But they make perhaps their strangest, most unexpected appearance in my long-postponed *The Stranger in Shakespeare* (1972), which I projected when I was young enough to know no better and finally wrote in grief and temporary exile.

I published in *Being Busted* (1970) a rather reticent account of the events which made me first an advocate of legalizing marijuana, which I do not smoke; then a felon, convicted of a crime which does not exist; and at last led me to seek refuge in England, a country which I do not love (departing, I wrote an essay called "There'll Never Be an England!"), but where in self-defense I began the required book on Shakespeare I swore I would never do. Divided into four sections—"The Woman as Stranger," "The Jew as Stranger," "The Black Man as Stranger," and "The New World Savage as Stranger"—that book examines the way in which Shakespeare sometimes ironically undercuts, sometimes slavishly accepts the stereotypical attitudes of his time toward the relationships of male and female, black and white, Jew and Gentile, Old World "culture" and New World "barbarism."

The Stranger in Shakespeare ends, therefore, though it is in fact the only book I have entirely written abroad, by bringing me back home again; which is to say, to Prospero's island and that prototypical American, Caliban. Not only does that "Monster" in relationship to the "Master of Arts" represent the fate of the Indian under the yoke of European imperialism, but he foreshadows the plight of white Americans as well: those refugees from Europe whose consciousness was altered by the confrontation with an alternative way of being human into something new under the sun—different from and profoundly troubling to the European mind. "Ca-Ca-Caliban, / Have a New Master, / Be a new man," D. H. Lawrence quotes from his chant, suggesting that it has remained the theme song of America ever since; and James Joyce in *Ulysses* refers snidely to the immigrant Irish as "Patsy Caliban, our American cousin"— both illustrating the persistence of that mythological figure at the heart of European anti-Americanism.

In part, no doubt, because of its concessions to pedantry, *The Stranger in Shakespeare* has been chiefly read by professional Shakespeareans, interested in *Othello, The Merchant of Venice* and *The Tempest* as texts for classroom analysis, rather than general readers, more interested in what they have to say about misogyny, anti-Semitism and xenophobia. And such scholars have responded in the main —as they have in fact to all of my work—by publicly vilifying it, while storing away its insights for future use, without acknowledgment, of course. It is a major mystery of my career (of which I have been reminded recently by a young East Indian just finishing a Ph.D. dissertation on my criticism) that I have come to be regarded as a "seminal" if "controversial" critic even though almost every one of my books has been more scorned than praised in the academic and literary reviews; and I have graduated, in the view of my critics, from the status of *enfant terrible* to that of "dirty old man" without passing through a decent maturity. I have long since ceased reading such responses, but my best friends insist on telling me all about them, and I have ended with a sense of needing to get through or around the official critics to my proper audience: those who return over and over (as I do) to popular authors like Twain and Stowe and Dickens, but never read anything labeled "criticism" which deals with those authors.

It has occurred to me that one way to do this is to bypass print by returning to the "archaic" public lecture, the Chautauqua—or even better, by taking advantage of what persists of that older popular form in the newer media, particularly the talk show on TV. There was a moment during the '60s when the format of the *Merv Griffin Show*, for instance, had come to include—along with an aging actress, a current pop music star, and a stand-up comedian—a visiting "nut," at that point usually Allen Ginsberg or Norman Mailer, or occasionally, as it turned out, me. After all, I had learned to communicate, beginning at age thirteen or fourteen, on a street-corner soapbox, and I have always enjoyed lecturing to large classes inside the university, where the sense of public speech lives on. Moreover, it seemed to me, after having published four or five books, that I was beginning (despite my invariable practice of never writing down a sentence until I have listened to it in my own head) to lose the sense of addressing a living, listening audience. Not that I have ever ceased venturing outside the classroom, addressing anyone who would invite me, book study groups in Whitefish, Montana, for instance, or monthly meetings of organizations with names like "The As You Like It Club," where everyone in attendance was likely to be knitting furiously as I talked about, say, *Finnegans Wake*.

But somehow television came closer to giving me the sense of a connection with a responsive nonacademic audience that I had experienced for the first time when someone in a heterogeneous group of listeners (it was in a park, as I recall, on the South Side of Chicago) screamed, "Now you're preachin', brother. Go right on preachin'." But television ran out for me after a while; perhaps when some clown clapped me on the back after I had sat hopefully for an hour in the Green Room, only to be canceled out of the show because that night's comedian had been especially hot, and said (I swear it), "Well, that's show biz." Or maybe it was the obnoxious business agent who bullied me into joining the American Federation of Television and Radio Artists after my second appearance on prime time. Still, being a member of AFTRA meant being paid "scale," so that before I quit I was able to buy a large-screen color TV for my kids, whom I made promise in return (I was then still the victim of vestigial elitism) that they would never watch me on it.

Eventually I stopped paying my union dues and, though I never ceased entirely talking to the cameras, returned to the college lecture circuit. At that point I had become incapable of committing anything to paper which I had not previously tried out *viva voce* several times, but I felt the need of doing so before auditors able and willing to talk back, as a studio audience typically does not. Students and teachers, even when they do not really listen, make responsive noises; and besides, they, like me, are accustomed to fifty- and sixty-minute presentations rather than the three-, four- or five-minute *shtik* television format demands. For such reasons among others, I feel at home with university audiences, even in remote places like Japan and India and Brazil, where more and more I have tended to wander (Europe having somehow used up its cultural usefulness to me) whenever I temporarily leave my own country.

That I had nonetheless not really escaped "show biz" I did not realize until a couple of lecture agents recruited me, upping my fees and making it possible for me to deliver my same old talks before church groups, social workers and dermatologists, as well as at "star"-studded symposia on The Urban Experience, Aging, Child Abuse and The Influence of D. H. Lawrence—held often enough in colleges, but subsidized by federal agencies, foundations, sometimes, indeed, the CIA. Actually, I had written by 1963 a novel called *The Second Stone* about a World Congress on Love held in Rome under American auspices, which is doubly disrupted when the wife of the theologian-organizer falls in love with an expatriate American loser, a writer who does not write, and the deliberations of the assembled critics, poets, shrinks and gurus are drowned out by the shouts of demonstrators, convinced by the Italian Communist Party that the whole thing is a CIA plot. It turns out

that American intelligence has indeed, without the knowledge of the organizers, picked up the tab for reasons which
no one is ever able to understand—not even I who wrote
the book.

What I was, however, beginning to understand then, and
what has become clearer to me since, is the equally ironic
fact that one does not cease being an "entertainer" by leaving lowbrow talk shows for highbrow symposia. The TV
cameras grind away even there, since, however elitist in
their aspirations, such assemblages are a part of that "popular culture" which, to be sure, sometimes these days they
rather condescendingly discuss. Even before the fashion
changed, I had been dealing with such matters, publishing
in the 1950s what I fondly believe to be the first apology for
the *Superman* comics. Yet like my colleagues then and
now, I too condescended to, when I did not actually deplore or scold the producers and distributors of "commodity" art. Admittedly, I made the occasional exception—for
ukiyoe, for instance, the popular woodblock engravings of
whores and actors mass-produced in Japan after the middle
of the eighteenth century, and for the best-selling novels of
Richardson and Dickens and Mark Twain. But the latter I
would not confess for a long time, even to myself, were as
much "mass culture'" as Grade B movies, TV sitcoms—and
my own platform performances.

Nonetheless, I found myself dealing more and more with
unequivocal, unredeemed printed "pop": pulp science fiction, hard-core pornography, the fairy tale, as well as fiction
by novelists never accepted into the canon of okay art, like
Conan Doyle, Bram Stoker, Rider Haggard, L. Frank Baum
and Margaret Mitchell. Nor have I ignored the post-Gutenberg "media," from the semi-iconic comics to Grade B movies (celebrating, for instance, Russ Meyers' atrociously
wonderful *Beyond the Valley of the Dolls*) and the daytime
serials on television. It was during a public argument with
Lionel Trilling on the "soaps" that I became fully aware,
first, of how obsessed I had become with such uncanonical
literature; second, of how I had passed from snide analysis
to passionate apology; and finally, of how equivocal the
position of elitist critics of the "media" had become, particularly if they were teachers in the mass American university. The occasion of my argument with Trilling was
especially revealing, since we spoke side by side with a

crew which included *inter alios* three Nobel Prize winners, a radical feminist, a black insurgent and Truman Capote at a symposium on The Future of Almost Everything, sponsored by ITT—in the interests, I gathered, of real estate development in Florida.

I have written and talked all my life under the sponsorship of anyone willing to let me publish what I believed at that moment (my not-so-secret motto being "Often wrong, but never in doubt") and to pay me for my effort. Such sponsors have ranged from a magazine later revealed as subsidized by the CIA to the magazine which revealed that fact to institutions funded with money left by America's robber barons and the Writers Union of Rumania.

LITERATURE AND LUCRE

It was not until 1980 that I found myself first talking publicly, then publishing an essay, about the connection between money and literature in my own life and those of the authors I most loved. I am not suggesting that I did not from quite early on associate money with the arts I practice and for which I am these days more often than not paid. Indeed, I can scarcely separate the one from the other, since from the moment I was possessed by the desire to become a writer, I have been aware that the process—in our society at least—is inextricably involved with making money. By "becoming a writer" I do not mean just getting out onto paper what I could no longer contain in my bursting heart and head, which is to fully consummated writing mere masturbation or *ejaculatio praecox*. What I yearned for was to be published, to be read, "to be great, to be known" (in the words of a poem by Stephen Spender which I have never forgotten), to open communication with an audience, to exist for others: utterly alien others, bound to me—unlike family or friends—only after the fact of having read me.

How hypothetical that audience, those alien others, might remain, and consequently how unreal, how impalpable the recognition, honor and love, I did not at first realize. To be sure, like other writers, even at the beginning of my career I received reviews in the press, plus after a while, as happens to almost anyone who lives long enough, testimonials and ceremonies of recognition. But for a long time, money (the one fiction of universal currency) is the only, and indeed always remains the most reliable, token that one has in fact touched, moved, shared one's most private fantasies with the faceless, nameless "you" to whom the writer's all-too-familiar "I" longs to be joined in mutual pleasure. "I stop somewhere waiting for you" is a sentence not just from Walt Whitman's but from every writer's love letter to the world. It is only when the first royalty check arrives in the mail (an answer as palpable as a poem) that the writer begins to suspect that the "you" he has invented in his lonely chamber, in order to begin writing at all, is real, and that therefore his "I" (not the "I" to which like everyone else he is born, but that fictive "I" which he, in order to be a writer, must create simultaneously with the "you") is somehow real too.

But this means, as all writers know, though most of us (including me) find it hard to confess, that literature, the literary work, remains incomplete until it has passed from the desk to the marketplace; which is to say, until it has been packaged, huckstered, hyped and sold. Moreover, writers themselves (as they are also aware) are reluctant virgins, crying to the world, "Love me! Love me!" until, as the revealing phrase of the trade has it, they have "sold their first piece." What scorn, therefore, the truly published, fully consummated writer has for those *demivierges* who publish themselves—turning in spinsterish despair to (again the customary phrase is significant) "vanity presses."

The fully published writer, however, feels not just scorn for the half-published and pity for the unpublished, but a kind of guilt, rather like the guilt of those who live by tourism or selling their own bodies. In his case as in theirs, that guilt breeds resentment against the intermediaries and accomplices who have made possible what he himself has desired. Just as the Western organizers of rodeos hate dudes, or whores and gigolos their pimps, johns and aging benefactors, the commercially successful writer hates agents, editors, publishers, reviewers and the M.C.'s of TV talk shows—hates finally the poor audience itself for buying what has been offered for sale. That guilt and resentment I must admit I share, though by admitting it I only compound my plight.

I spoke the original version of this meditation at a symposium on Literature and Lucre: a setting which both symbolized and aggravated that guilt and resentment, since I had been paid to attend and testify; and I was present therefore perhaps not *just* for the sake of the lucre involved, but for that reason among others. Indeed, I should like to think that the subject which I am treating is one so important to me and the community to which I belong that sooner or later I would have felt obliged to deal with it, even if somebody paid me *not* to do so. But this has not been my fate, so how can I be sure?

In any case, taking it up again in print for further payment makes me aware that I am communicating not as one talks (or writes) to an old friend, or even to someone he sits beside on a plane or at a bar, but because there is a contract between me and my audience, because we are joined briefly by a cash nexus. In some sense this, if it does not quite falsify, at least uncomfortably modifies the nature of our discourse, creating real possibilities of distrust and misunderstanding, since one of the participants is being paid to talk or write, while the other has paid to listen or read. The latter therefore feels free, if the former does not keep up his end of the bargain, neither entertaining nor enlightening his audience, let's say, to grumble and complain; but he *cannot,* in any case, get his money back—not from the one who talks. It is a strange business, an enterprise which promises profit without risk.

But this is precisely the situation in which I have written and spoken for all of my professional life: as a novelist, poet, teacher, scholar and critic-pedagogue. Like other critic-pedagogues, I am not only paid for public performance, but I get free books for which other people pay hard cash, and am invited to attend without paying admission plays and movies for which others must buy tickets at the box office. Moreover, I and my peers, or at least those among us who have access to commercial journals, are rewarded a second time by being paid for registering in print our opinions of those books, movies and plays: opinions which *must* be (I sometimes uncomfortably suspect) radically different from the responses of those we address, precisely because, having bought the book or paid their way into the theater, they have an investment to protect.

Even scholar-pedagogues who, out of snobbishness or a

desire to remain "pure," refuse to publish in paying journals like the *New York Times Book Review,* the *Times Literary Supplement* or, God forbid, *Esquire* and *Playboy* (in all of which, I must confess, I have appeared) cannot really escape the commercial trap. Unless willing to perish, they must publish *somewhere,* if only in journals of high prestige and low readability, like the *PMLA,* to which I have never contributed. But though such journals pay nothing, appearing in them guarantees tenure; and tenure guarantees to its holders that they will be paid more for repeating in the classroom what they have already published, or rehearsing what they hope to publish next. Eventually, moreover, such articles are gathered together, revised and expanded to make scholarly books, which have to be subsidized either by their authors or the schools in which they teach, since they are bought only by university libraries, from whose shelves (a recent study has discovered) some seven percent of them are *never* taken out.

Nonetheless, when these already oversubsidized pedagogues have persisted long enough in producing goods for which there is a reward but no market, they are likely to receive grants and fellowships, the most prestigious funded from carefully invested money, originally accumulated by the Rockefellers, the Guggenheims and the Fords—which is to say, the filthiest American lucre of all. Furthermore, when they have attained seniority and prestige (or sometimes long before, while they are still only needy and promising) they may be asked to compile, collaborate in or merely lend their names to freshman texts. Carefully tailored to maximum classroom demand as determined by market analysts, such texts are the academic equivalents of blockbusting best sellers by Jacqueline Susann or Harold Robbins. Think, for instance, of Brooks and Warren's inordinately successful *Understanding Poetry,* at once smugly elitist and happily profitable.

But is this not better, after all, than "selling out to Hollywood" like that backsliding Ivy League professor Erich Segal, or leaving the respectable sponsorship of Princeton University Press for the fleshpots of Simon and Schuster, who are not only the publishers of my own most recent book, but (I reassure myself) of Joseph Heller's *Catch-22,* a novel "taught" by some of my anti-commercial colleagues? Indeed many, perhaps the great majority, of the books taught by even the most snobbish and genteel among us were written by men shamelessly involved with the marketplace: Shakespeare, Richardson, Balzac, Dickens, Twain, Fitzgerald, Faulkner, Hemingway, Arthur Miller, Norman Mailer and Saul Bellow, to name only the first that come to mind. Moreover, in the last three or four decades many writers we "require" in class have compounded their complicity by becoming teachers themselves, i.e., secondary as well as primary hucksters.

But, I remind myself, only a generation or two ago "serious" creative writers (the heirs of modernist elitism and Marxist politics) considered employment in the university —that front for what our own students were still calling in the sixties "the military-industrial complex"—a kind of "selling-out" comparable to taking a job with an advertising agency or MGM or Henry Luce: a search for low-level security in place of high-risk ventures in the arena of High Culture. Not in Grub Street, be it understood, but in Bohemia: that anti-marketplace, in which, after the invention of the avant-garde and the raising of the slogan *Épatez la bourgeoisie*, "true artists" were imagined as starving, while pseudoartists flourished.

Even in the heyday of modernism, the legend of *la vie bohème* did not deceive everyone. Sigmund Freud, for instance, remained faithful enough to the reality principle to argue that *all* artists were driven by fantasies of becoming beloved, famous and rich. And George Bernard Shaw, always the enemy of pious hypocrisy, ironically made the same point in his famous argument with Samuel Goldwyn. "The trouble," he is reputed to have said, "is that you, Mr. Goldwyn, think about nothing but art, while all I think of is money." He is less likely to have been influenced by Freud, however, than by his true-blue English predecessor Dr. Samuel Johnson, who is on record as believing that money is the "purest" of all motives for writing.

In America, however—perhaps precisely because among us commerce is officially more honored than art—our eminent writers have not typically spoken with equal candor on the subject of literature and lucre. Certainly, the great novelists of the mid-nineteenth century, celebrated in F. O. Matthiessen's *The American Renaissance* and D. H. Lawrence's *Studies in Classic American Literature*, chose self-pity over irony or frankness in talking about their relationship to the marketplace. The classic statement is Melville's: "Dollars damn me . . . all my books are botches." And implicit in this melancholy cry from the heart is a belief, as strong and pertinacious as any myth by which we live, that the authentic writer is neither drawn to nor confirmed in his vocation by the hope of marketplace success, the dream of becoming rich and famous, but can only be seduced by lucre, led to betray or prostitute his talent.

Yet American culture came of age at the very moment when old aristocratic sponsors of the arts were being replaced by the mass audience and the masters of the new media, who profit by responding to its taste. The first of these media was print, and the first truly popular genre, the novel, the American form *par excellence,* in which the first American authors received worldwide fame for themselves and the culture which nurtured them. A commodity, mass-produced and mass-distributed, it offered its practitioners the possibility of growing rich as well as famous. But from the start, that possibility remained more promise than fact, at least for writers like Charles Brockden Brown, Edgar Allan Poe, Nathaniel Hawthorne and Herman Melville, who thought of themselves as producing "literature."

Before the first of these sophisticated novelists (all male) had begun to write, "best sellers" were already being turned out by other, more naïve, less pretentious authors (largely female), whose taste and fantasy coincided with those of the popular audience, itself largely female. Even over the long haul, the books loved by most Americans have not been *Moby Dick* or *The Scarlet Letter* or even *Huckleberry Finn,* which live now chiefly as assigned reading in classrooms, but a series of deeply moving though stylistically undistinguished fictions, which begin with Susanna Rowson's *Charlotte Temple,* reach a nineteenth-century high point with Harriet Beecher Stowe's *Uncle Tom's Cabin* and a twentieth-century climax with Margaret Mitchell's *Gone With the Wind.* The last, though never approved by "serious" critics and seldom required in "serious" courses in literature, is still sold in paperback reprints and, translated into the newer, more popular post-Gutenberg media of film and TV, is probably known to a larger worldwide audience than any other American fiction.

For a century and a half, those writers who aspired to

critical acclaim and an eternal place in libraries have therefore felt compelled to struggle not just for their livelihood
but for their very existence against the authors of "best
sellers," whom they secretly envy and publicly despise.
This cultural warfare may seem at first glance a struggle of
the poor against the rich, the failed against the successful.
But the situation is more complex than this, since, in terms
of culture rather than economics, art novelists and their
audience, "fit though few," constitute a privileged, educa-
tionally advantaged minority, while popular novelists and
their mass readership remain a despised *lumpen* majority,
whose cultural insecurity is further shaken when their kids
learn in school to question their taste.

The struggle of High Art and low has, moreover, been
perceived as a battle of the sexes. Referring to the writers
who had preempted the paying audience before he ever
entered the scene, Nathaniel Hawthorne called them a
"horde of damned female scribblers." And indeed, from
Mrs. Rowson to Jacqueline Susann, the authors of monumental, long-lasting popular successes have continued to
come from the sex which thinks of itself as otherwise exploited, oppressed, dominated in a patriarchal society. Consequently the novels and poems of which we are most
proud, and the critical/autobiographical works written on
them, reflect the myth of the "serious" writer as an alienated male, condemned to neglect and poverty by a culture
simultaneously commercialized and feminized.

There are prototypes of this myth in remotest antiquity:
the legend of Euripides, for instance, first avant-garde artist
in the West, having been hunted to death by a pack of angry
women (or, alternatively, dogs); while behind even that is
the primal image of Dionysus, torn to pieces by bacchantes,
eager to still his singing and exact revenge for their slighted
sex.

That image of the true artist destroyed by a money-grub-
bing society begins with the mythifying of Edgar Allan Poe.
Though originally the hybrid offspring of Southern American self-hatred and the French contempt for everything in
our culture except its presumed victims, the myth throve in
the New World. After Poe it is perhaps most notably exemplified by Herman Melville, whom we rejoice to imagine drudging away his last unhappy years in the Custom
House, unpublished, unhonored, forgotten; and Scott Fitz-

gerald, dying in shabby surroundings in a Hollywood which preferred Mammon to literature, and had no sense that this failed alcoholic scriptwriter was destined to outlive in glory the most celebrated producers, directors and actors of his time. That Poe and Melville and Fitzgerald failed not because they despised lucre and shunned the marketplace, but precisely because they were so desperately committed to the American dream of "making it," the legend does not permit us to remember.

We know that Fitzgerald began by producing best-selling novels and peddling hastily written short stories to family magazines at prices which mounted with his fame, and that he ended by squandering away a larger fortune than ordinary Americans can imagine earning in a lifetime of backbreaking work. Poe, too, though never as successful, even momentarily, spent his brief career as a hack writer and editor of commercial literary journals in pursuit of the common reader and the quick buck. Indeed, the fantasies which drove them both are betrayed in stories like Poe's "The Gold Bug" and Fitzgerald's "A Diamond as Big as the Ritz"—the dream of innocently acquiring guilty treasure, and the nightmare of losing everying.

Similarly, the mad, metaphysical quest in Melville's *Moby Dick* begins as a carefully planned commercial venture, with Ishmael bargaining for his fair share of the profits. And why *not*—in light of the fact that Melville's mad, metaphysical career began with the best seller *Typee*. Indeed, he never ceased trying to recapture his initial rapport with the popular audience. Even *Pierre,* whose underlying theme is the plight of the alienated artist in America, he assured his publisher (and perhaps believed himself) was "a rural bowl of milk," i.e., a domestic romance as palatable to the large female audience as to the somewhat smaller male one which had admired his adventure stories.

The pathos of such writers, whether they ended in insanity and withdrawal like Melville or in premature death like Poe and Fitzgerald, is not that they nobly refused to provide what the marketplace demanded, but that they tried to do so and failed. But this is not the story which the American mass audience likes to be told, since it needs to be assured that the writers it chooses only posthumously to honor (if not read) in some sense died for its sins: its lack of sensibility, mindless pursuit of profit, indifference to art —but not to artists, particularly failed ones, after they are dead. Realizing how in our world nothing succeeds like failure, certain lesser writers, from Rufus Griswold to Budd Schulberg, have produced parasitic best sellers about the tragic fates of Poe and Fitzgerald.

It may have been booze that destroyed Poe and Fitzgerald, but the great public prefers to believe it did the deed with its little hatchets, thus feeling at once powerful and guilty: a potent emotional mix for all true Americans. Certainly, we do not seem to derive as much satisfaction from contemplating the careers of eminent writers who have made it, dying, like Harriet Beecher Stowe, honored and rich—though cheerfully batty. It is, for instance, Mark Twain's final loneliness and melancholia we prefer to dwell on, or his many failures along the way. Yet, though Twain went bankrupt as often as any other capitalist entrepreneur of the Gilded Age, at the end he was able to support a splendiferous house and a set of expensive bad habits. He had finally grown so wealthy, indeed, that the only people he felt he could talk to as equals were Henry Rogers, vice president of Standard Oil, and Andrew Carnegie, whom he addressed as "St. Andrew" in letters signed "St. Mark."

Ironically, his fortune was based on the continuing success of *Huckleberry Finn,* which is to say, the classic version of the American anti-success story. We are asked to love Huck (and to prove our love by buying the book in which he appears) for running away, not just from school, church and family, but money as well: that guilty-innocent treasure which he and Tom had stumbled on at the end of *Tom Sawyer,* but which he, unlike Tom and the hero of Poe's "The Gold Bug," ultimately rejects. What Twain never wrote was a fictional account of a boy like himself, who, instead of "lighting out for the territory ahead of the rest," stayed home, grew up (as he would not let Tom grow up), permitted himself to be "civilized" by his wife and daughter, and at last got rich by writing about an eternal child who made all the opposite choices. Before the middle of the twentieth century, in fact, there is no respectable American book which portrays sympathetically an author who made good. Even Horatio Alger's disreputable juveniles, though they portray striking it rich as a truly Happy Ending, deal with boys who rose from rags to riches by becoming not writers but merchants or bankers.

Only in the last decades of this century did it become

possible, first in fact, then in fiction, for a novelist highly regarded by critics (Norman Mailer is an example) to become wealthy long before his death by having his books chosen as major book-club selections, then signing million-dollar paperback contracts, and finally appearing on TV talk shows, where (becoming, as it were, his own Griswold or Schulberg) he played the mythological role of the writer for the benefit of an audience which had not read, never would read his work. Even novelists who shun all publicity, like J. D. Salinger and Thomas Pynchon, accumulate royalties comparable to those earned by such critically despised darlings of the populace as Harold Robbins and Jacqueline Susann. Only Saul Bellow, however, Nobel Prize winner and laureate of the New Conservatism, has thus far dared translate this new-style Happy Ending from life to literature. And this is perhaps why his *Humboldt's Gift* has been universally (willfully, I suspect) misunderstood by its critics.

It seems, at first, a rather conventional elegy for a *poète maudit:* the last, somewhat improbable heir to the tradition of Poe, Melville and Fitzgerald, reborn this time as a failed New York Jewish intellectual—a super-articulate, self-defeating *Luftmensch* who has died abandoned and penniless before the action of the novel begins. It has been suggested by many, including Bellow himself, that the model for Humboldt was the poet Delmore Schwartz, who had indeed come to such a shabby end. But while there is a great deal of Schwartz in Humboldt, he is finally the portrait not of any single individual but of a whole generation of Jewish-American losers: including, surely, Bellow's one-time guru and lifelong friend, Isaac Rosenfeld, also dead before reaching forty, his handful of stories and essays remembered by a shrinking coterie of aging admirers; and perhaps Lenny Bruce as well, that hipster and stand-up comedian who O.D.'d in 1966. Reading of Humboldt's fate, I cannot, in any case, help thinking of *all* those mad, bright, young Jewish-Americans, still caught up in the obsolescent myth of the Artist as Victim, and dead before they had lived long enough to realize, like Bellow, that in prosperous America it was no longer necessary to end as a Beautiful Loser.

In any case, Bellow's book is called not *Humboldt* but *Humboldt's Gift*, and the recipient of that gift, that not-so-beautiful Winner, Charlie Citrine, is its real hero. For a little while, Citrine (who at times seems scarcely distinguishable from his author) finds in Humboldt's death and his own survival an occasion for guilt—the guilt we have long been trained to think of as the inevitable accompaniment of making it. But in the end, he succeeds in convincing himself that Humboldt has died for him, that all such losers die for all winners; leaving us as a heritage not empty regrets but a salable story: his story once, our story now, the book we are reading. Properly exploited, that story can (in the fiction we read) be sold to the movies, or (in the larger world outside) clinch for its author the Nobel Prize; make us survivors, in short, rich enough to meet the obligations of the prosperous living: alimony, mortgage payments, credit card debits, fifty percent income taxes. And if we weep a little, remembering those others whom we loved and betrayed and by whose death we profited, we can (as the old saying has it) cry all the way to the bank.

TOWARD POP CRITICISM

Though I have not struck it quite as rich as Citrine, I have been doing all right. And though it took me so long to speak out publicly about such matters, I have long ceased to be troubled by the fact that I have been paid for what I continue to believe I do out of love. What has troubled me is the question of *why* my manifold sponsors have been willing to pay up, what they are paying me *for*. It has taken me decades (I am a slow learner, though a fast teacher) to realize that like other entertainers I have been paid to allay boredom—in my case, by making our country and our culture seem more interesting and amusing than most academic accounts would lead us to believe. What has bugged me, however, ever since I have come to realize this is the fact that most of the readers of, say, *Love and Death in the American Novel* are likely to encounter it on assignment and in a classroom: a context which falsifies it as much as does reading *Huckleberry Finn* under similar circumstances.

Nor have I, alas, succeeded in breaking out of that trap with my fiction; yet surprisingly enough, I began to do so with my last long nonfiction work, *Freaks: Myths and Images of the Secret Self* (1978), a book so equivocally "interdisciplinary" that library catalogers did not know whether to classify it under "psychology," "sociology" or "literary criticism." Actually, my model for it (a secret guessed by one acute reviewer) was Richard Burton's *Anatomy of Mel-*

ancholy, which would make it, I guess, what used to be called belles lettres; though it has, in fact, intrigued chiefly "soft" and semi-"soft" scientists, longing to rejoin the humanities. The last couple of times I have talked about it in public, at any rate, I did so at a meeting of the Association of Medical Schools and before a group of professional sociologists—with whom most of my own colleagues believe we have no language in common. Nonetheless, though it delighted me to have escaped the church of True Believers, English majors, fellow teachers and literary critics, I am a little distressed by the fact that my auditors were academics still.

Before that, however—under the auspices of my superhype, hard-sell publishers—I had spoken about that same book on the *Dick Cavett Show,* the *Today Show,* the *Tomorrow Show,* the *Phil Donahue Show* (where I appeared side by side with actual freaks), plus God knows how many others on radio and TV. There, sweating in my makeup under hot lights, I had to discuss what I had written with interviewers, few of whom had read *Freaks* and some of whom did not even know my name, though they (or their more literate assistants) were aware that it had been reviewed not only in respectable literary journals like the *New York Review* but in the more popular press, including the New York *Daily News, Penthouse, Hustler* and *High Times*—the last, by the way, convincing my fifteen-year-old son for the first time that I was to be taken seriously as a writer. Moreover, it turned out that a fledging writer-director-producer of a G-rated fantasy-romance was watching a local L.A. interview show in which I confessed that I had always thought of myself as an actor and was getting tired of the single role of professor I had been playing for forty years; as a result of which I ended up joining this time not AFTRA but the Screen Actors Guild, and before my three weeks as a screen actor were over had been mentioned in the gossip column of the *Hollywood Reporter.*

The movie in which I play, appropriately enough side by side with a dwarf, has not yet been released, and may remain bogged down in "post-production difficulties" forever. But what media attention my brief film career attracted has confirmed the worst fears of certain high-minded colleagues, who had already begun to think of me as an apostate from High Art: a self-styled critic who had forgotten how to be "rigorous" (they are not amused when I remind them from time to time that the extreme form of rigor is *rigor mortis*), i.e., how to deal, in language accessible only to initiates, exclusively with "great books"—or even better, pure literary theory. Lacking such rigor, they assured each other, I was doomed to end up as a Pop Critic!

But this is, indeed, where I was headed from the start. Consequently, once I had realized that "required" books like *Moby Dick* and *Huckleberry Finn* no longer moved the mass audience as myth moves them, I determined to deal with popular, "optional" art forms which do, especially freak shows. In such shows the archetypes which inform printed texts are, as it were, made flesh, palpable and visible. I decided, therefore, to keep them so in my own *Freaks* by making the book an illustrated one; or, rather, one with an alternative iconic text: a visual gloss for the benefit of those who read pictures better than type.

As a result, it is possible to look at nothing but the illustrations in that book and have a real sense of what it is about. It might be said *Freaks* seemed destined from the start to be reborn without any printed text at all—and it was in fact optioned by a documentary film producer. But once the shooting had begun, the shape of the proposed movie kept changing so rapidly that long before even a rough cut was finished, the producers had decided to release it under a different title and without any mention of my name. But this is, of course, only "show biz" once more, and should scarcely have surprised me, who, even while I was still calling myself "Leslie A. Fiedler," had already begun pondering the nature of the popular arts.

As early as *Love and Death in the American Novel*, that is to say, I had felt obliged to come to terms with certain best-selling novels and their movie spin-offs, ordinarily passed over in silence by more consistent champions of High Culture, since I could not deny that, like millions of others, I had wept over the sorrows and thrilled at the triumphs of their protagonists. But I had felt obliged still to refer to them as "ready-made masturbatory fantasies" and to point out how their executive ineptitude and imprecision of language made them different in kind from the "classics" of our literature. Indeed, long after I had pointed out in "Archetype and Signature" that mythopoeic power was independent of formal excellence, I was able to write still in an insufferably arrogant essay called "No! In Thunder!" that in the realm of fiction, "to be inept, whether unwittingly or on purpose, is the single unforgivable sin. To be inept is to lie; and for this, time and the critics grant no pardon."

It was not a matter of my never having responded passionately to Mark Twain or Charles Dickens, James Fenimore Cooper or Harriet Beecher Stowe, even when in formalist terms they wrote least well; I had tried to identify what in them moved me at their egregious worst. "Myth" and "archetype" I called it, but I had still no language for analyzing and evaluating it without falsifying it, since literary criticism, my teachers taught me (and, alas, most of my students still believe), represents an attempt to speak logically, rationally, objectively about the *mythoi* which lie at the heart of all works which please many and please long. And this makes criticism *logos*, not *mythos*, does it not, philosophy rather than poetry; or to put it in more modern terms: science rather than art?

To be sure, it is science of a particular kind, like depth psychology or anthropology or linguistics rather than physics or geology or chemistry: a strategy for rationalizing the irrational by converting myth to mythologem. Like those "soft" sciences, then, literary criticism flourishes best in societies theoretically committed to transforming all magic into explained illusion, all nighttime mystery into daylight explication: alchemy to chemistry, astrology to astronomy, demons into mechanisms of the psyche or, better still, electrical impulses in the brain. "Where Id was Ego shall be," said one of the best-intended defender-betrayers of myth, Sigmund Freud; and similar demythifying impulses motivate the latter-day formalist critics who would convince us that literature is words on the page or a "text" explicable in terms of structure or semiotics.

How Did It All Start?

For literature, however, that process had begun centuries before Roland Barthes or Jacques Derrida, when Aristotle attempted—with what we must assume to have been the best of intentions—to defend the popular drama of his time against the attacks of his master, Plato, who distrusted both poets and their mass audience. Poets, he believed, were essentially unreliable fellows, moved by irrational impulses to produce works which they could not rationally explain and whose morality they could not rationally justify. To be sure, they were loved by the populace, i.e., the elements in society too gross for dialectics and metaphysics, who found especially in the theater a dangerous kind of titillation, using it as an excuse for indulging rather than repressing (as he thought they should) the disruptive emotions of pity and terror.

Childishly, inexplicably, it seemed to Plato, grown men and women found pleasure in scaring themselves silly over imaginary atrocities counterfeited by actors. "Shadows of shadows" he called such representations, and "watering the emotions" the effect they produced on their spectators. More specifically, he argued that by teaching (he assumed that the basic function of art was education) adult males in the audience to give way to pity and terror, it made them less efficient citizen-soldiers, more likely than they might otherwise have been to fear for themselves and feel sympathetic toward the enemy when called on to defend their city in war. For this reason, among others, he urged that in a perfectly just and rational society, all poets should be banned; even in a second-best community, like the one he lived in rather than merely dreamed, they should, he believed, be controlled and censored by, of course, philosophers, or at least by guardians of the state educated by philosophers, rather than miseducated by poets.

Artistotle, on the other hand, was temperamentally inclined to explain rather than condemn. Moreover, he was convinced that whatever institutions men invent must have social utility. He sought, therefore, to identify the psychosocial uses of tragedy, its positive value to the state, and contended that though the most admired plays of the age did indeed depend for their effect on stirring in the audience emotions subversive of law, order and proper civic behavior, they did not merely evoke them. By some mysterious process, found only in proper "poetry," they finally purged or purified, mitigated or neutralized them, thus leaving the beholders not less but more able to control themselves when confronted by the threat of mutilation and death, or the necessity of inflicting such atrocities on others.

To suggest the nature of this process, he employed the medical term *katharsis*, about whose exact meaning commentators have been arguing ever since. Yet finally it does not matter precisely how catharsis is defined, since what is most important in Aristotle's argument is the suggestion that literature *qua* literature is *not* incitement to action (like rhetoric, for instance), and therefore cannot be judged by the "goodness" or "badness" of what happens in its plot, much less whether its characters provide "good" or "bad" models for the audience. The suggestion that poetry is in this respect uniquely different from all other forms of speech marks the beginning of literary criticism, at least as I understand and practice it. I myself have never forgotten (distrusting all so-called critics who do) that the art we practice was born in conflict, out of an attempt to dissuade those who would control or ban poetry as socially and morally dangerous.

Nor has that conflict and its challenge to apologists for poetry ever ceased. Always, particularly in its more popular manifestations, literature has come under attack by social reformers, do-gooders, and commissars, as well as presbyters and priests, all of whom consider themselves experts on morality and therefore on the moral effect of literary art, about which they know nothing. Even this would be of little moment, however, except that their self-righteous clamor tends to drown out the voices of writers as well as the critics who argue that without first knowing what literature is, what it does, how it works and why we need it, it is impossible ever to understand why so many of the poems, plays and stories which have pleased many and pleased long have offended the prudential, no matter what their ethical codes.

What Plato already referred to as "the ancient quarrel between poetry and philosophy" was renewed, for instance, with especial virulence when Christianity replaced the wisdom of the ancient world with a new morality based on a new mythology, and recurred even more alarmingly when the Protestant revolt divided Christendom into a thousand competing sects. Though secular literature survived, many of its masterpieces were irrevocably lost in the burning of the great library at Alexandria and the campaign against "bloodshed and bawdry" in the popular arts which culminated in the closing of the theaters in seventeenth-century England. Nor has the "death of God" and the secularization of Western culture ended the onslaught against literature. Driven back but not destroyed, the fundamentalist sectarians manage still to mount attacks against freedom for the arts, and disconcertingly, they have been joined by "freethinkers" and "progressives" whenever the latter have felt *their* deepest pieties challenged by what they consider reactionary or decadent fictions.

In my own lifetime and my own country, I have twice confronted wholesale onslaughts against literature and the popular arts, once during the 1950s and again in the late '70s and '80s. The first of these, very much like Plato's campaign against the poets, began as a protest against violence —but this time not in stage tragedy (Sophocles, Euripides and Aeschylus, who were to the Greek philosopher the chief offenders, had become classroom "classics" immune to reproach) but in the comic books, which laid no claim to being "art" and were theoretically intended for children. The fact that during World War II they had been the favorite reading matter of men old enough to have been drafted was scarcely mentioned by anyone, though it may indeed have exacerbated the situation.

What the censors of that age of repression preferred to talk about was the corruption of the very young, the presumably helpless victims of unprincipled entrepreneurs. Interestingly enough, however, what such latter-day book burners contended was not, as Plato had argued, that exposure to excessive violence in the arts made people less effective soldiers, but that by providing models for justified aggression, it threatened to turn innocent boys and girls into rowdies and criminals, or at the very least, potential dupes of fascist warmongers. After all, the Bomb had been dropped on Hiroshima only a little while before, and the nightmare of World War III had begun to haunt the bad conscience of America.

There has been no hard proof, as behavioral scientists define it, that either of these contentions is true, or for that matter, false. Subsequent studies by sociologists and psychologists have been inconclusive, and they seem to me in any case irrelevant, since the belief that violence in the arts makes their audience either more or less aggressive is based on faith beyond evidence. Or to put it another way, the advocates of both positions are motivated by unconscious drives—a fear of fantasy, a distrust of myth, an unacknowledged hostility to all emotion and art itself; though they are not, of course, on a conscious level hypocrites. Moreover, they are not on any level utterly wrong when they charge the popular theater or comic books with subverting the values to which they subscribe, *whatever those values may be.* Such works of art are subversive of all unequivocal allegiances, all orthodoxies—being in essence equivocal, ambivalent.

Like our personal dreams, myths or communal dreams tend to express the repressed: especially the dark side of our ambivalence toward what any status quo demands we believe, and more often than not, think we do. In patriarchal ages, therefore, literature pays tribute to the matriarchal, even as in Christian times it gives the Devil his due. In societies that honor heterosexual bonding and the nuclear family, it allows us to acknowledge men's hatred of women and women's contempt for men, along with the desire of parents to possess utterly or to destroy their children, and the corresponding Oedipal dream of those children. Whatever is officially defined at a given moment as abhorrent to civility and humanity is what such art celebrates, and what is most generally banned is therefore its most nearly universal subject: the impulse to cannibalism, for instance, and incest, the lust to rape and be raped.

This fact disturbs moralists everywhere, who, eager to deny their own unconscious impulses to lawlessness, think of the popular arts as causing what they only reflect. But literature which transgresses our taboos teaches us that the impulse to do so preexists in the deep psyches of us all. Once translated into song and story, however, the released repressed triggers another primeval response: the fear of the unconscious and its tyranny over our bodies as well as our dreams; and by the same token, of the art which simultaneously releases and neutralizes its darker aspects.

So long as mythmaking is practiced, so also will mythocide, which is to say, censorship will flourish; and so too will the theory by which censorship is typically rationalized: the contention that art is incitement rather than therapy, reinforcing whatever a given era considers socially undesirable or morally reprehensible. Knowing this, I was not surprised that the arguments of fifties liberals against violence in the popular arts were, despite their anti-totalitarianism, not so very different from those of the father of all totalitarianism. Therefore, since it seemed to me still that only Aristotle had made a viable libertarian rebuttal of Plato's position, I wrote in 1955, with Aristotle as a model, an apology for the superhero comics as myth and catharsis.

I must confess that I was more than a little troubled by the fact that no other reputable critic had risen to their defense, since I myself shared with all reigning schools of criticism—the Marxist sociological critics, the proto-fascist "New Critics," the super-academic "neo-Aristotelians" of the University of Chicago—the elitist definition of what literature was that led them, more consistent in this respect than I, to consider such "trash" unworthy of analysis, much less praise. Nonetheless, I reassured myself, the most vociferous opponents of "lowbrow" *Superman* also condemned certain disturbing "highbrow" art which I admired, and I persuaded myself that in attempting to rebut the "middlebrow" (it was a sign of my vestigial elitism that I still used such terms without irony) enemies of both I was not really betraying the cause of High Art. But I found few allies.

The single other essayist for whom I had any respect at all who had dealt with comic books was Gershom Legman.

Yet he too, though a longtime professional outsider and disturber of the peace, came out *against* them—apparently undisturbed by the fact that those who disagreed with him on almost every other subject, particularly his defense of sexual pornography, agreed with him on this. To be sure, his *Love and Death* (a book whose title I appropriated for my own quite different ends in *Love and Death in the American Novel,* thus making a lifelong enemy) was violent and abrasive and full of "dirty" words. But like the more genteel conservative or liberal censors of the popular arts, this loud-mouthed radical who began by fulminating against such "trash" as *Superman, Captain Marvel* and *Wonder Woman* (whose well-filled jockstraps and brassieres he apparently found as offensive as their flagrant brutality) and *Gone With the Wind* ended by condemning the critically esteemed short stories of Ernest Hemingway. All these works, whatever their canonical status, he argued, vilified women and repressed healthy sexuality in favor of sado-masochistic fantasies.

Similar charges were made by various eminent psychiatrists, most notably perhaps by a certain Frederic Wertham. Ironically, however, his best-selling diatribe against horror comics, *The Seduction of the Innocent,* so vividly demonstrated (with copious illustrations) the phallic symbolism and brutality of the genre that it became one more source of pornographic titillation for the not-so-innocent kids, who would sneak it off the bookshelves of their pious parents and pass it from hand to hand, along with the comic books it condemned.

Meanwhile those same genteel parents, joined by dutiful teachers, irate congressmen, newspaper columnists and radio commentators with fewer degrees than Dr. Wertham but even louder voices, were crying out (in a typical phrase used at a protest session on "Town Meeting of the Air") that "comic books were the marijuana of the children." It is a phrase which reminds us that, though not all opponents of the favorite junk reading matter of the young were totally repressive, this was a time in which almost everything that especially moved tots and teenagers was under attack by someone. In addition to pot, favorite targets were left-wing politics, rock music, "Beat" literature (Allen Ginsberg's *Howl* was suppressed and Jack Kerouac's *On the Road* scorned), and especially J. D. Salinger's *Catcher in the*

Rye. For teaching such works, high school teachers found themselves without jobs—thus proving once more that freedom in the Republic of Letters is as elsewhere indivisible.

But on this subject, too, critics were once again silent; except, of course, for me, dreaming of becoming an Aristotle sufficient unto my own day by identifying the *mythos* that informed the superhero comic books. What he had done for the incestuous parricide Oedipus, I fondly assured myself, I could do for the *schlemiel* savior in long underwear, who could fly but not (in either of his avatars) make it with a girl, and though able to deliver Gotham from rampant evil could never even get promoted at his job. And why, I went on to ask, might not the fantasy embodied in that myth—the dream of innocent violence in humble disguise—serve as psycho-social therapy in a troubled age when the very notion of heroism in peace or in war, indeed, of any effective individual action, seemed about to disappear?

The orgy of self-righteous repression moved inexorably toward ultimate absurdity. The first target of the censors (even before they had set their sights on *Superman* and *Wonder Woman*) had been the flagrantly sado-masochistic E.C. Comics, against which a quite plausible case could be made, and actually was to a congressional investigating committee—which in those oddly naïve times was considered the proper body for passing judgment not only on Americanism, the morality of gambling and prostitution, but on the limits of literature. Needless to say, the assembled members of Congress reacted in horror when they were shown the cover of one issue of that most outrageous of all comic books portraying a bunch of boys playing a baseball game in which the bloody head of one of their decapitated comrades served as the ball and the bases were marked with his torn-out guts.

The Communist Party and even the Mafia survived similar public inquisitions, but the E.C. Comics did not. Yet, though they were eventually driven out of existence, much of their staff (the most skillful craftsmen as well as the most subversive fantasists of their generation) went off to found the long-lived and much loved magazine *MAD*—suffered to exist, I suppose, not merely because its extravagances are somewhat toned down, but because it appeals to the eternal adolescent rather than the immortal child in us all.

Having tasted blood, the censors went after such surviving comic books as *Batman, Archie* and *Donald Duck.* They did not destroy the genre, to be sure, or even quite eliminate the sadism so essential to its appeal, but forced the publishers to accept the infamous Comic Books Code, pledging to avoid excessive violence (whatever the adjective might mean), along with cuss words, sex, bad grammar and the mention of any controversial subjects, most notably dope. Yet this too did an inadvertent service to future popular culture, since in the sixties the so-called head comics would find in everything which had been forbidden by the code their proper subject matter, all the more titillating to the dropouts and the dissidents of the cultural revolution for having been banned.

All that, however, was still a decade away, and things were destined to get worse before they got any better, especially after timid voices began to be raised suggesting that it was pointless to snatch violent comic books from the hands of kids if at the same time they were being read—or taken to Walt Disney animated cartoons at the movies to see—even more horrific fairy tales by Andersen and the Brothers Grimm. Surely, among those reminding parents of how terrifying were the fantasies of "The Juniper Tree," "Little Red Riding Hood" or "The Little Mermaid," a few must have sought not more but less censorship. Alas, the results were exactly the opposite.

Once alerted, some "enlightened" parents, determined that their kids at least would never drop another bomb or lynch another black man, but unwilling totally to starve their imaginations, demanded and were provided by subservient publishers with bowdlerized versions of "Little Red Riding Hood," in which both that errant girl and her grandmother are never eaten by the wolf at all but escape into a conveniently located closet—so they do not have to be delivered to the Happy Ending by the woodcutter's *ad hoc* Caesarian section. Others forbade such reading completely, depriving two generations of the young of the pleasures of old wives' tales, or at least postponing that mode of satisfying their deepest and darkest ambivalences until late adolescence or early maturity, when, once more thanks to the cultural revolution, they could rediscover (stoned out of their minds more often than not) fairy tales in the original, in Disney replays, or as retold by J. R. R. Tolkien and his imitators.

Earlier folk literature, in prose and verse, demoted to second-class citizenship by the invention of printing and scorned by moralists and exponents of High Literature alike, had managed to survive in the nursery. But even this ghetto asylum was assailed by the censors of the fifties, alerted by pop Freudianism to the critical importance of childhood experiences. At last, only one hitherto unsuspected source of insecurity and aggression was left, the nursery rhymes. But they too were eventually banned or bowdlerized: "Rock-a-bye Baby" forbidden, ostensibly to prevent a lifelong fear of falling, and "Three Blind Mice" completely rewritten, in order to avoid unseemingly references to the handicapped or descriptions of animal mutilations. The "blind mice" became "kind mice," and the farmer's wife instead of cutting off their tails with a carving knife cut them slices of bread.

Even in the fifties there had been writing about "popular culture," or in the fashionable phrase of the time, "mass-cult." It was chiefly produced, however, not by proper literary critics but by journalists, sociologists or ex-political activists, deprived of their causes by history (Dwight Macdonald is a typical figure), and they tended to condescend to or scold the lowbrow entertainers for "flattering the ignorance of the young" or yielding to the exigencies of the marketplace.

In the sixties the situation improved, though that decade was by no means the era of an unchallenged "permissiveness" which we now think we remember, some of us with nostalgia, some with regret or indignation. The censors were by no means utterly silenced, and in fact scored some local successes, particularly against William Burroughs' *Naked Lunch* and, in the area of the popular arts, the stand-up comedy of Lenny Bruce, which managed to offend all the pieties of the age. But it was by and large a time of opening up, of expanding First Amendment freedoms, from which in the late seventies a retreat began that in the eighties threatens to turn into a rout. Not that our own repressive decade has repeated the absurdities of the fifties, preferring to invent new ones.

To a certain degree we have, in fact, in the last decades of this century *institutionalized* certain breakthroughs of the sixties, requiring rather than banning (in accord with the good old totalitarian principle that whatever is not forbidden should be required) much that was censored in the fifties. Not only do we, a little condescendingly perhaps, recommend *Catcher in the Rye* to the young, but we now teach courses in fantasy, sometimes compelling those enrolled to see horror movies in order to get class credit. Similarly, we collect old E.C. Comics for fun and profit, drag our kids to the moving-picture version of *Superman,* whether they want to go or not, and read them fairy tales out of our once proscribed copies of Grimm and Andersen. After all, Bruno Bettelheim has recently given them the psychiatric seal of approval in his *Uses of Enchantment,* assuring us that such childhood classics (he is much less approving of latter-day schlock out of, say, the Disney Studios) are *good* for them, and for us in our relationship with them.

Meanwhile, however, the Old Right has reappeared with renewed chutzpah, conducting, chiefly under the auspices of the self-styled "Moral Majority," a campaign to the death against godlessness and "secular humanism" as it manifests itself not only in textbooks dealing with evolution and sexual mores, but in literature as well, particularly in novels assigned for class reading or displayed in school libraries. Just as Salinger was the favorite target of the enemies of art in the fifties, Kurt Vonnegut is right now. His *Slaughterhouse-Five* is probably the most banned book of the last several years and, along with his collected short stories, *Welcome to the Monkey House,* has, in scenes reminiscent of the Nazi terror campaign against *Kulturbolschewismus,* been publicly burned in the schoolyards of small Midwestern towns. It is, moreover, included in the list of nine books banned from all high school and junior high school libraries by the school board of the Island Trees School District of suburban New York (the decision has been appealed at various judicial levels and is still in the courts).

Clearly, what disturbs the guardians of morality in Island Trees about Vonnegut's youth best seller is not only the fact that the young passionately respond to it, though this seems always to disturb a certain kind of parent, but its antiwar stance, its critical attitude toward the United States and its implicit atheism, as well as its sexy episodes, erotic fantasies projected into the remote future and outer space. It is the latter which the book burners prefer to talk about for publication, labeling Vonnegut's book "garbage," their code word for what the law calls "pornography" or "obscenity." But apparently politics offends them too: anti-black politics, or at least fear of the blacks' anti-white politics, in the case of two more of the forbidden books, Piri Thomas's *Down These Mean Streets* and Alice Childress's *A Hero Ain't Nothing But a Sandwich.* And perhaps the otherwise incomprehensible inclusion on their list of Bernard Malamud's *The Fixer* is due to the feeling of the board that, because its membership includes genteel Jews as well as Gentiles, anti-Semitism is a subject best left entirely unexamined.

But politics seems finally of secondary importance, since the censors of the eighties include in their ranks not just conservatives and racists, but the "progressive" defenders of blacks and Jews (as well as of other abused and stigmatized groups, including gays, women, Poles, Hispanics, the handicapped, etc., etc.), who in the interests of what they consider socially desirable have not only driven from college campuses Nazis, anti-abortionists and believers in racial differences in intelligence, but have prevented the showing of Shakespeare's *Merchant of Venice* and D. W. Griffith's *Birth of a Nation.* Most recently they have succeeded in banning from class use Mark Twain's *Huckleberry Finn,* that book out of which, as Hemingway once remarked, all subsequent American literature has come.

Even more confusingly, the two sides, each of whom believes the other a threat to society, have joined in an unholy united front against violence on TV, driving from the air some of my own favorite cop shows, including *Baretta, Kojak* and *Starsky and Hutch.* One wing of that successful campaign included the PTA and the AMA, solid middle-class citizens terrified by all violence and, indeed, any manifestation of antinomian or dionysiac impulses. But the other was made up of many who considered themselves defenders of civil liberties, yet acceded to denying the privileges guaranteed by the First Amendment to the writers of programs which in their eyes vilified the criminal poor and glorified cops contemptuous of Miranda rights.

Successful on this front, both sorts of enemies of freedom are now moving in on pornography—picketing "sex shops," encouraging the police to bust the operators of X-rated movie houses, attempting to ban by city ordinance cable services which provide R-rated films to those willing to pay and, by organizing boycotts of their sponsors, trying to drive from the air a whole range of sexy sitcoms from sleazy T-and-A shows like *Three's Company* to truly hilarious spoofs of conventional morality like *Soap*. What makes the campaign against pop particularly dangerous at the moment is the newly forged alliance between Bible Belt fundamentalists and radical feminists, convinced (despite the fact that some of the best works of the genre have been created by women, including Pauline Réage, Edith Wharton and Anaïs Nin) that all pornography is a vilification of their gender and an incitement to rape. It is a conjunction of forces quite like that which just after World War I succeeded in imposing on America the Eighteenth Amendment, prohibiting the sale of alcohol, and like that earlier pious campaign is launched by those who on both sides remain ignorant that beneath their overt rationalization lurks an underlying fear of freedom as well as a contempt for the popular arts.

The contradiction between their avowed and covert motivation, along with the hypocrisy it breeds, is betrayed by the fact that many of the same parents and teachers who try to protect their children against cop shows on TV urge them to follow such serial orgies of sado-masochistic voyeurism, involving interethnic rape and flagellation, as *Roots, Holocaust, Shōgun* or *Masada* because they possess "redeeming social values," i.e., are educational or pious or both. Clearly, what the self-appointed censors have always objected to in the plays of Euripides and Shakespeare, in the E.C. Comics and *Starsky and Hutch,* is not really, *really* the fact that they are violent or lubricious but that they are —or at least have been considered at one time or another— junk, trash, schlock. Almost invariably the targets of the book banners and burners have been unpretentious entertainment, relished by an audience which includes the naïve as well as the sophisticated, often children as well as adults. If that audience has been willing to pay to see such spectacles, clearly that is not because they teach history or morality, but because they provide the shameful pleasure we all feel (though often hesitate to confess) in contemplating images of terror and pain, with or without erotic overtones—indulging, vicariously, in the dangerous and the forbidden.

Most popular literature tends, moreover, to be weak on

the cognitive and formal levels, so that we cannot pretend even to ourselves that we relish it because it makes us wiser, subtler or more delicately responsive to beauty. In prudential terms, it makes us—by identification with men and women more brutal or lustful than our ordinary selves —worse: more at home with, in tune with, the darker, more perilous aspects of our own psyches, otherwise confessed only in nightmares. Yet an examination of works which we consider lowbrow or vulgar in our own time can reveal to us something of which we may remain otherwise unaware in what we have come to treat as "classics." Such honored works as Sophocles' *Oedipus Rex,* Euripides' *Medea,* Shakespeare's *Henry IV* and *Macbeth,* we thus realize, have persisted not merely because they instruct us morally or delight us with their formal felicities, but because they allow us, in waking reverie, to murder our fathers and marry our mothers with Oedipus; to kill a king with the Macbeths, or our own children with Medea; to lie, steal, cheat, deceive and run away from a justified and necessary war with Falstaff—and to glory in it!

What all truly popular writers seem to know, or perhaps better to intuit, including not just Shakespeare and Sophocles but Bram Stoker and Edgar Rice Burroughs, is that the burden of any system of morality becomes finally irksome even to its most sincere advocates, since it necessarily denies, represses, suffocates certain undying primal impulses which, however outmoded by civilization, need somehow to be expressed. And this release of the repressed, all art which remains popular, whatever its critical status, makes possible—symbolically only, to be sure; but the joy and terror we feel are *real.*

Once I had become aware of this, I no longer found Aristotle an adequate guide to understanding the nature of poetry or a model for how to defend it against its enemies. On the one hand, his notion of "catharsis" or purgation had come to seem too demanding a metaphor for the liberating effect of literature, with its suggestion that—like castor oil or a dose of salts—poetry is not good in itself but only a distasteful means to a good end. On the other hand, Aristotle's commitment to rationality as the supreme good led him to falsify tragedy radically. However lofty his motives, he ended by describing drama of great mythological power (his favorite play, as everyone knows, was *Oedipus Rex*) in terms of paradigms from which any trace of the mythic or magical had been quite removed. And by doing so, he established a tradition of defending art on the grounds of an extremely narrow sort of social utility, i.e., its compatibility with rationally determined ethical ends. But even worse, he left to his successors the perilous notion that works of literature were to be judged either by their content, themes and ideas, which he called *dianoia*, or their form, which he referred to as *architektonike*, or by some uneasy combination of both.

Exactly how either of these criteria, alone or in combination, was compatible with the notion of catharsis, Aristotle never quite worked out—at least not in what of the mangled text of his *Poetics* has survived. But in any case, it is the former rather than the latter that his Roman successors emphasized as central to literary evaluation. In his *Art of Poetry*, Horace gave its classic formulation to the theory that poetry must instruct and/or delight, and was therefore to be judged on ethical as well as aesthetic grounds. Yet even the ethical, he assumed, was the province of critics rather than philosophers, priests or political rulers; though in his own time, the state insisted on banning certain works as subversive or sending their authors into exile. And with the triumph of the Christian establishment, matters grew considerably worse.

For a long time, in fact, all song and story was regarded as contraband except that canonized by the hierarchy of the church, i.e., declared inspired by God and therefore to be classified as privileged "scripture" rather than mere "literature." But even at the height of ecclesiastical repression only manuscripts or, later, printed books fell under interdict; the oral/aural song and story of the folk flourished, as it were, behind the backs of the fully literate. Though censorship by state and church has never quite ceased (even the Index of Forbidden Books of Roman Catholicism has never been abolished), eventually in most of the Western world secular literature revived, and with the invention of the printing press became available to an ever-growing audience. The revival of such literature brought with it the rediscovery of classical criticism and an attempt to apply the Aristotelian-Horatian formula to contemporary song and story.

Though never quite adequate to certain loose Renaissance forms with roots in folk culture, like Elizabethan drama, for instance, such neoclassical criticism worked well enough as long as the reigning genres were those with prototypes in the ancient world: epic, verse tragedy and comedy, lyric. But criticism had to be—without at first quite realizing it—radically altered with the dominance of a new literary form in the West and the creation of a new mass audience, to many of whom it was the only familiar genre. It is that modern or bourgeois criticism (just now coming to an end, perhaps) which has ever since contended with church and state for the right to judge literature, distinguishing between canonical and uncanonical or, as it has come to say, high and low. But to understand why such criticism came into existence and in what sense it has outlived its usefulness, we must first try to understand the new reigning genre, the novel.

W**HAT WAS THE NOVEL?**

The modern novel, as invented once and for all in the middle of the eighteenth century by that extraordinarily anti-elitist genius Samuel Richardson, is the first successful form of popular art to have entered a culture more and more dominated by such sub- or quasi- or para-literature. It must be clearly distinguished, therefore, from old-style aristocratic art (an art dependent on limited literacy) as well as from folk art (an art dependent on mass illiteracy). It is related not to such forms as the epic, on the one hand, or the folk ballad, on the other—in fact, to nothing which precedes it, but to much which follows: the comic strip, the comic book, cinema, TV.

Like them, the novel is an art form which tends to make the classic distinction between literacy and illiteracy meaningless—or at least challenges it in ways disconcerting to traditional humanists; for it is a product both of the Industrial Revolution and of the political shifts in power which have replaced class-structured societies by one version or another of the mass society. In such highly developed, classless societies (which have destroyed the *myth* of class, however strongly analogous distinctions persist in fact), it seems possible and desirable to mass-produce forms of narrative not only for proper literates, but for quasi literates as well, i.e., for those who have acquired the mechanical skills of reading without being inducted into the elite culture which was their original context. The new electronic media have gone a step further by substituting images on the screen for words on the page, thus further reinforcing the disjunction between being able to apprehend a tale and acquiring the "standards" associated exclusively with books for judging its "value." Works of this kind tend to be successful or unsuccessful rather than "good" or "bad," to be sold or scrapped rather than canonized or rejected.

The development of the novel, at any rate, was from the start connected to the development of modern technology and modern means of mass distribution. The printing press was one of the first mass-production devices, and the novel the first literary form invented to be thus mass-produced. It has changed, therefore, as Gutenberg technology has changed, responding to the invention of stenotyping and linotyping, and to breakthroughs in papermaking and binding as well. It was, for instance, the discovery of procedures for producing cheap paper in the nineteenth century which made possible the serial "penny novel" with its new appeals to a new mass audience. Similarly, the development of less expensive means of binding encouraged the appearance in the United States just after World War II of mass-distributed paperbacks, and eventually led to the development of the "paperback original," as disposable as Kleenex.

Distribution as well as production has been essential to making the novel the closest thing possible within the limits of literacy to a mass art. The early invention of the circulating library and its evolution into the public library represented a first step in this direction. But an even more radical departure from traditional ways of making books accessible was the creation of the railway-station bookstall in England. Obviously, stagecoaches with their dark interiors and jolting motion made reading difficult if not impossible, but the train provided exactly the setting (and the airplane has perfected it with focused reading lights) for the leisurely consumption of expendable brief books intended to lighten the particular tedium of travel. Finally, the railway-station and airport bookstall became the model for the bookrack in the supermarket, on which novels appear as the commodities they are, ready always for the impulse buyer—and competing in allure against soapflakes and breakfast cereals with their bright jackets and catchy slogans.

It seems possible at this moment that even as print technology created the novel, post-print technologies may destroy it—or so Marshall McLuhan, among others, always insisted. Clearly, his most dire prophecies are not being fulfilled. We continue to read books, including his own, sometimes in front of the television screen itself. Yet the novel is in some sense changing in response to media which appeal to a wider audience than can ever learn to read words on the page with ease and pleasure. Even among those with superior Gutenberg skills, the prestige of books has been undercut by radio, television and the movies, which transmit speech to the ear and images to the eye without the intervention of print.

All this, however, was unsuspected by the emergent bourgeoisie, who remained for a long time unaware that insofar as they controlled the machines which reproduced works of literary art, they controlled that art too. Nor did they suspect that the marketplace, which was also in their hands, would come to determine which of those works would persist and be remembered. They were blinded by obsolescent mythologies, which envisaged "poetry" as the creation of a lonely genius and his Muse, rather than the product of industrial society and its technology. They thought therefore of literary "survival"—or as they still insisted on calling it, "immortality"—as the result of critical consensus rather than the workings of the marketplace. Consequently, they appointed "experts" to prepare themselves by the study of the classics and to tell them (to "brief" them, we would say these days) whether novels were okay in general, and if so, which were more okay than others.

Obviously, they did not always take the good advice they sought. Often, in fact, they continued to read what their critical mentors had taught them to regard as "trash"—defiantly in the case of sentimental trash, shamefacedly and secretly in the case of pornographic trash, even if they did snatch such work from the hands of their children, especially their daughters, when they caught them reading it. In the light of this, it is clear that the function of modern critics was from the start rather like that performed by the writers of etiquette books, dictionaries and grammars: they responded to the cultural insecurity of the eighteenth-century middle classes by providing "rules" or "standards" or guides to "good behavior." The new rich wanted to know which fork to pick up; how to spell things right; when, if at all, it was proper to say "ain't"; and also what books to buy for display in their libraries or on their coffee tables.

In establishing such "standards," literary critics had at first to compete with the clergy, who were also entrusted by their uncertain masters with the task of guiding them in this area. Not only was it unclear on both sides, and doubly unclear to those caught in the middle, into whose territory literature properly fell, the critic's or the parson's, but as long as those critics continued to maintain that literature must "instruct" as well as "delight," it proved impossible to separate the domain of Art, in which critics were the "experts," from that of Prudence, in which the clergy traditionally had the final word. And who, in any case, was to mediate between aesthetics and ethics: the critic or the pulpit moralist?

Since in the hierarchal value system of the bourgeoisie the ethical ranked higher than the aesthetic, it was more than a century before any critic dared confront the power of the church head-on by asserting the creed of "art for art's sake." More typically, critics tried instead to beat the moralists at their own game, by dividing all of art along crypto-Christian lines into what was serious, elevating, uplifting and of high moral purpose, on the one hand, and what was trivial, debasing, vulgar and of no redeeming value, on the other.

LITERATURE AS AN INSTITUTION

The notion of literature as an institution responsible only to itself has haunted the mind of Western writers ever since the Renaissance attempted to set song and story free from established religion. At first, however, this meant little more than changing masters: becoming not independent, but dependent on the needs and demands of the court rather than the church. But with the invention of printing, the growth of literacy and, especially, the appearance of a "free market" for the exchange of cultural commodities, literature seemed on the verge of total emancipation. To be sure, some huckster writers found in the new economic context an occasion for a new kind of subservience, making the commodity books which they produced—or so at least critics began to insist—subliterature, para-literature. "Real literature," the critics went on to explain, was something quite different, responsive not to the laws of supply and demand but to the "standards" they were in the process of establishing.

By the last decades of the twentieth century, however, those critics, once able to think of themselves as the all-powerful legislators of the invisible Republic of Letters, have themselves been co-opted by the university, as completely as the hucksters they despise have been by the marketplace. Though some of us continue to speak of the "great books," as if humanism were still a living movement instead of one more classroom subject, we all know in our hearts that "literature" is effectively what we teach in departments of English; or conversely, what we teach in departments of English is literature. Within that closed definitional circle, we perform the rituals by which we cast out unworthy pretenders to our ranks and induct true initiates, guardians of the "standards" by which all song and story are presumably to be judged.

Yet the penetration of academia by critics (as opposed to scholars and literary historians), along with the living poets and novelists which they analyze and evaluate, did not occur until a generation or two ago, within my own lifetime in fact. Robert Frost was, I believe, the first official writer-in-residence at any American college, and he arrived at the University of Michigan in 1927, only a few years after his verse had been accepted as a teachable subject in the curriculum. Yet even after colleges in the United States had legitimized contemporary works in the mother tongue, the prevailing academic definition of literature was still very different from that which moved most leading writers of the time.

The former definition was sustained by succeeding generations of old-style professors: the sons, or less often the daughters, of the original American ruling classes, sometimes eccentric but always genteel. Typically, they had been trained in German universities, whence they returned convinced of the virtues of rigorous Teutonic *Philologie*. Their taste in books was determined, however, not by "scholarly" criteria, which afforded them no guidance in this area, but by the values of Victorian England, which had reigned in the world of their growing-up. These parochial values—the product of a brief moment in the history of the upper classes of Great Britain and its colonies—they believed to be universal and eternal. Yet such "standards" were already being challenged before the outbreak of World War I by certain nonacademic exponents of a rival definition of literature.

Most of these self-styled "modernists," "avant-gardists" and "experimentalists" came from the same privileged WASP castes as their academic opposite numbers, but they sought to deny their bourgeois origins by passing into the non-class or meta-class of "bohemians" or "intellectuals." Moreover, though the first generation of "New Critics" who penetrated the university to challenge the "Old Scholars" came from their own ranks (think, for instance, of R. P. Blackmur, John Crowe Ransom and Allen Tate), they were in the beginning by and large resolutely extra-academic. Their occasional brief flirtations with the classroom ended typically in such comic denouements as Ezra Pound's expulsion from the faculty of Wabash College for having harbored "strippers" in his room. They prided themselves on being amateurs, dilettantes; or if professionals at all, journalists, book reviewers and especially contributors to, founders and editors of "little magazines," adversary literary quarterlies.

Often transient, occasionally more long-lasting, such journals ranged from some as catholic in their approach and appeal as *Hound and Horn* to others which took their stand on the political Right, like *Criterion* (whose editorial columns spoke more favorably of Fascism than Communism), *Southern Review* (subsidized by the reactionary populist Huey Long), *Kenyon Review* (in some sense its successor) and *Furioso* (one of whose editors became a CIA agent); or paid allegiance to the Left, like *New Masses* (whose staff consisted largely of orthodox Stalinists) and *Partisan Review* (which began with a Trotskyist split-off from Stalinism).

What they all had in common, making it possible after a while for some contributors to pass back and forth between, say, *Kenyon Review* and *Partisan Review*, was a commitment to "modernism" and a hatred for the bourgeois middle: middle-class morality, middling politics, middlebrow taste. Not even on the extreme Left did the extra-academics or their epigones object fundamentally to the elitism of the Old Academy. Rather, they accused the professional establishment of inadequate elitism: a failure to spot certain kinds of pretentious or genteel kitsch, and a complementary blindness to the merits of experimental, highbrow literature. This situation prevailed well into the fifties, after the emergence of a second, non-WASP generation of modernist critics (including me), who this time typically *did* enter college teaching, sitting in hostile silence as year after year the presidents of the Modern Language Association, all members of the *ancien régime*, ritually deplored the incursion of people like us into university departments of English.

On a more personal level, I can recall finding myself

homeless in 1953 in Bloomington, Indiana, where I had gone to teach a summer course. I had made arrangements well in advance, but discovered that the house I had assumed safely mine had been snatched away from me at the last moment by its landlord, a local "scholar" who had belatedly learned that I was "one of those others," i.e., a "critic." What made it even worse was the fact that I had been invited to Indiana University not as a member of the English Department proper, but as a visiting lecturer in the School of Letters, that oddly hybrid Trojan Horse, out of Philip Rahv by John Crowe Ransom, in which M.A.'s were awarded for "criticism." Fifth columnists like me had by then begun to swarm in alarming numbers out of the bellies of such treacherous machines into beleaguered academia.

And what a motley crew we were: not renegade WASP bearers of infectious aesthetic doctrines, but many of us the offspring of non-English-speaking stock, with a veneer of Anglo-Saxon polite culture no more than a generation thick. It was, however, a rearguard action that the defenders of the Citadel were fighting. By the last years of the fifties, we former outsiders had established ourselves as insiders. The end of World War II had seen the influx into colleges and universities of vast hordes of government-subsidized students, ex-G.I.'s, many the first in their families ever to have been exposed to higher education. To teach the succeeding waves of the continuing invasion, new faculty had to be recruited out of the first waves. Sons and daughters of working-class or petty-bourgeois parents, not even predominantly North European, much less *echt* Anglo-Saxon, after a while overwhelmingly East European Jewish (and, to make matters worse, graduates of land-grant universities or city colleges), such cultural *arrivistes* more often began their critical careers by contributing to the by-then-established "little magazines" than to scholarly journals.

But they were, alas, elitist still, though their elitism was necessarily quite different from that of the old-line scholars they had displaced. At first, indeed, it seemed possible to think of the program of the new academics as anti-elitist. After all, the triumph of "modernism" seemed to be opening up the restrictive canon by introducing into the classroom, even sanctioning Ph.D. dissertations on, writers like Pound and Eliot, Proust, Mann and Joyce, formerly considered too trivial, ephemeral, obscure, obscene or eccentric to be integrated into the "tradition." It ended, however, by merely substituting a new canon for the old, and one which, ironically, turned out to be even more self-consciously exclusive, more self-righteously narrow.

Consequently, two or three generations of students and teachers were brainwashed (as Eliot's *ad hoc* apologies for the literary practices of himself and his friends became an orthodox aesthetic credo) into believing that the only acceptable poets were those distinguished by "ambiguity" and "serious wit": the nineteenth-century French *symbolistes*, the seventeenth-century English "metaphysicals" and, of course, the "New Poets" themselves. Such formerly sacrosanct "great poets" as Milton and Shelley were downgraded in the name of an ill-defined "classicism"; but the special targets of the "modernists" were formerly best-selling makers of verses like Scott, Byron and Tennyson in England, Longfellow, Lowell and Holmes in the United States, who had managed to hold together to the very end of the nineteenth century the minority and majority audiences. If the old-line scholars of the early twentieth century had taken seriously such demipop laureates, with their banal verse forms and conventional themes, this was, the invaders argued, due to their lack of professional rigor and the laxity of their "standards."

Similarly, in the area of fiction, the apostles of "modernism" subverted the reputations of novelists who had managed to move both the popular readers and the soft-hearted, soft-headed critics of their own time. Martin Turnell, for instance, in *The Classic Moment* dismissed Hugo and Balzac to the outer darkness. And F. R. Leavis, in the first fury of his super-elitism, excluded from the "great tradition" of English fiction, along with Fielding, Sterne, Scott and the Brontës, the whole *oeuvre* of Dickens, except for his uncharacteristically austere *Hard Times*. Indeed, only six novelists made it to full canonical status, and of their works only a handful of selected books. For years now, therefore, dutiful graduate students have continued to grind out studies (driving me at least to bored distraction) of George Eliot's *Middlemarch* and D. H. Lawrence's *Women in Love* —with the sense that of all nineteenth- and early twentieth-century English fiction scarcely anything else is worthy of their time and effort.

Similar attempts to define a new canon of American fiction have been made, temporarily eclipsing authors available to the most naïve readers, like Edgar Allan Poe and Harriet Beecher Stowe, while immensely inflating the reputation of Henry James (whom F. R. Leavis had already claimed for his "great tradition"), especially the dense and forbidding later novels, about one of which Mark Twain is reported to have said, "I would rather be damned to John Bunyan's heaven than read that." But for reasons which I hope eventually to make clear, this proved an impossible task. Nonetheless, once they had become securely ensconced in academia, the new professoriate *tried,* one extreme elitist among them even attempting to prove that when judged by standards appropriate to the "accepted masterpieces of literature," Mark Twain, "however gifted a raconteur, however much genius he had as an improvisor, was not, even in *Huckleberry Finn,* a great novelist."

What such obdurate wrongheadedness in the name of "standards" finally indicates is, it seems to me, a need on the part of latter-day academics to prove by demonstrating their superior rigor their right to the positions they occupy. To their forerunners, born of upper-class parents, educated at quality schools and sustained by inherited wealth or marriage to money, a career in the university represented merely another, marginally acceptable gentleman's vocation. But to the newcomers it was a way of making it into a position of unaccustomed prestige, if not power: a strategy for social climbing without seeming to "sell out" to the worlds of hucksterism or venal politics.

I am not suggesting that they (we, I suppose I should say) were fully aware of all this; but it was at least subintended, and, in any case, it worked! Worked so well, in fact, that after a while those initially regarded as upstarts and interlopers began to seem more at home in the university than anyone else. Indeed, by the late seventies the few remaining extra-academic literary critics still publishing tended (in an odd reversal) to be primarily WASPs, whether piously moralistic defenders of the "eternal verities" like John Gardner or snide exponents of high camp like Gore Vidal. Yet, however self-serving the case made by these two novelist/critics against the academization of American fiction, they were responding to a genuine problem. Not only are most of the novels prized by academic critics the work of writers who have sought shelter in the university, but their chief readership consists of teachers and students who "study" them in the classroom.

There they are translated into semiotic or structual formulae, which is to say, finally experienced not as words on the page but diagrams on the blackboard. Similarly, the books despised by academics are typically experienced by their audiences not in print but only after conversion into images on the screen. Consequently, fewer and fewer novels of both kinds any longer function as ends in themselves; rather, they represent transitional stages on the way toward two quite different final forms.

WHAT WAS THE ART NOVEL?

It was not teachers of literature who initiated that split but, as we have seen, certain "modernist" writers, beginning with Flaubert in France and Henry James in England and America, who attempted to produce novels intended not for the marketplace of their own time but for the libraries and, as they did not yet suspect, the classrooms of the future. But this *is* the future, and though such "art novels" have become a part of "required literature," an increasing number of novelists and critics have begun to realize that they are no longer viable models for living fiction. Some writers, particularly in America, have even begun to suspect that the very distinction between "serious books" and "best sellers" upon which conception of the "art novel" depends was an error from the start.

It is an especially unforgivable error for American writers to have made, since the culture of the United States is favorable to perspicacity in this regard, being from the beginning "popular" beneath a thin overlay of imported European elitism. Our national *mythos* is a pop myth and our Revolution consequently a pop revolution, as compared, for instance, with either the French or the Russian, which originated in high-level ideological manifestos and debates. Our War of Independence was rooted in concrete grievances rather than abstract ideas (though after the fact certain homegrown ideologues dreamed up philosophical apologies to account for grown men dressing up as Indians and dumping into Boston Harbor that supreme symbol of effete European civilization, British tea). It was an event, that is to say, cued by a boy's dream, then translated into the highfalutin phrases of the Declaration of Independence by Thomas Jefferson, himself a lifelong small boy in love with gadgets, though he fancied himself a displaced *philosophe.*

From that moment, in any case, we proposed a "revolutionary" model of politics and culture, challenging to all civilizations with graveyards or museums to defend—to whom, therefore, the past is reassuring and the future a threat. Moreover, whatever has become of us in the area of politics, in the realm of the arts we have remained such a challenge to this very day. When Europeans—and other non-Americans from the elite classes of cultures which have not yet completely opened their universities to mass enrollment or their media to consumer control—speak of the incursion into their midst of pop forms, like rock music, country-and-western, comic books, schlocky TV sitcoms and cop shows, they tend to refer to it as "creeping Americanization." Especially where the official guardians of culture have not yet recognized our claims to eminence in High Art (England, for instance, where the critical establishment still regards Ernest Hemingway as a pretentious upstart, and Oxford University did not appoint a professor of American literature until the late 1970s) but cannot hold the line against our mass culture, this charge is leveled with special vehemence.

Nonetheless, though those who use "Americanization" as a synonym for vulgarization perpetuate a stereotype (remotely descended from Shakespeare's *The Tempest*) of the United States as a land of Calibans, half-educated fugitive slaves, the cast-offs of Europe, Asia and Africa, they speak a kind of truth. It is a truth, moreover, which bears repeating, since a considerable number of our own genteel and elitist academics (typically Anglophiles, willing to watch TV only when it speaks with a BBC accent) are unwilling to confess that the pop culture, which has by now not merely spread worldwide but has triumphed in every land where it is not forbidden for political reasons, *is* essentially American. Much of it is more particularly a part of the American youth culture, but then all Americans like to think of themselves as young (it was Mark Twain who remarked that in his dreams at least he never grew old) and their land as really, *really* the Fountain of Youth sought there by the early explorers.

Almost all of it came originally from sources outside the United States (jazz from Africa, science fiction from England, hot dogs and hamburgers from Germany), but before being exported again, it was remade in terms of the peculiarly American dream, which eventuated in the creation of those two peculiarly American institutions, the supermarket and the land-grant college, where all are permitted access and everything is made available. That dream imagines a slow, inexorable evolution toward an egalitarian community in which everyone, rich and poor (the native tradition can conceive of equalizing everything but wealth), will speak the same classless dialect of their native tongue, hear the same music, read the same books and periodicals, see the same movies and television programs, as well as drive the same cars, eat the same food and wear the same clothes.

Finally, for the first time in history, there will exist a cultural democracy in which no one can be identified and placed—and be therefore condescended to or envied—by how he talks, walks and dresses, or what he consumes to satisfy his hunger, slake his thirst and re-create his spirit. It is fitting, I think, that the same refugee Jewish immigrants who grew rich manufacturing ready-made garments which made it impossible to tell an aristocrat from a commoner at a glance ("Who was then the gentleman?") invested their profits in making Hollywood movies, which replaced simultaneously the folk entertainments of the illiterate poor and the courtly pastimes of the literate rich.

Certain products and commodities in our world, I am suggesting, are intrinsically *leveling* in their effect; and though, where capitalism prevails, they make money for the few who own the instruments of production, they also represent for the majority who are their consumers a kind of fulfillment of the populist dream. I am talking now not only of the popular arts but of mass-produced and mass-marketed items which it is customary in some quarters to malign, though their images possess us as once holy icons did our ancestors. I mean (and it is interesting how often the names of their original "authors" are attached still to such endlessly reduplicated creations) McDonald's ham-

burgers, the Colonel's Kentucky Fried Chicken, Levi
Strauss's blue jeans, Pepsi-Cola and Coca-Cola. The worldwide dominance of such products represents not merely a
triumph of advertising (which after all can only sell what is
perceived as satisfying a need) but evidence of an archetypal appeal to something less of the body than what used
to be called the "soul."

Like wine, beer, whiskey, coffee, and tea (but for everyone and, therefore, without class connotations), Coke has
become as much symbol as beverage: the occasion for a
secular ritual, a celebration of the human spirit, attuned to
mass culture; so that the slogan "Things go better with
Coke" is no idle and meaningless boast, significant only to
the Madison Avenue firm that grew wealthy inventing it,
but an unwitting revelation of a deep truth about, if not
what we really are in late industrial society, what we aspire
to become. It would repay us, therefore, to see in the context of such mythological soft drinks and fast foods other
great American pop products, similarly vulgar yet refresh-
ing to the spirit, like Tarzan, Mickey Mouse, the Wizard of
Oz, Superman, Batman; as well as certain characters like
W. C. Fields, Marilyn Monroe and John Wayne, who began
as actors but ended as full-fledged myths; and Natty
Bumppo, Huckleberry Finn and Moby Dick, since the
novel, which began at almost the same moment as the
United States, is also (in origin) hopelessly pop and (by
adoption) American.

Certain contemporary American critics, including not a
few of my own academic colleagues, would deny this relationship between our classic novel and other forms of
American pop. But they are disqualified from speaking on
the subject, since they prefer European *haute cuisine* and
haute couture, see only art films, preferably foreign ones
dubbed into English, forbid their children, whom they
send to private schools and Ivy League colleges, to watch
anything but educational TV at home—and have themselves not read Tarzan or science fiction or comic books
since they were kids. Yet American novelists have from the
start demonstrated a clearer understanding than those of
any other culture (except perhaps the British, by fits and
starts, in all the books left out of F. R. Leavis' *The Great
Tradition*) of the essentially popular nature of the genre
they practice, its necessary hostility to the modes and can-

ons of High Art. Certainly, before there was a respectable novelist, a self-conscious literary "artist," in the United States, we had produced hosts of best sellers (cf. the long gap in time between Susanna Rowson and Hawthorne or even Charles Brockden Brown). Moreover, the careers of our most eminent novelists even after Brown have been dominated by the pattern of first flirting with, then rejecting, the temptations of High Art.

The history of James Fenimore Cooper is typical in this regard; he began by imitating Jane Austen but quickly lapsed into providing for the unsophisticated the thrills of captivity and escape in the wilderness. And more recently our most talented fictionists have begun by emulating the European avant-garde, only to seek refuge in the American popular press. Think of how quickly Faulkner and Hemingway moved from "little magazines" to journals catering to the mass audience, which Scott Fitzgerald never turned away from at all. It is instructive in this regard to remember what literary histories seldom record, that the greatest of all Faulkner's stories, "The Bear," first appeared in the *Saturday Evening Post*, at a point when that journal appealed to the lowest and broadest level of popular taste. Moreover, the version of Faulkner's story published in those pages, and edited to suit precisely that taste, is in some ways superior to the final version expanded in the interests of "art" as understood by a small-town provincial.

Examples could be multiplied indefinitely of careers which, like Hemingway's, begin in the pages of elitist magazines and end in a special issue of *Life.* Most exemplary of all is the case of Nathanael West, who started by imitating the *surréalistes* in *The Dream Life of Balso Snell* but in his three later books turned to boys' fiction, bleeding-hearts journalism and the Hollywood scene in quest of a more authentic subject matter and style. *A Cool Million, Miss Lonelyhearts* and *The Day of the Locust* are not merely about pop culture, they *are* pop culture, their structure and tone modeled after the comic strip and the burlesque-show "blackout."

To speak to the people means to speak in the language of the people rather than in some artificial tongue invented by academicians precisely for the purpose of creating an elitist or hermetic art. And in this regard too, Americans have a marked advantage over more homogeneous cultures like that of France. Ever since the final decades of the last century, ours has been an ethnically various community in which no single dialect has ever managed to maintain special authority among all the others. The American school system has tried desperately—particularly in classes in "English," all the way from kindergarten to the freshman composition course in the university—to brainwash generations of more recent immigrants into accepting as their own the dialect spoken by a handful of White Anglo-Saxon Protestants in a few Eastern Seaboard cities, but this attempt has conspicuously failed.

No eminent American novelist, at any rate, has ever forgotten the necessity of speaking to and for, not the ruling or established classes (linguistically as well as ethnically distinguishable in the United States), but to everybody, and *for* one or another of those minorities who, generation after generation, represent the emergence into daylight of hitherto repressed elements in the American psyche. And to do this he has to borrow from the least reputable dialects of the excluded—or to contrive a dialect of his own even more disreputable and anti-WASP.

The American novel—ever since Theodore Dreiser surely, perhaps ever since Mark Twain—has used this counter-language to attack the WASP values of our earliest ruling class, which is to say, the imported Christian humanism of New England. By the same token, it has spoken first for a later North European migration that bypassed the old urban centers of culture in Boston, Philadelphia and New York on the way toward the Midwest (Dreiser himself is an example, as are Hemingway and Steinbeck); then for the children and grandchildren of the defeated Confederacy, the Scotch-Irish planters and peasants of the South (Faulkner plays such a role, along with Truman Capote, Katherine Anne Porter and Carson McCullers); and almost at the same moment for more recent immigrants to the big cities, old and new: the Irish, the Italians, and especially the Jews (Saul Bellow and Bernard Malamud are conspicuous examples) and the Negroes, who had not yet learned to call themselves blacks (James Baldwin is such a spokesman, as are Richard Wright and Ralph Ellison and even LeRoi Jones up to the point where he renamed himself Amiri Baraka, Moslem-style).

Even more important, however, than the actual breaking through to speech of such minorities—elected generation after generation to say what their ethnic predecessors had found too dangerous or alien to utter—has been the attempt to represent the Alien Other, along with what seems most foreign in their own souls, by members of long-established or recently successful groups in the community. Especially notable in this regard has been the effort on the part of the most gifted white American authors to project—through a kind of magical ventriloquism—the authentic voices of those two non-European groups in whose presence and on whose backs, as it were, transplanted Europeans have built American culture: the voices of Indians and Negroes, red men and black. In what we think of as the "great books" of America, these non-European voices can be heard in dialogue with the voices of certain runaway ex-Europeans, creating an interchange as vital to our culture as the conversation of Kings and Fools in the literature of the High Renaissance.

It all begins with Chingachgook in James Fenimore Cooper's *Leatherstocking Tales* (if Twain taught our writers how to talk American, Cooper long before him taught them to dream American), with the release of the voice of the expropriated Indian. And the process continues when, for the first time, the mute black slave is heard crying out in rage through Babo in Melville's "Benito Cereno," or praying in faith and humility through Harriet Beecher Stowe's Uncle Tom, or pledging an impossible and perfect love through Nigger Jim in Mark Twain's *Huckleberry Finn*. When Cooper reimagines himself as Chingachgook speaking to Natty Bumppo, or Mrs. Stowe pretends she is Tom addressing young Marse George, or Twain projects himself as Jim talking to Huck, it is not merely as if they were two kinds of Americans sundered by exploitation and hate, but also as if two halves of the long-sundered American soul had found a way to communicate. No wonder that this is the point at which our authentic literature begins, and no wonder that the dialogue continues to this very day.

Yet, for a little while during the reign of "modernism"—the age of Proust, Mann and Joyce, of T. S. Eliot and the belated cult of Henry James, the time of the New Criticism with its odd blending of fascist politics and aesthetic formalism—these basic facts of American life and art were forgotten. And during the first four or five decades of the twentieth century, many of our most talented writers took themselves off to the cafés of Paris or the universities of England in order to learn certain "modernist" modes of High Art: first an anti-bourgeois and disreputable experimentalism, an elitism redeemed partly at least by the risks it entailed; then the Eliotic tradition, in which the avant-garde had turned wan and genteel. In both cases, however, the "alien" voices evoked tended to speak European: sometimes actual literary French or British English, sometimes medieval Italian or Confucian Chinese; though from time to time, the inflections of Boston Irishmen or New York Jews or Alabama blacks emerged in a kind of counterpoint—condescended to or broadly burlesqued.

By the sixties, however, there was everywhere in the United States a sense that the neoclassical critical modes stimulated by Eliot and practiced by such Southern agrarians as John Crowe Ransom, Allen Tate and Cleanth Brooks had exhausted their small usefulness. Their analyses, it became clear, had made possible some reforms in pedagogy, and had even illuminated a handful of neglected lyric poems, chiefly by John Donne. But they had done nothing to explain the great novels of our own tradition, or to encourage any new achievement in that genre. Indeed, even in poetry, their example served to inhibit rather than to spur new experiments after 1955. There occurred simultaneously, therefore, a reaction against the example of T. S. Eliot in verse, and that of his preferred novelist, Henry James, in prose.

Looking back over the past couple of decades from the vantage point of the 1980s, when we seem to have reached another dead end in the development of fiction, I find that the most interesting work of the period occurred in what I described then as the anti-art art novel or the death-of-the-novel novel. That form seems to me to have been best exemplified in Vladimir Nabokov's *Pale Fire* (1962) and John Barth's *Giles Goat-Boy* (1966): a strange pair of books really, the former not quite American and the latter absolutely provincial American. Yet they had in common a way of using typical devices of the "modernist" art novel, like irony, parody, exhibitionist allusion, redundant erudition and dogged experimentalism, not to extend the possibilities of the form but to destroy it.

Such novels are the literary equivalents of those auto-destruct sculptures built to blow themselves up: infernal machines intended not to explode a barracks or factory or palace but the very notion of "Art" which they embody. We may begin by thinking that *Giles Goat-Boy* is a satire intended to mock everything which came before it, from *Oedipus the King* to the fairy tale "Three Billygoats Gruff." But before we are through, we realize that it is itself which it mocks, along with the writer capable of producing one more example of so obsolescent a form, and especially us who are foolish enough to be reading it. It is as if the art novel, aware that it must die, had determined to die laughing.

W HAT WAS THE DEATH OF THE NOVEL?

When, more than twenty-five years ago, I announced boldly (as I announce every new insight boldly) that THE NOVEL IS DEAD, I was not yet aware that some practicing novelists were ready to agree with me. I was, in fact, initially greeted with howls of derision from certain insecure fictionists of the time, who found especially offensive, I guess, my confession that after finishing a group of new novels by them and their friends, I had slipped off to the movies for refreshment and relief. A little later, I began to hear from those who concurred with me, making clear what I should have surmised: that though grateful for my support, they did not need me to tell them that the genre their fiction travestied was obsolescent. To be sure, they, like me, knew quite well that long prose narratives were still being published and read, as they have been ever since the mid-eighteenth century, when the genre came into existence and almost simultaneously critics began announcing that it was dying or dead.

Nonetheless, not until the second half of our own century did a considerable number of novelists introject an awareness of the death of the genre into the novel itself—which is to say, begin to write self-confessed posthumous novels. This development coincides with, perhaps is in part cued by, a change in the way in which novels have come to be distributed and consumed. Printed and bound in boards or paper, they continue to be borrowed from libraries and bought in bookstores. But transmogrified, they also lead a second life, or rather two kinds of second life. On the one hand, they are assigned in classrooms in schools and colleges, becoming in the process a part of required culture, a duty and a chore rather than a diversion or an escape, while on the other hand, and for quite another group of readers, incapable of assimilating words on the page with ease and pleasure, they are translated into images on the screen, made into movies and TV series—the watching of which is often regarded as suspect by the guardians of culture.

Occasionally, the same books make it both ways, Ken Kesey's *One Flew Over the Cuckoo's Nest,* for instance, being simultaneously or successively transformed into classroom material and popular films—products of what moviemakers like to call "the Industry," show biz, in short. But by and large, novels tend to fall into one or another of these categories; not just after they are written and have been sorted out by self-conscious critics and/or the blind mechanism of the marketplace, but in their very conception, before the fact, as it were. This becomes increasingly true as more writers learn to anticipate falling into one of these mutually exclusive categories and begin, therefore, to write *as if* for the academy or Hollywood, that is, as if to be taught, analyzed and explicated—or to be packaged, hyped and sold at the box office.

In this sense, then, it is possible to argue that the novel is really dead—dead as a final form, an end in itself, requiring no translation into another medium or a different context. But only a small number of authors of the anti-art-novel art novel are aware that the traditional novel is even in this sense dead. They have, indeed, become so obsessed by their awareness of this fact that it has tended to replace the traditional subject matter of the genre (class, the relations of the sexes, the conflict between individuals and society) in their work. Yet even this subject begins to be used up, as I became aware trying to read my way through John Barth's recent book *Letters,* which may represent for him a step beyond *Giles Goat-Boy,* and is perhaps best understood as a death-of-the-death-of-the-art-novel art novel. And what further life can there be for fiction which aspires to the status of what used to be called "literature" beyond this triply involuted awareness of its death?

•

Other writers identified with what is sometimes called "post-modernism" seem not yet to have realized that we are approaching the end of "surfiction"—that it becomes finally a bore to be reminded yet again that the art novel is no longer viable, and perhaps never was. I am thinking not only of Robert Coover, Thomas Pynchon, Donald Barthelme and William Gass—whose long-drawn-out experimentation with terminal fiction is redeemed variously by political indignation, an infatuation with pop culture, a kind of cutesy charm, or an obsession with the middle of the middle of our country—but of such fanatical devotees of the auto-destruct novel as certain members of the Fiction Collective, who seem to have accepted not just the death of the genre but of the audience which once sustained it. They are apparently content to write for each other, plus, I suppose, the captive audience of their students, since they are by and large teachers of writing and literature.

If the replacement of a readership for whom the novel is optional by one for whom it is required represents a final indignity for practicing novelists, they do not seem to think so. That this is the situation in the case of their own books strikes them as a final proof of what they have all along believed: that what they produce is of value precisely because it is nothing like what the mass audience has always thought of as a novel, i.e., a book with a plot, characters, and dialogue, as well as an author, concealed or intrusive, who speaks with final authority. That kind of novel is for them effectively dead. They may, it is true, go occasionally to see films made from commodity novels, or less often, perhaps, read certain subgenres of the kind, science fiction, let us say, or hard-core pornography; but they would in no case *write* such books.

Those who do, and profit immensely thereby, seldom suspect (though most of their profits come from film or TV versions of their work) that as a final form their kind of novel is also dead or ailing. They are as blithely unaware of this "fact" as born-again Christians or backcountry Baptists are of the "fact" that God is dead—indeed, that their God, the Judeo-Christian deity, died, for a minority of articulate and influential intellectuals, some two hundred or more years ago, just as the novel was beginning to establish itself as the reigning genre. Yet this difference of awareness which separates not just majority and minority writers but majority and minority audiences is evidence that the novel is, in yet another sense, dead: dead as a single genre—*the single genre* capable of unifying an otherwise fragmented society.

How likely is it that a novel will appear in, say, the mythological year 1984 or 2001 which, like Harriet Beecher Stowe's *Uncle Tom's Cabin,* can be read "with equal pleasure [the words of praise are Ralph Waldo Emerson's] in the kitchen, the parlor and the nursery"? But precisely such novels did appear with fair frequency from the middle of the eighteenth century to the end of the nineteenth: *Robinson Crusoe, Gulliver's Travels,* Richardson's *Pamela* and *Clarissa,* Cooper's *The Last of the Mohicans,* most of Dickens, particularly the earlier books, much of Balzac, Dostoievski, Tolstoi and almost all of Twain, from the weariest of potboilers, like *The Prince and the Pauper,* to *Huckleberry Finn.*

In its beginnings, as we have already noted, the novel was a popular, a demotic, a leveling form. Indeed, elitist critics were embarrassed from the start by its intimate connection with the commercialization and democratization of culture in an emerging mass society, and only begrudgingly did they grant it the status of real literature at all. They began in fact by trying to ignore it, but not only did it refuse to go away, it became—over their dead bodies, as it were—the reigning literary genre of the world, what young men and women dreamt of writing in their lonely chambers.

"If you can't lick 'em, join 'em," the critics decided at long last. Yet even after they had ceased dismissing *all* novels as vulgar entertainments for the half-literate, chiefly women and girls, they insisted on dismissing most of them as "trash," books to be read quickly and thrown away—as opposed to a very few considered worthy of being analyzed and preserved in libraries. For a long time most practicing novelists resisted this attempt at invidious categorization, and the climax of the ensuing great debate as to whether there were in fact two separate kinds of fiction received its classic formulation in the interchange between Robert Louis Stevenson, who states his position in "A Humble Remonstrance," and Henry James, who makes his case in "The Art of Fiction."

James was the first novelist to think of himself as writing in English the kind of novel read by a self-congratulatory minority audience, which in the name of the "standards" it embodies feels free to ignore books prized by the mass audience. Those books include not just Stevenson's *Treasure Island* and *Dr. Jekyll and Mr. Hyde,* but Rider Haggard's *She,* H. G. Wells's *The Time Machine,* Edgar Rice Burroughs' *Tarzan of the Apes,* L. Frank Baum's *The Wizard of Oz* and Margaret Mitchell's *Gone With the Wind,* many of which have never been out of print from their date of publication to the present moment. They are known, moreover, by a larger audience than has ever read them in their original format through comic-book versions, musical-comedy adaptations, movies and TV scripts.

Such popular novels, or rather (since the language in which they were originally expressed seems oddly irrelevant) their chief characters and plots, live on in the collective memory of us all. Unlike books assigned in school, they are read not for the virtuosity of their authors or the elegance of their structure or style, much less the precision of their language or their subtlety of thought, but for something quite other: their mythic resonance, their archetypal appeal. They are read, moreover, not only by members of the majority audience, who are their chief consumers, but by members of the minority audience, some of whom sometimes sneak off to enjoy them behind closed doors or with the shades pulled down. But most readers of the latter kind think of themselves as engaging with a western or detective story or current best seller in a manner quite different from that in which they encounter *Middlemarch* or *Gravity's Rainbow* or *Ulysses.*

And maybe, after all, it *is* misleading to use a single word to describe the diverse ways in which the two reborn forms of the dead classical novel are apprehended. Popular books are in fact responded to by all readers not as canonical art but as secular scripture, though the images which underlie them depend upon neither the Judeo-Christian mythology sanctioned by the competing churches to which most of us belong, nor to the Greco-Roman body of myth which informs most of the "classics" we study in school. More than a century ago Walt Whitman cried out to his fellow Americans, "Cancel out please those long overdue accounts to Greece and Rome. . . . Post 'to let' on the walls of Jerusalem." And the whole world has heeded him in the American century.

But *what* has in fact replaced the older pantheons, the critics did not foresee; imagining, perhaps, like Matthew Arnold, that "serious" poets and novelists would create, for an audience pledged to "high seriousness," "serious" new gods and demigods. Instead, we live in a world whose deepest aspirations and fears are for most of us (worshipfully hushed before the screen in the darkness of the theater, or in a thousand dusky living rooms before the flickering TV set) embodied in *daimones* like Frankenstein's Monster, Dracula and Mr. Hyde, inhabitants of pop fairylands like Oz and the erotic daydreams of shopgirls made flesh in characters like Scarlett O'Hara and Rhett Butler. Though creatures of print, they occupy the same psychic space as Popeye and Archie Bunker, a space utterly alien that preempted Stephen Dedalus and Buck Mulligan, Albertine and the Baron de Charlus, Hyacinth Robinson and Lambert Strether. To that space we have also relegated Odysseus and Achilles, Little Nell, Oliver Twist, Huck Finn and the Brothers Karamazov, though in the beginning they existed in the former.

Since the sixties the latter have been rejected by younger readers, who in their quest for the marvelous have turned away from the canonical works of High Literature to less respectable popular books, ranging from Tolkien's *Lord of the Rings* to Richard Bach's *Jonathan Livingston Seagull.* Anything a traditional critic has to say about such cult favorites seems to their hierophants not merely impertinent but sacrilegious, as was impressed on me when I tried vainly one day to persuade a student admirer of *Jonathan Livingston Seagull* of that book's pretentious banality, only to be greeted by the howled protest "Man, it changed my life." Or was it "changed my head"? I have heard both comments over and over ever since—but never, even in the grimmest backlash of the late seventies and the just-beginning eighties, in reference to *The Ambassadors* or *Paradise Lost* or Barth's *Lost in the Funhouse.*

Such responses are typically cued by books which are fantastic in mode, and if not downright naïve in form, at least reassuringly old-fashioned. Such novels, resolutely nonexperimental and anti-mimetic, have constituted the favorite reading matter of a couple generations of younger readers, turned away from the avant-garde by its canonization in the classroom, and hungry for fantasy, of which many of them were deprived in childhood by the grim, reality-oriented parents of the repressive fifties. Such books belong, in short, to the category of youth best sellers: which did not come into existence until the emergence in those 1950s of a self-conscious generation of adolescents well-heeled enough, on the one hand, to buy whatever they liked, and convinced, on the other, that their life-styles and values were different enough from those of their parents and teachers to require another kind of commodity culture.

The earliest youth best sellers differed sharply from one another (think, for instance, of William Golding's *Lord of the Flies*, J. D. Salinger's *Catcher in the Rye* and Jack Kerouac's *On the Road*), some of them, indeed, aspiring to the status of High Art. But finally the makers of the cultural revolution of the late sixties seem to have decided that what they needed was a form of popular fiction. It had, however, to be different not only from the kind of books which the book clubs were still bringing their bourgeois mothers: novels of domestic sentiment and exotic-erotic romance verging on soft porn, what had once been the best seller *par excellence;* but also from the masculine protest pop which had long pleased their fathers: specialized subgenres read not as literature but as anti-literature, including adventure stories, spy thrillers, mysteries, westerns, hard-core pornography and science fiction.

The last, however, unlike the rest, the young finally adopted rather than rejected; in part, perhaps, because science fiction was the most recently invented, but also, I suspect, because a generation of rebels, largely male and at least covertly misogynist, needed some form of masculine protest literature to call their own. In the beginning they made do with kidnaping, against their will, as it were, certain old-line hacks like Robert Heinlein, who, informed of the bewildering vogue of his *Stranger in a Strange Land* among the dissident young, is reported to have cried out, "But I hate even my grown-up readers!" After a while, however, they managed to win over to their side such writers ripe for conversion as Kurt Vonnegut, who had begun by trying to make a buck by producing s.f. pulp stories for middle-aged males, but ended by providing the young in fantasy form answers to the ultimate cosmological questions. And finally, they have begun to produce out of their own ranks heirs to the patrimony of science fiction—most notably, perhaps, Samuel F. Delany.

In any case, the youth best seller has become as established a commodity in the marketplace of pop culture as the women's best seller, though it has not, of course, driven the latter out before it, any more than it has displaced the older types of masculine protest literature. In the supermarket of mass culture where it is always possible to open a new department to satisfy a new consumer demand, the favored books of the young coexist with the preferred genres of their elders, even as their favorite drugs, pot, for instance, are consumed, not instead of, but along with booze and beer.

What has happened over the last couple of decades, however, is that the mass audience has not grown closer to the elite audience (as I predicted in a hopeful but utterly mistaken essay called "Cross the Border, Close the Gap," first published in December 1969) but has been further subdivided in itself; which is to say, has become ever more atomized as the forms of pop fiction have become ever more various and parochial. When God dies, the Death-of-God theologians have been discovering recently, the gods are reborn—monotheism being replaced not with atheism but polytheism. Similarly, when the novel dies, it leaves behind not a vacuum but a proliferating swarm of competing subgenres, each clamoring for recognition.

The fact was publicly and officially acknowledged by the Association of American Publishers, which in a document dated August 6, 1979, announced that henceforth it proposed to give, instead of a single award for fiction, separate prizes for best "Children's Book," "Science Fiction," "Mystery," "Western," and "First Novel." Greeted, however, by howls of execration from elitist writers and critics, along with some who merely aspired to that status, they backed down—giving science fiction, for instance, back to the hard-core fans. But they have insisted on maintaining a new way of judging the candidates for what used to be called the National Book Award, lest more traditional (and popular) fiction be passed over entirely in favor of postmodernist fiction, as it had been not long before when a panel of highbrow judges (including ambivalent me) had given the award to John Barth's *Chimera*. Not only had that "experimental" novel proved—despite the consequent publicity—commercially unviable, but read properly, it suggested what publishers are understandably reluctant to confess: that in all of its forms the novel may be approaching death.

The Association of American Publishers does not propose, of course, to rig things so that what they themselves consider unredeemable schlock will be chosen in the years ahead, *Love's Savage Embrace,* say, or *Passion's Fury* or *The Burning Dawn.* Indeed, though these are perhaps the most salable of all books, crowding everything else off the racks in the supermarkets, the association did not even include in its list of proposed new fictional subcategories the women's romance, of which they are examples. It is rather the kind of novel which I once called "middlebrow," and for which I have found no satisfactory new name, that they would prefer to see given the award: the work of "serious," undisturbingly respectable authors, who remain as unaware as they that traditional narrative fiction is obsolete.

This category includes much that is fashionable these days for reasons more ethical and political than aesthetic: feminist novels, black novels, Jewish-American novels, all of which tend to be old-fashioned in form, autobiographical, mimetic, philosophical and technically unadventurous. For that very reason, such novels have been preferred by the notoriously conservative Pulitzer Committee, and even the Nobel Prize judges, when they have sought to honor American literature, have typically selected works of "social realism," by authors like Sinclair Lewis, Pearl Buck and John Steinbeck, scorned by elitist critics. Other, later American Nobel laureates, like Faulkner and to a lesser degree Hemingway, have seemed "modernist" and "experimental" enough to escape their scorn, but not so the two latest: the Jewish-American Saul Bellow and the American-Jewish Isaac Bashevis Singer.

Such critics have been especially hard on Bellow, whom they consider a belated nineteenth-century writer, a lesser, latter-day Dostoievski, who after learning much from the early modernists has ended by publicly disavowing their "negativism" and "alienation." Nor is he redeemed, like Steinbeck or Buck, by "progressive" social ideas. Indeed, identifying himself with the tradition of Western "civility" and scared by the "barbarism" of the sixties, he has become a spokesman for the New Right, vilifying the young, blacks and insubordinate women.

Ironically, however, he is at the moment by all odds the

favorite contemporary American novelist throughout most of the rest of the world. Not only is he read in Europe, South America, Asia and Africa by younger readers, to whom their own countries' fiction seems dull and irrelevant, where it exists at all, but he has become the favorite subject for Ph.D. dissertations wherever the prejudice about dealing with living authors has gone down before the spread of mass higher education. There are scores of such theses being written in Germany, for instance, and hundreds, it sometimes seems, in Japan and India. The few Americans, however, who undertake similar projects are likely to be dull plodders, at odds with those of their "postmodernist" contemporaries who dream of becoming imaginative writers themselves. Not that Bellow pleases the old-line authors of best sellers either, the Harold Robbinses and Judith Krantzes, who though they may be even richer than he (no movie, as far as I know, has ever been made from any of his books) wish they were as highly esteemed by the prize committees.

Bellow falls between the two extremes, and perhaps for this reason is particularly admired in developing countries, aspiring to make it culturally as well as economically in the post-industrial world, and eager therefore to import—along with our other mass-produced artifacts, from TV series to nuclear power plants—*all* forms of narrative fiction which have survived in the United States: not just the "experimental" novel and the best seller but, especially, the classic bourgeois novel, which they have not yet heard, or cannot afford to believe, is dead.

W HAT HAPPENED TO POETRY?

We have exported no comparable living "middlebrow" American poet, because there is none, the last contender for that title having been Robert Frost, whose most important work was done well before World War II. He was in fact the first poet whose work was ever distributed to its mass readership by the Book-of-the-Month Club, the only others having been Rod McKuen and Erica Jong. But McKuen is (in this case justly, I think) utterly despised by the guardians of High Culture, and Jong was dismissed out of hand as having been chosen only because just a little while before she had produced a best-selling "pornographic" novel. Even Frost, despite his undeniable merits and his early recognition by such gurus of modernism as Ezra Pound, was regarded with suspicion both for his conventional verse forms and for the very fact of his "popularity."

Yet no matter how "popular" Frost may once have been, he survives now chiefly in school anthologies. Indeed, in the United States there is at the moment no really large audience for *any* recent poet. To be sure, inside the university, it sometimes seems as if everyone is *writing* poetry, yet no one appears to be reading it—except, of course, on assignment. Outside of academia, the situation is even worse, since scarcely anybody will confess to being interested in poetry at all. Yet those, young and old, who claim that "poems" play no part in their lives are likely even as they say so to be listening to Muzak or a car radio or (in the case of real fans) a portable one clapped to their ear as they walk down the street.

They are, however, quite unaware that the lyrics, the words to the songs to which they listen (and sometimes sing), are themselves "poetry": a word which they associate only with bad experiences in classes in "English." That originally *all* poems were sung and that in periods when poetry throve best (in Elizabethan England, for instance, or nineteenth-century America) there was no difference between verse intended as lyrics and that destined to be printed, they have no way of knowing. If there is such a difference now, this is only because in recent years an unfortunate distinction has been made in the realm of song, as in that of story, between high and low. In the former case, moreover, the situation has been exacerbated by the fact that almost all poetry available to the majority audience is set to music and therefore typically not read, but heard on records, tapes and radios, or at concerts in which the words take second place to the (immensely magnified) instrumental sound and the body language of the live performers.

Meanwhile, the poetry considered appropriate for the minority audience is just as typically printed for classroom use, and if listened to at all, listened to at poetry readings, often organized after school hours under academic auspices. The audience which gathers on such occasions is likely to consist largely of students, many of whom have attended because they have been required to do so by their teachers. In the fifties, such readings were typically held in the seedy Bohemias on the outskirts of college campuses. Even when they moved onto the campus proper in the late sixties, they most often occurred under student sponsorship in fieldhouses or gymnasiums, or out in the open in the midst of "smoke-ins" or demonstrations against the war in Vietnam.

But such occasions, too, have been assimilated to the institution which subsidizes them; so that at present even the returning laureates of the defunct cultural revolution, an aging Gary Snyder, say, or a grizzled Allen Ginsberg, their work initially acceptable only because of what Herbert Marcuse called the "repressive tolerance" of the new academics, are now presumed to have met the "standards"

from which only extracurricular sung verse is—like extracurricular film narrative—exempted. But this is fair enough
insofar as their verse has all along conformed to the norms
of "modernism," established for "serious" English and
American readers at the moment when T. S. Eliot's "The
Love Song of J. Alfred Prufrock" (which is not, in any traditional sense, a song at all) appeared almost simultaneously with Irving Berlin's "Alexander's Ragtime Band."

Whether Irving Berlin was ever aware of T. S. Eliot, I
have no way of knowing, but I do know that Eliot was
aware of him and his ilk, parodying what he took to be their
betrayal of true poetry in verses which appear in *The Waste
Land:* "O O O O that Shakespeherian Rag— / It's so elegant
/ So intelligent." From biographical sources, I learn that
Eliot admired the music-hall singer Marie Lloyd, and that
he kept an autographed picture of Groucho Marx on his
office wall. But all this smacks to me of "camp" and condescension, suggesting that he only liked pop culture when
it "knew its place" (like the Irish, the Jews or other lesser
breeds), not when it competed with its betters, like Shakespeare—and Eliot. At any rate, ever since "Prufrock" we
have endured what seems to me an ultimately unendurable
split in poetic taste.

Even the few of us who have learned painfully in our
unnaturally extended schooling to prize minority verse
have never quite unlearned our initial addiction to majority
poetry, which continues to assail us everywhere: not just in
the lyrics we ourselves sing or dance to or listen to willy-
nilly, but in the pornographic parodies of those lyrics transmitted orally from generation to generation, the graffiti
inscribed in public toilets, children's game chants and
greeting-card verses. The norms of such poetry are, moreover, no matter how irreverent their themes, quite similar
to those of the sentimental verses we are most likely to have
got "by heart" from earliest childhood, and which therefore
ring still in our heads between sleeping and waking.

They range from the anonymous Mother Goose rhymes
no one ever quite forgets ("Hark! Hark! The dogs do bark,
/ The beggars are coming to town") to those earliest of
American poems which are part of our common heritage
whatever our level of education: some recited ritually at
festivals ("And laying a finger aside of his nose, / And giving a nod, up the chimney he rose"), and some sung around

the piano by family and friends, who may never have heard the names of Emma Hart Willard or Samuel Woodworth but can manage a stanza or two of "Rocked in The Cradle of the Deep" and "The Old Oaken Bucket." The names of other authors of majority verse are remembered still, if only in the nursery, like Henry Wadsworth Longfellow, James Russell Lowell and Eugene Field, whose "Wynken, Blynken and Nod" I can still recall, and whose "Little Boy Blue," I am shameless enough at this point to confess, even now moves me to tears ("The little toy dog is covered with dust, / But sturdy and staunch he stands"), though once, in the first flush of elitist pride, I used to read it to my freshman classes as an example of everything that poetry should *not* be.

So also when drunk enough I find myself reciting Rudyard Kipling's "Gunga Din" and Robert Service's "The Shooting of Dan McGrew," as I used to do to the applause of my admiring family when I was ten years old. To be sure, Service was considered from the start hopelessly "pop" by those in the know, while Kipling was always a borderline case. But others, like Longfellow and Lowell, whose pictures, bearded and austere, still hung on the walls of my own English classrooms, were once regarded as the "gray eminences" of that Anglo-Saxon Brahmin culture to which we little Jew boys were being taught to aspire.

Longfellow is a spectacular case in point, since as long as poetry on the page and the lyrics of popular songs were "poetry" in the same sense, he was equally loved by the mass audience and the guardians of critical standards. And why should they not have honored him, after all? He had studied at the best universities of Europe, whose culture he then transmitted to the children of our ruling classes as the first professor of modern literature at Harvard, the oldest and most distinguished of American colleges. Nor did it detract from his reputation that his poems were available to the common reader (when he was invited to the court of Queen Victoria, before bowing to the throne he was obliged to sign autographs for fans in the servants' quarters of the royal household).

Readers from all walks of life (of whom there were more and more as the ideal of universal education became reality), though some of them knew almost no other poetry, could recite his "The Children's Hour," "The Village Blacksmith," "The Wreck of the Hesperus" or "A Psalm of Life." I can myself recollect, for instance, being waked early in the morning by the sound of my children's not-very-literate great-grandfather tunelessly singing, as he went about his household chores, "Life is real! Life is earnest! / And the grave is not its goal." Moreover, even in my high school days, we all knew his work well enough to be amused by a parody of his "Hiawatha," an American "epic," which appeared in 1855 and became immediately a smash hit.

In that same year, Walt Whitman's *Leaves of Grass*, a long poem with similar epic intentions, was published and read by almost no one; indeed, even in the early 1930s only the most advanced of my fellow students were really familiar with that bulky, intricate work—and we were not quite certain whether or not we were supposed to admire it. What we did know and despise was "O Captain! My Captain!" which we had encountered in classroom anthologies, where it was included (we were sophisticated enough to be aware) precisely because of its uncharacteristic subject, patriotic and sentimental, plus its conventional meter and rhyme. Though this single attempt of Whitman at regular stanzaic form was halting and inept, the mere effort had sufficed to win for the poem the undying affection of the popular audience—which, by the same token, continues to ignore everything else written by Whitman in the free forms he, ironically, believed more appropriate to a mass society.

But the majority audience has, in these post-modernist times, also come to ignore the poetry of Longfellow, which they once loved. To be sure, his name in a weary joke or two ("The man sat in the balcony / His feet were in the orchestra." Longfellow) was told to each other, until quite recently at least, by kids who still knew the parody of "The Wreck of the Hesperus" ("The boy stood on the burning deck. / His feet were full of blisters. / He tore his pants on a rusty nail, / And now he wears his sister's"), but had forgotten the original.

Indeed, of all the nineteenth-century poets who were formerly able to hold together the majority and minority audiences, none survives in the memories of ordinary readers, except perhaps for Edgar Allan Poe, who lives on chiefly in a few lines of "Annabel Lee," "The Raven" and that tedious virtuoso piece, "The Bells," which for reasons elite critics have never been able to explain appeal to children as no other verse encountered in the classroom seems to do. Nor does the critical establishment deplore this disappearance from majority culture of once popular versifiers, since in the first flush of modernist exclusivism they relegated to the dustbin of history, along with unpretentious versifiers like Eugene Field, James Whitcomb Riley, Will Carleton and Ella Wheeler Wilcox, such erstwhile canonical writers as Longfellow, Lowell and Whittier.

In fact, the only American poet who wrote between the War of 1812 and the Spanish-American War whom they have wholeheartedly endorsed, making her a staple of the English curriculum, like the "anti-popular" novelists of the American Renaissance, is Emily Dickinson, since she possessed, among other virtues, that of having been almost entirely unknown in her own time. They have tended, indeed, to pass over the whole of our native poetic tradition in embarrassed silence, dealing instead, in such standard "New Criticism" texts as Cleanth Brooks' *The Well-Wrought Urn*, with British writers, more amenable to their "standards," from John Donne to Gerard Manley Hopkins. Influenced by them (though I would then have hesitated to admit it), I wrote my first long "scholarly" paper on Hopkins, and my Ph.D. dissertation on "The Medieval Backgrounds of John Donne's 'Songs and Sonnets.'"

It was not, however, until 1955, some fifteen years after I had begun teaching literature, that I dared deal with my own ambivalent relationship to Whitman, in an essay in which I attempted to deliver myself from the elitist attitudes toward him which had been brainwashed into me. True enough, such a leading spokesman for modernism as Ezra Pound had, after initially defining himself *against* Whitman, finally come to terms with him, declaring in a moving little poem, "I make a pact with you, Walt Whitman— / I have detested you long enough . . . / I am old enough to make friends." But T. S. Eliot, in his introduction to a volume of Pound's *Selected Poems*, was moved to comment, after confessing his own aversion to Whitman's "form, as well as much of his manner," that "I am equally certain—it is indeed obvious—that Pound owes nothing to Whitman."

Consequently, most of the later "New Critics," following Eliot's lead, have rejected Whitman as a model for "New Poetry." Yvor Winters, for example, spoke of "the impossibility of getting anywhere with the Whitmanian inspiration"; while R. P. Blackmur concluded a comparison of his influence and Baudelaire's by insisting that "the influence of Whitman was an impediment to the *practice . . .* of poetry." And finally William Van O'Connor declared that not just Whitman but all his followers (he was thinking chiefly of Carl Sandburg) were "away from the tradition which runs from Hawthorne and Melville through James and Eliot," which is to say, are outside the revised new canon, American-style.

Nor did modernist critics do much better with Poe. Henry James had set the tone of elitist condescension very early, by observing that "an enthusiasm for Poe is the mark of a decidedly primitive state of reflection," apparently untroubled by the fact that Baudelaire had been moved by precisely such "enthusiasm" to devote years of his life to translating and touting the American poet whom he described as *"un Byron égaré dans le nouveau monde."* But Eliot, who admired Baudelaire greatly, *was* troubled—reminding his readers that not only he, but other eminent French authors whom he thought of as his literary ancestors, like Mallarmé and Paul Valéry, also considered Poe the great American poet.

In an oddly cagey essay written in 1948, late in his own career, Eliot tried, in light of the undeniable influence of Poe on the development of French *symbolisme,* to give him his due. But try as he would, he ended by condescending to him throughout, speaking, for instance, of Poe's "slipshod writing" and his "puerile thinking," then suggesting of his poems in particular that they possess "perhaps more of the character of good *verse* than of poetry." He further contended that the "cultivated English or American reader" (meaning, no doubt, himself and his friends) remembers Poe for "a very few short poems which enchanted him for a time when he was a boy," but which he is unlikely to return to, finding when he does only "the memory of an enjoyment which he may for a moment recapture."

But what has annoyed the few second- and third-generation "New Critics" who have, despite their master's reservations, tried to redeem Poe for "High Literature" is Eliot's snide remark that neither Baudelaire nor Mallarmé nor Valéry "knew the English language very well" and that "it is certainly possible, in reading something in a language imperfectly understood, for the reader to find what is not there." Theirs is in any case a vain and foolish attempt, since, as the *Literary History of the United States* rather mournfully remarks, after reporting Baudelaire's high esteem for Poe, "no major American poet [which is to say, no one absolutely at home with the American language and its poetic uses] has yet affirmed his living value in such high terms." And this is indeed so, Lowell having thought him "two-fifths sheer fudge," Emerson having called him contemptuously "the jingle man," and even Whitman having described him as "brilliant and dazzling, but with no heat."

Yet, though almost universally denigrated by his poetic peers, Poe has been preferred to any or all of them by the majority audience, which, as indifferent to his declared contempt for the "mob" as they are to Whitman's avowed love for the common man, have spurned the latter and taken the former to their fickle hearts. Poe cannot be credited with having played the kind of role in establishing a new genre of pop poetry that he did in introducing into pop fiction the detective story and science fiction. But he did singlehandedly create the lowbrow equivalent of what was to become in the hands of the alienated French poets, who thought they were emulating him, *"poésie pure."*

In the realm of majority literature, however, he had no successors, except possibly (as both Eliot and W. H. Auden have observed) for Edward Lear, who more parodies than emulates him. Though there is always somehow the suggestion of hoax in Poe's work, he is, finally, as deadly serious as a child at play, writing not frankly humorous nonsense verse but a kind of higher "non-sense." His incantatory song, without in any sense tickling our risibility, blurs all meaning to indistinction, so that what themes or pseudo-themes, what narrative or pseudo-narrative, are present become at last as elusive and incoherent as a dream. But serious as he is, Poe is not quite serious enough to suit modernist or post-modernist taste, which, though it is tolerant of the most extreme incoherence (how else to explain the inflated reputation of a poet like John Ashbery, who has a talent for nothing else), insists that it be high-toned, learnedly allusive and obtrusive enough to put off the ordinary reader.

This last is perhaps the most important criterion for inclusion in the modernist canon, into which almost any poet ranging from Robert Bly, William Stafford and Allen Ginsberg to David Ignatow, Frank O'Hara and Robert Duncan will be accepted, so long as his poetry serves to *épater la bourgeoisie* by challenging their preconceptions about what is "poetic." It scarcely matters if some of those poets are members of cliques with conflicting theories of poetics, like the "Iowa school," for instance, and the "Black Mountain school." They are all represented in anthologies with titles like *The New Naked Poetry*, from which they are taught by the new academics in courses called "Creative Writing" or "Contemporary Poetry." Indeed, some of those courses are presided over by one or another of those very poets, who over the past couple of decades have been entering the academy, just as contemporary novelists have, though, it would appear, not to such an extent. But even those who do not enter the sanctuary of the university are likely to live largely on the poetry circuit, which in turn is subsidized by departments of English or associations of students, urged by their teachers to support "living poetry."

The definition of what is truly "living" has, it is true, altered slightly in recent years, as certain early modernists have been replaced as models by others: T. S. Eliot and Wallace Stevens, for example, by William Carlos Williams and Charles Olson. But Ezra Pound has from the very beginning of the institutionalization of modernism been included on the list of required readings, and in his name aspiring young poets have been taught fanatically to avoid rhyme, as well as traditional or, indeed, any clearly identifiable, easily scannable meters. "Break the iamb," their teachers cry, and though formulated before the birth of many of them, that threadbare Poundian injunction still seems to have for the young a revolutionary cachet.

In the fifties, for a little while, traditional stanzaic forms seemed to be making a comeback at the very heart of the American modernist-academic establishment— partly under the influence of W. H. Auden, a thirties British poet, who after World War II tried to turn himself into an American one. The new formalists did not, however, turn themselves into pop poets by adopting sentimentality and simplicity along with meter and rhyme, but remained as allusive, ironic and sometimes as hermetic as Eliot himself. By the end of the sixties, in any case, though a few diehards like Richard Wilbur were still producing elegantly patterned verse, most of them, including Robert Lowell, the most distinguished of all, had opted for more "open" forms. But every zig must have a zag, and another version of formalism returned a decade or so later under the banner of post-modernism. Called "concretism" or "concrete poetry," it has had, to be sure, a long prehistory in "modernism," most notably in the United States, perhaps, in the work of E. E. Cummings, or as he characteristically insisted on inscribing himself, e. e. cummings.

The patterns of such poems, unlike others in the modernist canon, distinguish themselves at first glance from prose, their unique patterns being indicated, or rather, I suppose, dictated, by typography, the relationship between print and blank space on the pages of a book or a magazine. They constitute therefore the first truly post-Gutenberg poetry, not merely reproduced, but in some sense produced, by movable type. But they represent also the first poetry to accept as given and irremediable the split between poetry for the eye and for the ear. They cannot be read aloud, and exist therefore not as recorded speech or music, but as untranslatable icons. Actually, this is the final *reductio ad absurdum* of a tendency implicit in modernist aesthetics from the beginning and classically formulated in the edict once known to every aspirant to twentieth-century High Culture that poems should be "palpable and mute"—like Oriental calligraphy or a well-wrought Grecian urn.

But the metaphor "concrete" betrays openly what the aesthetes had all the time been covertly meaning: hostility to song and submission to technology. After all, the fixed Gutenberg icon is at the furthest possible remove from any association with dance, or loving subservience to the exigencies of a tune which exists outside of and before meaning, whether that tune is actually heard or only implied. Such flight from song is, however, only one restrictive aspect of modernist poetry, though as fundamental to it as the flight from story is to modernist prose narrative. What was also essential to the "New Poetry" from the start, and will remain so as long as the modernist tradition survives, is the avoidance of excessive feeling, the substitution of irony for sentimentality and pathos. But most essential of all, perhaps, is the fear of banality.

"Make it new!" Ezra Pound enjoined his fellows long

ago. But even as he said it, that revolutionary injunction was in the process of becoming an iron restriction: a key slogan of what the eminent French critic Jean Paulhan has called "la Terreur" in a classic monitory study of modernism entitled *Les Fleurs de Tarbes*. His title, *The Flowers of Tarbes,* refers to a garden in a small city of Provence, on whose gates he had discovered a sign reading: IT IS FORBIDDEN TO ENTER THE GARDEN BEARING FLOWERS. This Paulhan equates with the modernist ban against bringing into new poems lovely commonplaces, long-honored phrases, language blessed by association with earlier poems, everything traditionally known as "poesy": IT IS FORBIDDEN TO ENTER THE GARDEN OF POETRY BEARING THE FLOWERS OF POESY. The use of the phrase "the Terror," ·evoking the French Revolution at the point when its original liberating impulses had begun to turn repressive, seems apt enough under the circumstances, for the Jacobins of modernism, precisely like their political forebears, have enjoined for all time, with that special sort of self-righteous rigor possible only to one-time advocates of freedom, any return to a past antecedent to their own, thus foreclosing the future.

It seems to me, however, high time for that future to begin, since modernism in poetry has reached a dead end and the attempts of the so-called post-modernists to escape its limitations are doomed to failure so long as they continue to pursue originality, require irony in the place of pathos and forbid song in the name of "free verse," "breath rhythms" or visual patterning on the printed page. For a while in the heyday of the sixties, it seemed as if the irreverent youth audience that was imposing its taste on their scarcely older and considerably less secure instructors in "literature" might succeed in closing the gap between poetry written for print and that intended to be sung.

I even dared hope that they might rescue from the obscurity to which he was condemned by academics contemptuous of popular song the only nineteenth-century American "poet" (but I, long brainwashed, find it difficult to use that word for him) whose verses are known to a broader segment of the majority audience than even Edgar Allan Poe's. I mean, of course, Stephen Collins Foster, who —like Harriet Beecher Stowe and Mark Twain in the area of prose—tried to redeem the poetic diction of his time by teaching it to speak the language of the Negro slave, but who died, heartbroken and bankrupt, only twenty-three cents in his pocket and a scrap of paper inscribed with what seems the salutation of an otherwise unwritten letter to the world (or was it only another song title?), "Dear friends and gentle hearts . . ."

It is a tragic ending worthy of being remembered by the historians of our literature side by side with the similar deaths of Poe and Scott Fitzgerald. But it has not been so remembered, of course; nor have "serious" critics come to take seriously the greatest of our pop laureates who composed not for the reader's eye but the singer's voice. By the same token, they have continued to disregard those poets of our recent past who, though they did not make lyrics for songs, wrote for the printed page poetry governed by the same criteria and appealing to the same taste. Not only has the reputation of that truly passionate and daring spokesman for the *eros* of women, Ella Wheeler Wilcox, remained unredeemed, but even Henry Wadsworth Longfellow himself continues to be neglected, though (wrong again!) I wrote hopefully in 1970, in an essay called "The Return of the Vanishing Longfellow," "We are living . . . in the Children's Hour come round once more, and who can more appropriately be resurrected to serve as its laureate than the author who presided over a similar era more than a century ago?"

Over a decade later, however, it has become clear to me that the taste of the leaders of that latter-day Children's Crusade was too chic and erratic to be effective. Moreover, their interest in any poetry except the lyrics of rock music or soul or revived folk was too weak to make a real difference. I myself could not care less whether certain of their favorite printed poems ever make it into the canon or not: the ersatz mystical maunderings of Kahlil Gibran, for instance; or the rather wooden and unreconstructedly Victorian "songs" scattered throughout the *Rings* trilogy of J. R. R. Tolkien; or the vapid rhapsodies of Rod McKuen. Some of what has made it, though, I do indeed admire, including the work of platform performers like Allen Ginsberg and Gary Snyder, who have proved easily assimilable into the modernist mainstream, as well as the lyrics of more literate songwriters like John Lennon and Bob Dylan (who rebaptized himself, after all, with the name of an academic favorite of his time, Dylan Thomas).

Nonetheless, I recognize that including a handful of their lyrics in recent classroom anthologies or writing analyses of them in scholarly jargon has served less to open up the canon than to "co-opt" them to the academy. In any case, none of this has helped redeem the pop of earlier times, so that those of us who still enjoy undying sentimental chestnuts like "Gunga Din," "The Face on the Barroom Floor," "Little Boy Blue" or "The Children's Hour" must continue to do so in the closet. Nor is established criticism of much use to us even in understanding, much less resolving, our plight: the intolerable tension between what we like and what we are told we should, what we listen to of our own free will and what we read largely on assignment.

In terms of the "standards" of the critics, all song (especially if it appears in print), like all story, is still classified as "junk" or "mere entertainment" if it opts for sentimentality rather than irony, the literal rather than the symbolic, the commonplace rather than the recherché. On the level of style and structure, prose narrative must not just reject the conventional happy ending and the Maupassant–O. Henry "hook," but all undue emphasis on plot and character. Similarly, poetry must eschew end rhyme, regular meter and stanzaic form. In the end, the institutionalized elite taste of the late twentieth century regards as substandard almost everything which naïve and uninstructed readers are likely to recognize as a "story" or a "poem." But this means in effect the exclusion of anything which the children of such readers can comprehend, even after they have entered college, without the aid of a qualified teacher.

W HY WAS CRITICISM?

It should be clear, therefore, that whatever the *origins* of the definition of literature that determines the English curriculum, one of its functions is to guarantee to Ph.D's. opportunities for the display of exegetical skill. It is not entirely a one-way transaction, however, since what provides ego satisfaction to certain professors simultaneously affords a chosen minority of students—hard-core English majors and fellow travelers—the sense of being initiated into a self-made, self-perpetuating aristocracy of taste. For such teachers and students, literature is totally identified with the "texts," the "words on the page" they scrutinize together. They have consequently little difficulty in believing either that "the medium is the message" or that print is the ultimate medium. Any work, therefore, that calls this article of faith into question by proving translatable into post-Gutenberg forms without loss of effect and authenticity challenges their *raison d'être.* This is why they find themselves at the moment defending High Culture against the "media," meaning, simply, all ways of transmitting song and story more generally accessible than print.

But this was not the enemy against whom we were contending when we entered university departments of English. It was against our genteel predecessors and their obsolete notions of what constituted literary excellence that we sought to defend the modernist works we loved and a definition of "literature" which justified our taste. Though we are still defending that definition, qualified a little in light of certain post-modernist developments, we find ourselves battling not our old academic opponents but the mass audience, which reads best sellers and science fiction, or more often watches sitcoms, cop shows and soap operas on television—as a good many of us do, too.

I saw an article recently quoting an unreconstructed highbrow who boasted that she had never even opened a "best seller" and knew no one who had. But that is not a boast I can make, and I suspect that a large number of my academic colleagues, plus most of my students—sometimes openly, sometimes secretly—break their strict diet of required belles lettres in order to satisfy the hunger for irresponsible fantasy, concupiscence, tears and laughter which are released by popular fiction and verse. Yet we do not ordinarily face up to our hypocrisy in this regard; much less do we understand *how* we have been persuaded to accept a definition of literature which we are driven helplessly to betray.

Universal schooling, I think, lies at the root of it all. Originally fought for as a right, it has long since become required by the state, because it trains students in skills necessary to our economy and inculcates the values which sustain it. In the immigrant society of the United States, this has involved the homogenization of diverse peoples; and, of all courses in the curriculum, English has proved the most useful for the instant bourgeois WASPification of all new Americans, whatever their class or ethnic origin. In the primers of the early twentieth century, children of the foreign-born were taught, along with reading and writing, to change their underwear frequently and sleep with the windows open, to honor their mothers and fathers, respect the police, work hard and save their money.

Even now their children and children's children are presented with similar norms embodied in those insufferably pink-and-white, well-adjusted little WASPlets called Dick and Jane. At least they were still so called when my own sons and daughters were in the first and second grades, and I have no doubt that though the names and pristine suburban settings may have been changed, just such spotless smiling kids, plus their dog, cat and eternally adolescent parents ("OH, SEE FATHER RUN! FUNNY FUNNY FA-

THER!"), continue to stir envy and emulation in children like me, who had neither dog nor cat, only Yiddish-speaking grandparents and a father who never joined me at playing baseball.

Such behavior modification is continued in English classes up through grade eight and on into high school, where for many years—at the suggestion of certain old-line Anglophile professors—American teenagers were required to slog their way through pre-modernist masterpieces, presumably suited to their age: Scott's genteelly racist Tory romance, *Ivanhoe*, for instance, and George Eliot's heavy-handed Victorian morality, *Silas Marner*. Nor does this process cease in English grade thirteen, which even when "required" seems somehow not quite so oppressive in a college setting, where at least guards do not prowl the halls, exit doors are not locked to prevent truancy, and it has been given the new names "Freshman Composition" or "Rhetoric I." For a while in the late sixties, such courses were on many campuses abolished, made optional or turned into opportunities for free expression, self-examination and amateur therapy. But ten years later, the cry "Back to Basics" went up, and in response "research papers" returned in place of journal jottings or group-gropes; so that, even though certain superficial changes in manners have persisted (freshman teachers continue to sleep with their freshman students, and both to smoke pot), in all essential respects the *status quo ante bellum* has been restored.

Once more, that is to say, freshman comp has been openly revealed as what it has never ceased to be covertly: a last desperate attempt to brainwash us out of our demotic linguistic codes of home, street and schoolyard, and at the same time to make us ashamed of the demotic literary culture we have acquired outside the classroom.

In freshman courses in composition, the grounds for that rejection can be made clear, as, presumably, they have never been in high school, where most teachers of English are incapable of distinguishing between High Literature and low. *Here or nowhere,* beginning teachers of composition tend to think; *now or never,* we must teach these majors in nursing, engineering or business administration that popular culture affects us differently from High Culture, drugging rather than stimulating the mind, enslaving rather than liberating the spirit. And when our students resist

what seems to us so apparent, we are likely to blame not
the doctrine we espouse, but the philistine society which
rejects it.

I myself first taught comp as a T.A. some forty years ago,
and for fifteen or twenty years such courses constituted a
major part of my load. Yet I can remember dreaming all that
while that someday I would get to teach *real* courses in *real*
literature, as rigorous and difficult as those I had grimly
endured on my way to a Ph.D. I suspect that even now
young teachers of required comp keep telling themselves
that once they have come to preside over upperclassmen
and graduates they will no longer have to play the degrad-
ing role of thought police enforcing "standards" but will be
able instead, like kindly commissars, "patiently to explain," and thus convince mature men and women to accept freely the notion that political democracy does not
necessarily entail cultural leveling.

That dream is not altogether delusory. After a while, we
preach to students convinced, like us, that all literature is
divided into what panders to the ignorant many and what
appeals to the learned few. Yet the overburdened taxpayers
and generous alumni who make possible those classes and
sustain those libraries have utterly different assumptions
about the nature of literature. Why, then, do they continue
to subsidize not just the critical establishment but those
works which it calls High Art? Is it sheer hypocrisy—the
tribute vice pays to virtue? Or does it reflect a need on the
part of the majority to believe that what they read by preference is in some sense taboo?

To be sure, as we have already observed, the majority
who foot the bill seek on occasion to impose their will on
the minority who teach their children, trying to ban in their
zeal some works which the latter would agree are "trash,"
but others which they consider admirable High Art, like
The Tropic of Cancer, for example, or *Lady Chatterley's
Lover*. At such moments, the minority assume the stance of
defenders of freedom, though in fact they seek to impose
an equal and opposite tyranny—by, for instance, giving low
grades to or withholding degrees from students who refuse
to accept their standards of literary excellence.

Small wonder, then, if the parents of those students are
aggrieved, since the enforcers of such standards are to be
found in the multipurpose state universities, subsidized by

all taxpayers, as well as in private colleges, sustained by tuition and endowments from those who have themselves chosen to attend or to enroll their children in them. The former institutions are, moreover, typically dedicated to the egalitarian "land-grant philosophy": not merely admitting to their classes indifferently endowed applicants, once considered "unteachable," but offering courses once considered even in the United States (and still deemed in many European universities) unworthy of inclusion in the curriculum, like wood-gluing, instrument repair or, for that matter, "creative writing."

How, then, has the hierarchal view of literature survived in such schools, themselves a product of the mass culture which elitists deplore? It is partly because the process of accrediting teachers of literature assures that few if any potential dissenters from such standards will make it into the professorate. But the kind of people attracted to the profession in the first place by and large need no brainwashing on this score. Even the Marxists, who have achieved a token representation these days in almost every large department of literature despite their communitarian politics, subscribe to elitism in the arts.

This is revealed by the fact that their anti-textbook of academic dissent, *The Politics of Literature* (edited by Kampf and Lauter), when it appeared at the height of the "revolutionary" sixties, though it bravely attacked the "New Criticism" (already moribund at that point) and had a kind word or two to say for surviving folk art, made no defense of the post-Gutenberg culture preferred by the majority audience. Latter-day Marxists, largely urban types, have a sentimental pseudo-nostalgia for, say, country music —particularly when it can be adapted to their current political line, like the songs of Woody Guthrie. But they have no sympathy for what workers and their families actually watch on television.

This should surprise no one in light of the fact that Karl Marx himself devoted much of his first book, *The Holy Family,* to an attack on the idol of mid-nineteenth-century working-class readers, Eugène Sue. It was surely Sue's sensationalism which offended the genteel academic Marx, but even more, the spectacular marketplace success of *The Wandering Jew* and *The Mysteries of Paris.* Such success, Marx felt, could only be explained on the grounds of manipulation of popular taste by the interests who profited from its sale: "the masters of the media," as they have come since to be called. And his paranoid "conspiracy" theory has continued to haunt left-wing academics ever since, most especially, perhaps, Herbert Marcuse and the members of the Frankfurt school.

According to this theory, the "masters of the media" offer us in place of what "we" (whoever "we" may be) really want what "they" want us to want, think is good for us; which turns out to be horror, porn, trivializations of reality, soporific dreams, which otherwise we would theroretically spurn. But this is, it seems to me, palpably untrue. The boards of directors that control publishing and broadcasting, along with the international cartels that control them, detest and fear as much as any puritanical Marxist the horror and porn which are the staples of pop literature. I myself once was the target of intended censorship, after I had published in *Esquire* a story called "Nude Croquet," and I found it instructive that the campaign was initiated by certain officials of the Du Pont Company, who actually withdrew twelve or fourteen pages of advertising by way of protest.

Ordinarily, however, what those who pay for such advertising seek to provide is what they surmise the mass audience wants, even if it offends their own sensibilities. It turns out, however (think of the astonishing number of TV shows in which large sums of money have been invested that bomb each season), that they are more often wrong than right in their guesses. Far from manipulating mass taste, its so-called masters breathlessly pursue it, cutting each other's throats, risking bankruptcy to find images which the great audience will recognize as dreams they have already dreamed, or would if they could. No wonder they think of themselves as riding a tiger, as do the commissars of culture in societies where socialism has triumphed. What items of popular culture they have sought to ban, in the name of "progress" rather than profit—from jeans to rock-and-roll records—are traded in secret, the black market having replaced the free market as the dream machine of the masses.

Some less orthodox American radicals have been more perspicacious, Daniel De Leon, for instance, founder of the Socialist Labor Party, having translated Sue's *Mysteries of the People* for the edification and delight of his followers. But at the heart even of our native populist tradition there has lurked a yearning for High Culture and a corresponding contempt for mass culture. V. L. Parrington, for instance, most distinguished of its spokesmen, considered James Branch Cabell's high-tone pornographic fantasy *Jurgen* "real art" in a sense that Harriet Beecher Stowe's *Uncle Tom's Cabin* was not. Her best-selling book has proved, indeed, a stumbling block for all self-proclaimed "friends of the people," both revolutionary blacks and radical feminists having found it despicable.

Nor did the campus activists of the sixties, the avant-garde of the self-styled "youth revolution," do much better. To them the reform of the university, which, ironically enough, had provided them with a refuge from the draft, meant primarily its deliverance from the control of the "military-industrial complex." They were, in any event, less interested in literature than in pop music and movies, though they did press for opening up the English curriculum to certain novels which they had made "best sellers." They had surely ceased to read, as Marshall McLuhan asserted. I never saw, for instance, even in the sixties, an agricultural commune which did not possess a slim collection of highly prized volumes, which, however, should not be thought of as constituting in any traditional sense a "library." In their function and use, they were more like the household books of some pious seventeenth-century New England Puritan than the "great books" stacked on nineteenth-century study shelves or the latest selections from the book clubs piled on twentieth-century parlor tables.

In place of the Puritan's Bible, however, and Milton's *Paradise Lost* and John Bunyan's *Pilgrim's Progress,* one was likely to find a motley (but at last somehow standard) selection including some of the following: *The Tibetan Book of the Dead, The Whole Earth Catalog* and the *I Ching,* along with all three well-worn volumes of Tolkien's *Rings* trilogy, a macrobiotic cookbook, Kurt Vonnegut's *Cat's Cradle* or *Slaughterhouse-Five,* Castaneda's *The Teachings of Don Juan,* a couple of Hermann Hesse novels, and a complete file of the latest Stan Lee comic books. Plus, as I have almost forgotten, some pornography: a "head comic" by R. Crumm, or a more grossly masochistic one by S. Clay Wilson, or, perhaps, the *Kama Sutra.* The point is not merely that the scriptures of various alien cultures were given equal status with the Holy Book of Christianity, but that *any books which were read at all were read as a kind of scripture,* which is to say, not for information or "cultural enrichment," much less to pass an idle hour, but as guides to salvation.

It did not matter to such readers what the author of any particular text they adopted thought he was writing. He may have believed, like Robert Heinlein, for instance, with his *A Stranger in a Strange Land,* that he had written an easy entertainment to make a quick buck. But he could not stay the process which kidnaped his work for "sacred" ends, extracting from it a new "holy" verb ("to grock") and supplying the initial inspiration, as well as a passage or two, for Charlie Manson's syncretic black ritual. Furthermore, it is neither accidental nor irrelevant that *A Stranger in a Strange Land* comes from the world of joyous junk rather than that of solemn art, for the new "religious" who found his work "holy" were in quest of a pop religion. Not just pop fiction, but pop science as well, was raided in the endless search for pop scripture, since the distinction between literature and science, fiction and nonfiction, was meaningless to those young readers—as was the distinction between fact and fantasy, real and counterfeit.

Like all the believers, they cried defiantly, "I believe because it is absurd," thus scandalizing all who trust in reason, especially their own parents, who kept trying in vain to deliver them from "delusion" to "truth." But no "debriefer," no matter how impressive his academic credentials or skills at behavior modification, has found it easy to de-convert, say, a true believer in the palpable hoax of Scientology: the creation of L. Ron Hubbard, who was a hack writer of science fiction before he decided to peddle his fantasies as fact—thus becoming as rich as any robber baron or Park Avenue shrink. In an age of underground pop faiths, the underground faithful rejoice in leaders called "charlatans" and "liars."

But it is not charlatanism alone which produces scriptures, as is attested by the long-lived vogue of *The Whole Earth Catalog,* a product of the believers themselves rather than of those who exploit them. However secular in tone, it too became the bible for a sect dedicated to a cult of pop technology, as defined by that odd blend of technocrat, guru and nut inventor, R. Buckminster Fuller. His doctrine was oddly transformed by being translated from the urban centers he loved to the New Mexico countryside preferred by younger men and women, less sure perhaps than he that technology can solve *all* the problems it has created by becoming supertechnology. It is indeed a kind of *sub*-technology which the editors of *The Whole Earth Catalog* finally proposed: minimal technology, a technology of do-it-yourself. But they share Fuller's fundamental faith, the religion of gadgetry, and in 1972 their technocrat's bible was given, scandalizing some and gratifying others, a National Book Award.

The judges who bestowed that prize were attempting to certify as "literature" a collection of ads for goods considered kosher in a time of conspicuous underconsumption. But *The Whole Earth Catalog* had already made its way onto the shelves of readers who would never use any of the products it advertised—having no desire to build geodesic domes or erect prefabricated Indian tepees, but merely to read or own a holy text. How different has been the fate of the Sears Roebuck catalog, its prototype and predecessor, only esteemed and preserved when it grew obsolescent enough to seem proper "camp." The latter evoked no "holy" names like that of Buckminster Fuller, no "sacred" theory like his. But this is not the real point. In the declining twentieth century, what is chiefly prized is whatever is most debased, most utterly vulgarized, so long as it can be used for presumed sacred ends: turning on, returning to nature, dropping out, avoiding pollution of the environment, ripping off the establishment.

It has, in fact, always been true in the case of American pop religions, like Christian Science and Mormonism, that the low literary value of new scriptures has been taken as a warrant of their authenticity. And here precisely is where the reading of literature as scripture, as practiced by the children of the sixties, differed totally from the elitist "culture religion," whose apostle was Matthew Arnold. For Arnold, what made some literature secular scripture, i.e., a replacement for Holy Scripture in an age of declining faith and the death of God, was its aesthetic excellence. On the other hand, what makes some literature seem scriptural in an age of the revival of faith and the rebirth of the gods is its doctrinal content; in the light of which, excellence in aesthetic or formalist terms becomes not merely irrelevant, but offensive. Once more faith has driven out before it the criterion of taste, which could only have flourished in its absence.

Oddly enough, Buckminster Fuller, along with many other aging writers whom the young of the sixties considered their gurus, cared no more for any of the novelists they loved than he did for the music or films preferred by the young. Fuller was basically indifferent to all art, while others were elitists of the old school, like Marshall McLuhan, who had begun as an acolyte of the New Criticism and whose favorite authors were always Gerard Manley Hopkins and James Joyce. So too, Norman O. Brown remained in some sense an unreconstructed classicist, dreaming of Hesiod and Ovid; and Herbert Marcuse, despite his left-wing politics, was enough of a German academic to distrust pop to the end of his days.

Nonetheless, even before some of those young activists of the sixties had turned into middle-aged faculty members, books like A Stranger in a Strange Land had begun to infiltrate the curriculum. This opening-up was partly a matter of cold-blooded hucksterism, though it also suited the needs of certain aging professors who had grown as weary of their "areas of specialization" as the students themselves. They were joined by some of their junior colleagues, not too much older than the undergraduate apostles of the counterculture, and impelled therefore by sibling rivalry to claim such underground favorites as their own. After all, they reminded their students, it was they who had fought the good fight against their academic predecessors for yesterday's youth-cult books—Proust and Mann and Joyce, Fitzgerald and Hemingway and Faulkner, Nathanael West and Henry Roth; nor were they about to surrender their place at the head of the avant-garde.

As the job situation grew ever grimmer, however, it seemed to such younger faculty less important to please a constituency which changed every four years than to win the esteem of their tenured older peers. To do so they had to play the institutional game by its own rules: begin by publishing in "reputable" journals "rigorous" essays on canonical books, then produce a "major book," formidable enough to be issued under the aegis of a distinguished university press.

Consequently, those of them who have not completely

abandoned the contemporary have shifted their attention from novelists like Robert Heinlein and Robert Pirsig and Robert Adams, who provided the largest young audiences with immediate pleasure, to others who afforded much smaller groups the mediated satisfaction of classroom exegesis. John Barth and William Gass, for instance, have made their permanent homes in the university, but even those who have visited the academy only from time to time, like Vladimir Nabokov and Donald Barthelme, or have spurned it utterly, like Thomas Pynchon, seem to write *as if for* such exegesis. All of them, therefore, gifted though they may be, end up by addressing merely themselves and their post-modernist critics, who, in turn, address only each other.

"Autotelic" is what their modernist forebears, the "New Critics," labeled such criticism. But they were aware, at least, that the craft they practiced has not always been so self-referential. When first reinvented in the West by the self-styled "Humanists," it had (Sir Philip Sidney's *Defense of Poetry* is the classic example in English) addressed itself to living writers, to whom it gave, before the fact, formulae for literary excellence and, after the fact, good or bad marks. The prescriptive/proscriptive function of criticism has, however, been largely surrendered these days to classes in freshman composition, while the evaluative one survives on all levels of instruction in English, as well as in newspaper "book reviewing." But neither function is any longer performed by "serious" criticism.

Nor is the meditational or apologetic function central to the audience-oriented school which next rose to preeminence. Such early examples of the approach as the Marquis de Sade's *Idées sur le roman* and Wordsworth's *Preface to the Lyrical Ballads* responded to the split in the growing audience, which tended to divide along class lines, as literacy spread to groups not yet inducted into the traditional culture, and along generational ones, as radically new styles in prose and verse succeeded each other with confusing rapidity. Until the first decades of this century, most major critics were still desperately trying to put Humpty Dumpty together again, by explaining to a "philistine" public what was obscure or unfamiliar in contemporary art, or defending what seemed deliberately offensive. But in the end, their efforts proved futile. Larger and larger numbers of readers not merely continued to reject novels and poems highly prized by such critics, but ignored *them* as well—until, like the authors of those neglected works, they began to consider their exclusion a testimonial to their worth.

Nonetheless, the "New Critics" and their present-day heirs did not at first completely abandon the missionary goals of their predecessors. Instead, they narrowed them down, addressing only those alienated sons and daughters of the "philistines" who sat at their feet in classes in English, and in the process the New Criticism became the New Pedagogy, eventuating in such canonical textbooks as Brooks and Warren's *Understanding Poetry*. But as modernism yielded to post-modernism and even newer formalisms emerged, the audience came to seem as irrelevant to "serious critics" as the authors. All that mattered was the "text"—or rather, as the fashionable phrase has it, the "sub-text"; despite all of which, academic criticism is no longer truly autotelic, since the critic-pedagogues who produce it are paid for doing so by a society which considers them part of the "professional" cadre that turns raw English majors into the next generation of fully credentialed critic-pedagogues, capable of training a third generation, etc., etc.

Moreover, for a long time, academic critics have published out of economic necessity; first, in order to avoid "termination," then, to rise in rank. Even after they have reached the final level of vertical ascent, continuing publication makes possible lateral movement to more prestigious schools, more salubrious climes. Any challenge to the literary status quo therefore threatens not just individual teachers but the very structure of the university, along with the assumptions about professionalism, specialization and scholarship upon which it is based.

IS THERE A COUNTER-TRADITION?

Nonetheless, mine is not the only voice in the academy speaking out against indurated elitism, as my less sympathetic colleagues hasten to remind me. Often, indeed, they simultaneously dismiss my notions as heretical nonsense *and* point out that courses are being offered everywhere dealing with formerly extra-canonical genres, ranging from science fiction (first to establish itself in the curriculum) to westerns, comic books and pornography.

Besides, more than a few younger "scholars," they insist, are earning promotion and tenure on the basis of talks given before the Popular Culture Association and articles published in the journal it sponsors. But to this I am moved to respond that not only are such courses cynically instituted in response to sagging enrollments in the humanities, but those who teach them tend to be condescended to as second-class citizens. Moreover, I continue, just as the American supermarket can accommodate gourmet delicacies or health foods without losing its homogeneous character, or commercial American television find room for occasional ballet or opera "specials" without abandoning its mission, so can the American university, without betraying its hierarchal heritage, provide courses in both High and popular literature.

When I further point out that such courses are typically segregated, pop being taught only with pop, and High Literature with other High Literature, and that, worst of all, articles produced as spin-offs from the former tend to appear in "ghetto" publications like the *Journal of Popular Culture*, they seem scarcely to understand. It is all a matter of time, they tell me; everything is changing, even the *PMLA*. When I glance at that most staid and longest established of academic journals, I find indeed that its contributors are now citing more up-to-date names than when I looked last, including Roland Barthes, Jacques Derrida and Jacques Lacan, and that many of the essays are now written in the first-person singular instead of the once sacrosanct "objective" third. Far from having learned to speak colloquially as well as autobiographically, however, the contributors have merely replaced one jargon with another, and the new names are cited in the old scholarly form—as if to remind readers that what they are reading is responsible critical discourse rather than merely "imaginative" writing.

Yet I am convinced that if criticism is ever to be delivered from its long institutional bondage, those who practice it must not only themselves remember but constantly remind others that the authority of the critic, like that of the poet and the novelist, depends on the mysterious ability to compel suspension of disbelief rather than on the "rigor" of exposition and accuracy of citation. There is no generally accepted name for that quality, but the ones that occur to me (mythopoeic power, charisma, magic, charm) all suggest that it is, in any case, more gift than acquired skill or method.

In the English departments of the mass American university, however, there are not likely to be many teachers passionately engaged with literature and capable of responding in kind to its special use of language and evocation of image. Distributed along a normal probability curve, the populations of such departments (a little skewed, to begin with, in favor of those with a high tolerance for boredom and small capacity for risk) will inevitably include a majority who have to *fake* an effective response to song and story, or pretend in self-defense that such a response is inappropriate. Compelled by their jobs to confront daily the madness and terror implicit in literature, they need—like doctors, who seek with standardized terminologies and procedures to distance themselves from suffering and death—protection against the disruptive effects on normal consciousness of what they profess to "teach." For them, methodology is a godsend which, however limited, is at least available on demand.

It would seem, then, that literary criticism, except in institutionalized, self-parodic form, is impossible inside the university. Yet hope continues to glimmer in my heart, since, I assure myself, there has always been in the departments of English a counter-tradition, liberating rather than repressive. Indeed, such departments were invented in order to open up the traditional canon of teachable literature. The administrators of American colleges, following the European example, had once decreed that no literature in any living language be taught within their walls. Only the "classics" were considered worthy of inclusion in the curriculum, and they were to be read in the original Latin, Greek, Aramaic and Hebrew, the "dead" languages, as we used to say without intentional irony.

Even when—under pressure from populist, democratic or patriotic quarters—some English literature began to be taught, it was only books by dead authors; which turned out to mean chiefly British books, written in a dialect only approximately comprehensible to most Americans, whether the descendants of the original British settlers or the children of more recent immigrants. Not only were the English professors of the late nineteenth and early twentieth centuries hopelessly Anglophile, but felt the need to prove that in abandoning the "classics" they had not become philistines. By teaching with appropriate "rigor" books which despite being in English had to be glossed to be fully understood and to be "required" to be read *at all*, they hoped to persuade their more conservative colleagues that they upheld "standards" still. Moreover, they attempted to reintroduce courses in the "classics" of the ancient world in translation, even as they sought to establish certain canonical modern works as new "classics" by making them seem as securely "dead" as *The Aeneid* or *The Iliad*.

By the time I had entered graduate school toward the end of the '30s, such "required" poets as Spenser and Milton were presented not as potential sources of pleasure but formidable obstacles on the perilous path to the Ph.D. What was not required was not exactly forbidden, but surely discouraged; so that twentieth-century literature came to be thought of as a subject turned to as a last resort by inadequate scholars. And even nineteenth-century authors were regarded as best left to the lazy and the half-prepared, on the way to becoming "critics" rather than "scholars." Such "critics," however, not only prevailed but after a while urged that the revolution which had made "English" respectable be turned into a permanent one—by introducing into the curriculum formerly despised modernists, along with certain American writers hitherto neglected in the academy.

Whereupon the cry was raised once more: "Let such borderline figures in, in response to fashion and the taste of the vulgar, and all will be lost. Not only will the study of English be turned from a serious discipline into a pastime for the idle, an easy way to get good grades and shoddy degrees, but bad currency will drive out good. Milton and Spenser will be replaced first by Joyce and Eliot, then Saul Bellow and Norman Mailer, and God knows who. Where will it all end?"

But, of course, by the time such protests are raised, it is always too late. Like the first revolution, like *all* revolutions, the second revolution succeeded—and failed. In order to assure victory, its cadres had given away too much, betraying finally even some of the writers whom they had fought to include in the curriculum: when they pretended, for instance, that *Huckleberry Finn,* colloquial, comic-horrific, vulgar and available even to children, was really another difficult and uplifting "classic," like *Paradise Lost* or *The Aenied.* To prove it they had written studies in which Twain's novel, along with *Moby Dick, The Leatherstocking Tales* or "The Purloined Letter," is analyzed in whatever critical jargon is momentarily chic. Once started, the process never stops. What we have done for the novels of the nineteenth century we can do for those of the twentieth, whether *Herzog, V, The End of the Road, Portnoy's Complaint* or *Slaughterhouse-Five.*

Finally *(mea culpa!)* such books come to seem as hermetic, esoteric and inert as *The Faerie Queene* itself, indicating that the time for a third revolution in English studies is at hand. It is, as a matter of fact, long overdue. Already, by the mid-1960s, it seemed as if the departments of literature were preparing to extend the already much-extended canon, even at the risk of undercutting the distinction, which had survived two earlier revolutions, between true literature and mass culture. It was an age in which many traditional distinctions were being challenged—between the sexes, the generations, even Good and Evil—so that one more seemed scarcely to matter. Indeed, the university itself seemed on the verge of extinction—at least according to the shouting students in the streets and the hysterical reactions of the press.

But suddenly a decade and a half has gone by, and the university still stands. Required composition has been restored almost everywhere, and students themselves begin to cry out for stricter grading and courses relevant not to their revolutionary dreams, but to the facts of life and the marketplace. Consequently, the old alarmist cry is raised once more, this time in regard to the post-print media, especially television. Treat as "literature" sitcoms, cop shows and soap operas, stories told in pictures whose authors no one ever quite remembers, give students course credits for watching what they would watch anyhow, what takes no work to comprehend, the argument runs, and literary studies would become truly meaningless, our degrees really a joke! But this is precisely what an older generation had said about teaching Eliot and Joyce, Hemingway and Faulkner, is it not? Yet when told so, the latter-day enemies of the permanent cultural revolution answer that *this* time the situation is different. To take *this* additional step would mean a qualitative alteration rather than a mere quantitative modification of the "tradition," the death of "English" as we have known it.

It seems to me, however, that "English as we have known it" is not threatened with death by the new changes in the curriculum. It is already dead, destroyed by the last set of changes, or the one before that. It began dying at the moment that people like me were permitted to join the profession. I am not proposing, as some have charged, to "open the gates to the barbarians," since I *am* a barbarian, already within the gates. It becomes me therefore to urge that, having nothing to lose, we venture to find out what might be gained by abandoning our last and dearest snobbism, the conviction that print is inherently superior to movies and TV, even though everyone must presumably be taught (by *us*) to read words on the page, whereas no one has to be instructed in reading images on the screen.

To be sure, there have been in recent years attempts by

academic critics of cinema (they do not like to say "movies") to kidnap that vulgar form for classroom analysis, even to "teach" how to read it properly. But such *cinéastes* merely repeat—in a kind of unwitting parody—the old errors of elitist literary criticism: on the one hand, losing sight, in the midst of jargonizing about "montage," "tracking shots" and *"auteur* theory," of the fact that movies tell stories and embody myths, and on the other, making untenable distinctions between "box-office trash" and "art films," which turn out to be more often than not "experimental" and "non-narrative." Most of us, however (including not a few literary elitists), continue to think of movies as an extracurricular diversion, whose comprehension requires no more formal instruction than walking or talking. And this is all the more true of television, which we cannot help being aware can be watched while ironing, eating and drinking, or making love.

In any case, print is not the ultimate mode of transmitting poetry and fiction, an inestimable advance over pre-print or folk forms, or a peak from which the post-print or mass media constitute a decline. Words on the page are only one among several equally effective and honorable ways of transmitting song and story. As obvious as this seems to me and the great audience, however, I have had difficulty in persuading my colleagues of its truth. I was in fact attacked not very long ago by one such colleague, in the midst of a large professional meeting of his peers and mine. A Jewish-American academic *arriviste* like me, rather eminent in his own right but a little insecure, perhaps, because he had no Ph.D., he seemed driven by a need to be *plus royaliste que le roi.* He was, in any case, genuinely shocked by what appeared to him heresy, and he suggested that if I did indeed believe what I had been reported as saying, it was my duty to resign from the profession I was hellbent on destroying.

How could I have explained to him (fortunately, I was not present and did not have to try) that I was proposing a strategy to ensure the *survival* of that profession by suggesting that what is essential is not a particular curriculum, a fixed canon of okay books or films, much less a normative reading of each *one* of them and a set of "standards" for judging all? These have always changed, as they must; and will continue to change, as they should. What does not change is a commitment, an attitude, a way of living with living literature, amateur rather than professional. After more than four decades, one of the few things I believe I have really learned is that the teacher, that professional amateur, teaches not so much his subject matter as himself. If he is a teacher of literature, he provides for those less experienced in song and story, including the reluctant, the skeptical, the uncooperative, the incompetent, a model of one in whom what seemed dead, mere print on the page, becomes living, a way of life—palpable fulfillment, a transport into the world of wonder.

To do so effectively, he must show himself capable of responding not only to those works which his students are not likely to discover without his guidance, but also to those which have persisted in spite of critical disapproval. He must, moreover, teach such works in the same courses, as chronology or theme or his own whim dictates, thus avoiding even the semblance of celebrating already established works at the expense of those still despised, much less those preferred by an elite at the expense of those loved by the great majority. Only in this way will he be able to make clear the continuity of all song and story, pre-print, print and post-print, high, medium and low.

If we remain faithful not just to our students but to the works we teach, "English" will be alive and well in the next century, whatever happens to the "value of the degree" or, indeed, to the degree itself. I am not talking about English as vocational training, much less English as elitist brainwashing. I mean English for everyone: an introduction to works of the imagination over which all humankind can weep, laugh, shudder and be titillated; communal dreams, shared hallucinations, which in a time when everything else tends to divide us from each other join us together, men and women, adults and children, educated and uneducated, black and white, yellow and brown—even, perhaps, teachers and students.

WHAT IS TO BE DONE?

Meanwhile, I feel the need to take the first steps—outside the academy as well as in, on the lecture platform or the "tube," wherever anyone will listen to me—toward creating a new kind of criticism. To be truly new, however, it must not only confront the popular arts, but deal with them, and the high arts too, in a style consonant with a sensibility altered by the former. I began this study by confessing that I have long been moving in the direction of such criticism, though without quite knowing what I was doing or even whether I really wanted to do it. From the start, however, I have been sure that in order to survive, criticism must avoid the creeping professionalism endemic in our post-industrial world by eschewing jargon, the hermetic codes which secular hierophants use to exclude the uninitiated. The newest critics therefore must, like the oldest, learn to speak with the authority not of experimental science or systematic philosophy, but of poetry itself—in this age of mass culture, a colloquial, demotic poetry, vulgar enough to fear neither humor nor pathos.

   Their criticism should, moreover, be "generalist" rather than "specialist," setting literature in the broadest possible context by refusing to distinguish what is "intrinsic" from what is "extrinsic" to song and story. *Experienced* as images in heads, which exist in society, literature cannot be separated from history and biography, sociology and psychology. Recent critics, in any case, who have reached the widest audience have been "generalists" like Marshall McLuhan or Norman O. Brown. The former has set literature in the context of electronic technology, computer science, anthropology and the history of ideas, while the latter has drawn on Marxist political economy, Freudian psychiatry and the visionary perceptions of Christian mystics. To be sure, they have not satisfied the "experts" in the extra-literary disciplines into which they have wandered, being anything but "sound scholars"; but this is, of course, beside the point. What terms they have used are those already assimilated into mass culture, popularized in Sunday supplements, family magazines and informational programs on TV.

The only other literary critics who have recently attracted even small extra-academic audiences have been practicing poets and novelists, as different in other respects as D. H. Lawrence, T. S. Eliot, Ezra Pound, William Carlos Williams and Charles Olson. Their criticism has, however, too often been aimed at justifying their own practice, so that their followers tend to be obnoxiously reverent "groupies." Moreover, as writers they have made it into the ranks of okay literature, and as critics have turned out to be covertly or overtly elitist. Consequently, they have aggravated rather than mitigated the split between High Literature and low—as do older amateur critics I once took as models, from Longinus and Dryden to Nietzsche and the Marquis de Sade.

Indeed, the only critical study I know by a distinguished artist which rejects the exclusion of what pleases the many in favor of what is prized by the few, and itself functions as literature, is Tolstoi's *What Is Art?* At precisely the moment when apologists for modernism—or, more specifically, what Tolstoi calls "decadence"—were inventing the latest form of elitism, he launched a violent counterattack. He did not, however, dare to defend the actual mass culture of his own age, advocating instead a kind of anarcho-Christian folk culture, based on rapidly disappearing methods of agriculture and the worship of a God dying if not dead.

Furthermore, he did not urge closing the gap or building a bridge between majority art and minority art, but opted for the former rather than the latter, thus merely standing elitism on its head. Worse, there is something authoritarian in his rejection of any art (including all of Shakeaspeare,

Michelangelo and his own *Anna Karenina*) a taste for which separates the few from the many: a suggestion that in the ideal commonwealth such works ought not merely to be spurned but banned. At least he has been so interpreted in his own native land, in which cultural commissars have in the name of "popular taste" prevented the publication and showing of anything which has proven alien or disturbing to their own. In any event, Tolstoi's position represents not the voice of the mass audience, urging democratization of culture from below, but the bad conscience of an aristocratic elite, offering piously to make amends for yet one more injustice of a class-structured society.

But are there *any* models of grass-roots anti-hierarchal criticism? Certainly not that half-mocking proposal for a school of "pejorative criticism" suggested by certain of my own graduate students at the point in the sixties when they had come half seriously to think of themselves as "niggers" or an intellectual proletariat. According to its tenets, the criticism of the future should be brief, negative—and if at all possible, gross. The sole example I can remember (and I could not swear that there were even any more) is: "Milton's *Paradise Lost*—too fucking long!" While I find it possible to believe that "talking dirty" can be when discreetly employed as useful to critics as to politicians and stand-up comedians, I am also aware that we need no prophet to come back from the grave to tell us so.

Profanity has long been a well-established practice in England, where it is considered "underbred" in some circles to avoid the language of the barracks and barroom in speaking of books; so that it is quite possible to write for highbrow journals reviews beginning, "Everyone knows that so-and-so is a little shit . . ." Such studied insolence is used, however, not to open up literature to the vulgar, but to put down presumptuous members of lesser breeds, like Hindus and Americans. Indeed, amateur criticism in the British Isles has traditionally been the province not of cultural reformers but of "gentlemen" at ease in the world of culture—as they believe certain lower-class or foreign-born culture-climbers are not.

Only in the United States has there ever been a long-lived venture into non-elitist amateur criticism, and that uniquely American experiment would, it seems to me, repay close examination in terms of both how it succeeded and how it failed. I am referring to the "fanzines," those mimeographed journals in which, beginning in the early thirties, certain young admirers of pulp science fiction began to publish, for a minuscule audience who shared their enthusiasm for that pop genre, cartoons, illustrations, fiction not yet up to the level of the pulps—and, of course, naïve criticism as well.

It is curious and illuminating to realize that the fanzines dealt only with science fiction, along with the two closely related subgenres, fantasy and comic books. There are no comparable amateur publications devoted to other popular specialty fiction of the time, like the detective story, the spy novel, the western or the girls' romance. This is true in large part, I suppose, because the latter did not attract so impassioned, cohesive and exclusivist an audience, whose taste was defined by both a preference for a particular literary kind of fiction and a rejection of almost everything else, from the mimetic best sellers their parents read to the "classics" their teachers assigned.

Though most such journals proved ephemeral, some are still in existence, their contributors as smugly parochial as ever, which is to say, unaware of most contemporary books outside the closed circle of s.f. and uninterested in the critical methodologies invented in the last several decades. Not surprisingly, therefore, no new critical voice or point of view has emerged from their midst. They have, however, produced as an offshoot a series of vulgar critical books, which, though they have never quite made it to the level of real best-sellerdom, sell well enough to be displayed in mass paperback form on newsstands in airports and supermarkets. I am thinking of the numerous works, primarily celebratory, historical, biographical and anecdotal—but incidentally exegetical and analytic—which have grown up around the TV series *Star Trek*.

Canceled in 1967 after three seasons on prime-time television, that show has refused to die, surviving in endless replays, an animated cartoon version, and recently two successful feature-length films. First, however, it spawned fan clubs and fanzines of its own, largely composed of adolescent females; which in turn begot book-length volumes of eulogy and nostalgia, as well as anthologies of rewritten episodes from the defunct series, complete with introductions and other critical apparatus; and a series of spin-off novels by younger writers of s.f. Included in the by now formidable array of "fan" publications are *Letters to Star Trek, The World of Star Trek, Star Trek's "The Trouble with Tribbles," The Making of the Star Trek Conventions,* Leonard Nimoy's *I Am Not Spock, The Official Star Trek Trivia Book, Star Trek Spaceflight Chronology* and the not-quite-book *Fourteen Official Blueprints from Star Trek the Motion Picture.*

There is something touching about such naïve reinventions of criticism outside the academy, but something comic as well, since what they inadvertently parody is the patient documentation and mindless accumulation of fact which characterizes academic "research" at its deadliest. "What disease is affecting Miss Hedford in 'Metamorphosis'?" and "What caused the inhabitants of Talos IV to move underground?" asks *The Official Star Trek Trivia Book,* like some conscientious teacher of high school sophomore English. Doubtless the tongues of its compilers were tucked firmly into their cheeks, but many of those who bought it to test themselves and their friends were in deadly earnest. Nor did it occur to them that the whole thing was part of a continuing sales pitch, a "hype," an event in the realm of the marketplace rather than of literature.

As a travesty of traditional scholarship, an antidote to what the young endure in school, such a volume could be of use both to them and to their teachers. But I fear it appeals chiefly to the pedant in those for whom it works at all. *Star Trek* amateur criticism is, however, no more inadvertently self-parodic than the "professional" criticism produced by academics for reading to each other at meetings of, say, the MLA sessions devoted to science fiction, in which the recherché vocabularies of semiotics, Lacanian psychoanalysis and deconstructionism are applied to stories written by the same writers who did scripts for that TV series.

Such academics have, moreover, begun to rank s.f. hierarchically, as they had earlier done with what hard-core fans of that pop genre call "mainstream literature." So, for instance, a recent textbook has kind words to say for such favorites of the fans as Olaf Stapledon, Arthur C. Clarke and Walter M. Miller, but dismisses A. E. Van Vogt, whom such fans regard even more highly, with the contemptuous phrase "precisely the sort of writer who has given science fiction a bad name among serious readers." Yet this makes matters even worse, by instituting at the heart of what once seemed unredeemable pop a kind of invidious hierarchal canonization no longer viable even in the area of High Literature. Unhappily, that distinction survives everywhere, in the university and out, in bourgeois capitalist society and under socialist regimes, in the realm of High Art and low. But why? Is there nothing we can do about it? No way out of the trap?

To answer such questions, we must attempt to discover where it all began. Apparently, it was the Greeks who (even as the Hebrews were conceiving the notion of scripture) invented secular literature, along with the proto-university, in which gymnastics, pederasty and pedagogy were uniquely blended. Blake's condemnation of that homoerotic culture is perhaps too bitter to be taken at face value (" 'Twas the Greeks' love of war / Which turned Love into a boy / And woman into a statue of stone / And away flew every joy"). But it was in fact misogynist, reflecting male envy of female natural creativity and a desire to preempt it on a "higher plane." In a society in which men had reserved for themselves all other power, only the ability to bear life and nurture it from their own bodies remained the exclusive privilege of women, and art consequently represented (as the myth of the male poet impregnated by the Muse and bringing forth spiritual progeny betrays) an attempt to even the score.

I do not mean to suggest that song and story were first invented at that relatively late date. They are surely as old as speech itself, which may indeed have been song and story before it was anything else, *mythos* preceding *logos*. But before they could become "literature," two things had to be added: first, the notion that some fiction and verse were worth preserving "forever" and, second, the conviction that authors should be "immortalized" along with what they had composed.

The first notion implies the selection by a secular authority of a secular canon, a body of poetry and fiction felt to be worth preserving because it embodies true wisdom in beautiful form. Eventually the intuitive perceptions by which wisdom and beauty were determined came to be formulated "rules" or "standards," and lay rituals were created for honoring those who met them. Afterward, when public acclaim and a crown of laurel no longer seemed sufficient, poets and dramatists were subsidized, paid for their services to mankind, originally by aristocratic patrons, then (as society became democratic and mercantile) by the consumers who bought their works on the open market.

At this point, song and story came to be thought of as private property, fixed, signed texts protected by copyright from plagiarism. In the time of manuscript transmissions, only courtly or scholarly works deemed of the highest value were copied (along with Holy Scripture of course), and, more often than not, attributed to authors, mythological or real. Folk literature meanwhile remained anonymous, and changed as it was passed from mouth to ear to mouth, each performer altering and amending what was felt belonged not to an individual but to the whole community. Only the former was considered real "literature," though occasionally some artistocratic critic would commit to print a condescending word of praise for a tale or ballad of the folk.

There was, in any case, no possibility of confusing the two kinds, separated by a still unchallenged distinction between the different social classes that were their primary audiences. But with the invention of movable type, all song and story became words on the page: Greek and Roman classics, fairy tales from the Black Forest, oral poetry, popular drama, as well as post-Gutenberg works, high or low. Once mass production of literature had become possible (and the development of post-print media has exacerbated without basically changing the situation), all books, ranging from the "art novels" of Henry James or Marcel Proust, Thomas Mann or James Joyce, to "best sellers" by Jacqueline Susann or John D. MacDonald, Conan Doyle or Bram Stoker, are distinguishable from one another only after the fact.

We may think back on them differently, after we have been brainwashed by elitist criticism, but we absorb them, respond to them, in quite the same fashion—laughing, weeping, shuddering, losing ourselves in the alternate universes they create. To be sure, we are taught in some cases to be proud that we have been so transported and charmed, in others to be ashamed of, even publicly deny our infatuation. Moreover, what is unredeemably pop passes almost immediately into the public domain, its characters kidnaped and its plots reworked in the collective unconscious, reappearing in the dreams and fantasies of those who may not ever have read the original. Indeed, many popular novels are, like the romances of Alexandre Dumas, the Tom Swift books and Alex Haley's *Roots*, written in the first instance with the aid of ghostwriters or by anonymous committees.

What the reader of such books remembers are not "words on the page," but images which seem to exist somehow before and after, outside those words. At worst, the prose in which they are rendered is awkward or pretentious or both; at best, just adequate, and in any case, oddly transparent. And for this reason, the best of low fiction can move from medium to medium without loss of resonance or authenticity, sometimes, indeed, with considerable gain. It survives not just translation to the screen (where sometimes the director is a superior artist, as in the case of *Birth of a Nation*, sometimes an indifferent hack or series of hacks as in that of *The Wizard of Oz* or *Gone With the Wind*), but even the most perfunctory writing for TV and the interruptions, at intervals dictated by quite unartistic exigencies, of commercials and spot news.

Not only does *echt* pop reveal itself by its failure to meet aesthetic standards, its odd way of making them seem somehow irrelevant, but it does the same with ethical ones, offering on the level of full consciousness moralistic clichés about love and marriage, love and the family, usually a generation or two out of date, and beneath that pious veneer pandering in contempt of those clichés to desires and lusts repugnant to all do-gooders and social reformers. Even as minimal mimesis, the imitation of life as it is, rather than as it might or should be, pop proves untrustworthy, presenting undisciplined wish and fear in the guise of fact. Finally, however, lowbrow literature at its most authentic, the great Good Bad Books, identifies itself by its disconcerting characteristic of being loved by the majority audience generation after generation, without ever having been embraced by the minority one.

Confusingly, however, there are some works which suit both the untutored taste of the popular audience and the most exacting aesthetic and ethical standards, sometimes, indeed, entering the public domain even before being classified as canonical. All the plays of Sophocles, who won first prize by popular acclaim almost every time he entered a tragedy competition, fall in this category, as do some of Shakespeare's—*Hamlet,* surely, and *The Merchant of Venice,* along with both parts of *Henry IV.* Yet at least one of Shakespeare's dramas, *Troilus and Cressida,* bombed in the popular theater, and for nearly a century after his death hard-line neoclassical critics refused to accept *any* of his plays as equal to those of the ancients.

Indeed, his final canonization by his own countrymen, most notably Samuel Johnson, was surely due in part to their patriotic sense that whatever his contempt for the "rules," he was the only contender for "greatness" who had written in English. Yet, once he had been kidnaped by the respectable and made required reading in the academy, it was assumed that the "Bard" could do no wrong, so that even a play as ill-constructed, ill-written and fundamentally vicious in its sado-masochistic appeal as *Titus Andronicus* (I not long ago attended a production from which several genteel British suburban ladies fled howling—as they had every right to do) is treated as a work of art rather than the equivocal pop best seller it really is.

The case of Shakespeare is by no means unique. Many essentially pop writers have for one reason or another been smuggled into the realm of High Art—not by acknowledging the inadequacy of critical "standards" and adjusting or amending them, but by fudging, *lying:* hypocritically pretending that works which refuse to die but are woefully deficient in terms of both execution and "high seriousness" somehow *do* meet those standards. Mark Twain, it seems to me, falls into this category, as does Charles Dickens. Both in fact, though they occasionally produced works which in whole or in part satisfy the demands of elitist criticism (perhaps two-thirds of *Huckleberry Finn,* most of *Great Expectations* and all of *Hard Times*), in much of the rest of their work commit over and over the sins of "sentimentality," "banality" and "bad taste."

Some of their books, indeed, are so grotesquely and palpably awful by all orthodox measures, like, for instance, Twain's *The Prince and the Pauper* and Dickens' *Old Curiosity Shop,* that "serious" critics are driven to ignore them in favor of less characteristic works which meet their "standards." Other such writers, however, have produced no books which qualify, yet have been accepted all the same. One conspicuous example would be James Fenimore Cooper, whose faults Mark Twain (convinced that he had, however inadvertently, written "High Literature," and eager to separate himself from other popular authors who had not) identified in a jocular-serious essay called "Fenimore Cooper's Literary Offenses."

If there are indeed "rules governing literary art," Twain wrote, they must include "using the right word, not its second cousin . . . eschewing surplusage . . . not omitting necessary details . . . avoiding slovenliness of form . . . employing a simple and straightforward style." Since Cooper must, as Twain contends, be given bad marks on all these scores, how is it possible to deny his summary indictment of *The Deerslayer:* "A WORK OF ART? It has no invention . . . no order, system, sequence or result . . . no lifelikeness . . . no seeming of reality . . . its characters are confusedly drawn . . . its humor is pathetic; its pathos is funny . . . its conversations are—oh? indescribable; its love-scenes odious; its English a crime against the language." Yet, though Twain's little essay has been often reprinted, no "serious" critic has ever taken it seriously. After all, he presented it as a kind of extended joke, without the pedantry and grim rigor we have, alas, come to associate with proper literary criticism.

Moreover, Twain's final judgment of Cooper was challenged by more qualified critics even in his own time: a certain "Prof. Lounsbury," for example, declared *The Pathfinder* and *The Deerslayer* "pure works of art," while Professor Brander Matthews found Natty Bumppo "one of the very greatest characters in fiction." Even after their Victorian taste had been superseded by "modernism," so antigenteel an extra-academic as D. H. Lawrence called *The Deerslayer* "one of the most beautiful and perfect books in the world: flawless as a jewel and of like concentration." And that apostle of "classical" rigor, T. S. Eliot, concurred —as he did with scarcely any of Lawrence's other critical opinions. It is indeed difficult to understand why an exception was made for this singularly clumsy pop writer, as it was not for, say, the no more inept author of *Uncle Tom's Cabin,* which is still widely read, as *The Last of the Mohicans* is not—except on assignment in school.

No more than any of the other critics, Victorian or modernist, who have extravagantly admired *The Leatherstocking Tales* could Lawrence, I am convinced, have justified his judgment in terms of aesthetic standards—or for that matter, ethical ones. What they were all responding to, it seems clear to me, was not Cooper's "art," but an extratextual appeal which in their critical vocabularies did not even have a name. Whether they knew it or not (and their ignorance on this score was, I believe, necessary to their methodological peace of mind), what moved them in his fiction was its mythopoeic power—more specifically, its evocation for the first time in the American novel of the same myth which underlies later, more aesthetically and ethically satisfactory works, like *Moby Dick* and *Huckleberry Finn:* the archetypal story of interethnic male bonding, whose essential sentimentality (based as it is on an impossible dream of a love able to transcend the hostility of white and nonwhite Americans) did not disturb them, as did the domestic, female-oriented counter-myth of Mrs. Stowe. The former was, indeed, rooted in a fantasy and evoked a pathos already so deeply implanted in their own male WASP psyches that they took it for simple "reality."

What I am suggesting is that even in the heyday of elitist criticism, a dim sense persisted in many critics—betrayed whenever in contempt of their avowed "standards" they acknowledged a popular work which defied them—that some books possessed a third sort of excellence, different from either aesthetic appeal or ethical significance. But as long as that *tertium quid* remained unnamed and, as it were, preconscious, it was recognized only erratically: leading to the canonization of certain good-bad writers, like Cooper, while others equally gifted in this respect remained in perpetual limbo, like Mrs. Stowe, or were rejected for all eternity, like Edgar Rice Burroughs or Sir Arthur Conan Doyle. Nor could it be otherwise, since, like the Christians' Hell, the underworld of para-literature required that from time to time, preferably with fair frequency, someone be consigned to it. After a while, a theory of predestination developed: the belief that some song and story were from the moment of conception doomed to be cast into eternal darkness.

FROM ETHICS AND AESTHETICS TO ECSTATICS

Let me be clear. My quarrel is not with the notion that some literary works are better than others, which is to say, more moving, more lasting in their appeal. What seems to me untenable is the faith that one kind of book (which turns out to be, more often than not, fantastic, sentimental or pornographic, and in our culture written by women, blacks, Hispanics and other stigmatized minorities) is intrinsically bad, while another (usually mimetic or reflexive, and written by privileged generational, ethnic and sexual groups) is intrinsically good. I am not suggesting that the search for standards be abandoned completely and that evaluation be confined to noises of admiration or distaste, the simple "Wow!" or "Ech!" which seems to satisfy some of our students. Finally, I do not believe (influenced in part by an awareness of how my own preferences have changed with time and experience) that even in an open society like our own everyone is entitled to establish his own rank order of books based on personal preference, whether these lead him to rate *Jonathan Livingston Seagull* higher than *Huckleberry Finn* or vice versa. I *know* that the first is pretentious, banal and essentially stupid, while the second subtle and mythically resonant, yet capable of moving a child of ten. Consequently, I am resolved to discover a way of saying why this is so, more satisfactorily than the one I was taught in school.

Moreover, I am unwilling (as certain critics like Northrop

Frye are) to give up evaluation completely. If criticism is to survive its necessary transformation in the near future (and I am convinced that it will not, *must* not die, being a human response as ancient and essential as the song and story which prompt it), it must continue to make judgments. All men and women, boys and girls, leaving, say, a movie they have loved or hated, will shout to friends they see waiting in line for the next performance, "Lucky you, you're in for a treat!" or "My God, get out while you still have time!" If then they are challenged and go on to justify their reaction, they will have invented criticism as a form of discourse, a social act. Any critical writing, therefore, which tries out of some perverse impulse to eschew value judgments is likely to lose its audience, except perhaps for fellow critics of a like persuasion.

Once we begin to evaluate, however, we run a double risk. On the one hand, it is hard for us as the heirs of a long elitist tradition to avoid confusing "better" and "worse" with "high" and "low," which is to say, what appeals to the refined few and what pleases the vulgar many. On the other hand, as good little boys and girls who have grown up to be good citizens, we find it difficult to keep our judgments about art free from prudential considerations: rating works which we feel enhance life and "civilization" (however we may define these) more worthy than those which call into question our fundamental assumptions about man and God.

In the end, surely, the second is the great danger, for it tempts us inexorably toward censorship, while the first only leads us in the direction of snobbism. The latter is, in addition, more deeply rooted in the prehistory of Homo sapiens. Though Plato may have been the earliest writer to record the "quarrel between poetry and philosophy," he already referred to it as "ancient," and introspection suggests that the distrust of unregulated literature is as old as "civilization" itself, or the resolve which made us human that "where Id was Ego shall be."

For a while it looked as if a compromise had been reached between the enemies of literature and those driven to produce it by forces, Plato argued, as much out of conscious control as those which move the lover, the madman or the mystic. Mad, bad poetry seemed at the point of regulating itself, as the poets—instructed by theology and philosophy—paid lip service at least to the principle of law and order. Like "good niggers" they had apparently "learned their place," their proper function in the larger polity; which turned out to be, of course, "to instruct and delight," especially to instruct delightfully those not yet mature enough for more rigorous forms of mental discipline. Since nothing is forbidden to poetry, it is free, of course, to instruct and delight among other things; in some cases, indeed, it seems primarily dedicated to those two socially desirable ends.

Behind the obsequious smile of the "good nigger," however, often lies the subversive grin of the mocker, suggesting that art may have another function, in some sense antithetical to the first two. To instruct and to delight are not in any case the sole functions of song and story, whatever certain more solemn pedagogue-poets from Matthew Arnold to T. S. Eliot may have said on this score. Whenever, therefore, High Literature has reached a dead end, as at the moment of the invention of Romanticism, for instance, or of Dada, it turns to the popular arts (to the folk ballad, the fairy tale and Ossian, in the one case, to "Krazy Kat," Charlie Chaplin and the Marx Brothers in the other) out of an instinctive sense that clues to renewal and rebirth are to be found there. I do not mean to say that low literature is in this respect superior to High. Best of all are those works which, like Sophocles' *Oedipus Rex* or Shakespeare's *Hamlet*, satisfy both the guardians of Aristotelian-Horatian "standards" and the mass audience, which responds to the mysterious *tertium quid* which the former do not even deign to notice.

It would, in any event, be a mistake simply to stand the traditional rank order on its head by insisting that what pleases the many should be judged "good" and therefore be preserved, perhaps even taught, while that which is available only to the few, and therefore divides class from class, should be condemned, perhaps even banned. It is a position which tempts me, appealing to my deepest egalitarian commitments. Why, after all, I ask myself, in a polity where the most ill-educated and naïve have an equal voice in choosing their political leaders, and determining which brand of TV dinner, toothpaste or sanitary napkin survives in the marketplace, should they not have the right to make similar decisions about works of art? Once that vote has been taken, moreover, why should they not be entitled to impose their will on the minority? But since I am a libertarian even before an egalitarian, it gives me pause whenever the threat of majoritarian tyranny is posed, in the realm of culture as well as that of politics.

The point is neither to ban the low in favor of the high, as the Arnoldian position seems to me to imply, or the high in favor of the low, as the Tolstoian counter-position suggests. I resist both, not only because each in its own way restricts the full freedom of literature, but because each unconsciously *lies* about the works it seeks to defend. So Matthew Arnold falsifies the essential ambiguity, the radical skepticism verging on nihilism, in the plays of Shakespeare and Euripides by reading them as sources of "sweetness and light." And similarly, Tolstoi misrepresents Harriet Beecher Stowe and Dostoievski by ignoring their sentimentality, racism and sado-masochism in an attempt to prove them pure apostles of the brotherhood of man and the fatherhood of God.

Literature, both high and low, it seems to me, when it is most nearly universal in its appeal, no matter what its superficial ideology, on its deeper, more mythological levels is fundamentally antinomian, and therefore it reinforces *no* respectable pieties of any kind. If it asserts anything, it is the impossibility of unqualified assertion, the ambiguity of all moral imperatives and the ambivalence it breeds. In this respect, song and story are utterly different from the *logos* of preachers and teachers, but very like the primeval *mythos* from which discursive speech seeks to distinguish itself. There is a sense in which myth *as* myth survives in literature, as it does not in philosophical or pedagogical discourse. Low literature, indeed, whether in pre-print, print or post-print form, aspires to return to the condition of pure myth. Consequently, the critic who desires to do it justice in a way which emphasizes its resemblances to rather than its differences from High Literature must be first of all a "myth critic"—of, I hasten to add, a particular kind.

There have been in this century many critics who have called themselves, or were classified by others as, "myth critics," but none of them use the term "myth" quite as I do. I feel obliged, therefore, to make quite clear just how I *do* use it before moving on. I certainly do not mean by myth "a damned lie" (though it is, to be sure, like all fictions, not gospel truth), nor do I employ the term, as a good many others rather confusingly do, as a synonym for "ideology." No matter if used in the neutral sense of "a manner or the content of thinking characteristic of an individual, group or culture," or pejoratively to signify "a sociopolitical program ... constructed wholly or in part on factitious or hypothetical ideational bases," "ideology" always refers to thinking or ideas, i.e., what is conscious; whereas myth functions on an unconscious or preconscious level.

I further distinguish "myth" from "mythology," reserving the latter term for bodies of story of whose mythic basis we have become fully aware, and which because they are not for us "gospel," being products of cultures we consider archaic or naïve or "primitive," we condescend to as "only make-believe"—typically remanding them to the nursery. Once we have reached the point where we are able to ask of any archetypal story "Is it true or false?" rather than simply accepting it on a level before or beyond belief, it dies as "myth," and if we decide it is "false," is demoted to the status of "mythology." Sometimes, however, it withers away first into a cliché, which when widely enough shared and firmly enough established, we tend to take as self-evident fact.

It is not always easy to say when a living archetype becomes a moribund stereotype, particularly when we are dealing with contemporary popular culture. Among the myths of the American West, for instance, the nightmare vision of the native American as an irreconcilable enemy of white culture has long since frozen into the platitude "The only good Injun is a dead Injun." Yet for most present-day viewers, the duel fought by the Good Guy and the Bad Guy on the sunbaked set of a cowboy movie—like the love that joins Huck and Jim on the raft—is still living myth. We feel both, however, as somehow different from accounts of the wanderings of Ulysses or the Quest for the Holy Grail, which we encounter in the classroom, either in ancient texts or as allusions in such latter-day "classics" as Dante's *Divine Comedy* or Tennyson's *Idylls of the King.*

When they are evoked in more recent works, highly regarded by the critics, like Joyce's *Ulysses,* Eliot's *The Waste Land* or Pound's *Cantos,* they have become a special kind of "secondary mythology," not merely allegorized or euphemized, but ironized or parodied. But in non-elitist books produced in the same period, but typically ignored by the critics, like *Dracula* or *Tarzan*, what we find is not mythology once removed but primary myth. This is also true of certain earlier pop works, misleadingly assimilated into the canon of High Art, like *The Pickwick Papers*, *Huckleberry Finn* and *The Last of the Mohicans*, which allow both the authors and the readers for whom they are chiefly intended to remain unaware that they are anything but "good yarns."

Eventually, however, certain cryptanalytical critics identify the "mythic" import, in what the original audience is likely to feel is an act of desecration. I have played that dangerous game myself and have been responded to thus, particularly when I tried to raise to the level of full consciousness the archetype implicit in *Huckleberry Finn* and *The Leatherstocking Tales*. I was, I think, aware of the risks involved right from the start. Yet I could not resist the impulse to understand better not just those books themselves, but certain aspects of the American character and fate which they reveal: dark ambivalences about race and sex, ignored or denied by political spokesmen and deliberately propagandistic writers. In retrospect, however, I am driven to ask whether it was worth it after all. In some sense, surely, by doing so I helped turn living myth to dying mythology, if not archetype to stereotype. Nonetheless, I remain convinced that there is a chance of raising such material to the level of full consciousness without utterly falsifying it, as long as the critic who does so remembers that he is himself writing literature about literature, fiction about fictions, myth about myth. The only critical works which long survive (think of Nietzsche's *Birth of Tragedy* or Tolstoi's *What Is Art?*) are those which attempt not to prove or disprove, construct or deconstruct anything, but to compel an assent scarcely distinguishable from wonder, like the songs or stories which are their immediate occasion. Meta-myths themselves, they are written not with the methodological rigor of the sciences, soft or hard, but with the openness, the ambiguity and the contempt for logic or mere "truth" of the myths they subsume.

But even such a dedication to anti-method, though necessary, is not sufficient, since there are other ways in which the critic can betray the mythic in literature—most notably, perhaps, by attempting to apply to works whose primary appeal is archetypal "standards" invented for judging "formalist" or "realistic" works. The demand for elegance of structure is especially inappropriate, since hard-core pop, like primal myth itself, has no proper Aristotelian beginning or end—only an indefinitely extended middle. It is this characteristic which explains its affinity for serial publication, as in the novels of Charles Dickens, the "continued next week" movies of my own childhood, and the present-day "soaps."

Also irrelevant is the requirement of a distinguished style, in the Flaubertian or Jamesian sense; for style belongs to the "signature" element in art, the assertion of the individual as opposed to the communal, which is embodied in the archetype. Only after the emergence of a cult of personality in the Renaissance does it become customary, for instance, to identify a painting by its artist rather than its theme or genre; so that we refer not to "A Crucifixion" or "The Visitation" but to an El Greco or a Rembrandt. But this applies only to High Art, not to popular art, whether early or late, religious or secular; so that just as we are likely to describe the mosaic in a Byzantine church as "a *theotokos,*" we speak of the kind of picture hung in a twentieth-century barracks as "a pinup."

When pop is not anonymous to begin with, it tends to become so in the minds of popular readers, who when asked what they are reading are more likely to answer "s.f." or "a spy story" or "a romance" than "Isaac Asimov" or "John le Carré" or "Fern Michaels." And even when on occasion someone responds instead "a Harold Robbins" or "a Stephen King," the name is used as a kind of generic shorthand, like "Vaseline" for petroleum jelly or "Bayer" for acetylsalicylic acid. Think of the quite different way in which such an unsophisticated reader, improbably caught with *Hamlet* in his hand, would answer a similar query not "a Shakespeare" but "Shakespeare!"

Modern "hype" by turning certain best-selling writers into temporary celebrities has perhaps made some difference in this regard, but in the nineteenth century Edgar Allan Poe was still able to assert without any qualification that there were "two great classes of fiction": a "popular division," in which "the author is lost or forgotten," and a more elite one, in which "even when the works perish, the man survives." But the phenomenon he describes seems to me to be attributable to two kinds of audience rather than two kinds of literature, since Shakespeare, for instance, has endured both of these presumably exclusive fates, one with the majority audience and the other with minority readers.

That majority audience is, moreover, as indifferent to the verisimilitude of plot and character as it is to the beauty of structure and style. Intuitively aware that the mode of the books they prefer is fantastic rather than mimetic or analytic, ordinary readers do not demand that their protagonists be psychologically credible, or indeed that they have any "inwardness" at all. Inwardness is what they represent symbolically or by projection in "characters" which function like the split, doubled or disguised actors in our dreams. Consequently, as in such dreams, the actions those "characters" perform take place in a realm where probability and rationality are no longer relevant.

It would also be misguided, therefore, for critics to ask of gifted oneiric writers that they demonstrate an understanding of human nature or the functionings of society. In the daylight realms of psychology and ideology, they are likely to prove trivial and banal, even pathological or perverse. Nor does it matter. They move us viscerally rather than cerebrally, at a level where "both/and" displaces "either/or," and we can have our cake and eat it too. Consequently, we find it possible (to the distress of high-tone critics and earnest moralists) to respond passionately to the triumphs of Tarzan and the sufferings of Scarlett O'Hara, even as we are being repelled by their authors' politics.

If we are interested in discovering *how* pop moves us, it would repay us to look closely at the four forms of subliterature which have most troubled elitist critics, even as they have most pleased the mass audience. These are (1) sentimental literature, particularly as it has developed from the novels written by the first female imitators of Samuel Richardson, through such late nineteenth-century best sellers as Maria Cummins' *The Lamplighter* and Susan Warner's *The Wide, Wide World* to the daytime serials on television; (2) horror literature, from, say, M. G. Lewis' *The Monk*, through *Frankenstein, Dr. Jekyll and Mr. Hyde* and *Dracula* to the horror comic books, *The Rocky Horror Picture Show* and *Carrie* out of Stephen King by Brian De Palma;

(3) hard-core pornography, from Cleland's *Fanny Hill* and the Marquis de Sade's *Justine,* through Frank Harris' *My Life* to Pauline Réage's *The Story of O* and *Fritz the Cat;* (4) low comedy or hilarious desecration, from Aristophanes' *Lysistrata,* through Mark Twain's *Those Extraordinary Twins* and Jaroslav Hašek's *Good Soldier Schweik* to the "black humor" of Lenny Bruce and Monty Python.

There is a real sense in which all four of these can be regarded as "pornography," since they titillate by infringing deeply revered taboos and impel us toward some kind of orgasmic release, ranging from tears to a scream, from uncontrollable laughter to actual ejaculation. Some forms of pop can indeed stir all of these responses, like the "Bombay movies," those popular films exported worldwide from India which make their audiences cry, shudder, guffaw and grow sexually excited in a three- or four-hour span. Different segments of any population, however, depending on age and sex, respond with special enthusiasm to one or another of these appeals; though such differences seem finally less innate than learned.

In Anglo-Saxon culture, for instance, women have traditionally preferred sentimental, or, as it was called in the nineteenth century, "handkerchiefly," porn. To this day women constitute the majority (though by no means all) of the audience for the TV soaps, in which suffering and illness, betrayal and desertion, are the central themes, and the beholders are constantly being called on to cry over the troubled plight of humanity, while deploring the evil in the human heart.

On the other hand, men until recently have reserved for themselves the exclusive right to erotic porn. It is, in any case, written by males from the female point of view, providing for its preponderantly male readership the illusion of knowing what it feels like to "them" to be made love to —often by force, and seldom without sado-masochistic overtones—by "us." This is true not just of hard-core porn like *Justine* or *Fanny Hill,* but of the explicit sexual scenes in "classic" novels, ranging from Richardson's *Clarissa* to Joyce's *Ulysses* and Lawrence's *Lady Chatterley's Lover.* Some types of erotica, moreover, are limited in their appeal not just because they represent the fantasies of men about women, but because they tickle the fancy of a particular class, educated to a particular level; like "dirty limericks," for example, which apparently appeal almost exclusively to well-educated male bourgeois.

For a while, however, especially in the later sixties, women seemed about to claim, along with other "equal opportunities," the right to produce and consume erotic porn. But by the late seventies and eighties, more radical feminists had switched from a demand for free access to the least reputable of popular genres to a crusade against it as essentially misogynist and, indeed, a kind of moral or aesthetic equivalent of rape. Horror, however, they object to only when the female is its chief target; nor do they spurn even the grossest burlesque unless it is directed against old maids, nymphomaniacs, castrating women, witches or other traditionally stigmatized creatures of their gender. Yet in the comparatively recent past, those of their grandmothers still proud to be called "ladies" considered the literature of both violence and sacrilegious humor something not just for "gentlemen only," but for "adults only" as well.

Children, however, have always responded positively to all these tabooed genres, except for erotic porn, since pre-pubescents are incapable of coming to terms with any love scene, whether romantic or explicitly sexual. Certainly this was true of boys in their "latency" period during my own childhood, when I and my friends would close our eyes and hoot loudly to drown out what we called the "mushy love stuff" at the Saturday matinee. It was bloodshed we wanted or belly laughs.

To be sure, there are some kinds of outrageous comedy unavailable to children, who have still too little conscious stake in the sanctity of marriage to be moved by farces about cuckoldry, or in science and reason to find Books III and IV of *Gulliver's Travels* hilarious. Books I and II, however, *do* tickle them, as do all jokes about the relativity of size or the absurdity of those in authority. But they find most appealing "grab ass" or "slapstick," like the films of Abbott and Costello, Laurel and Hardy and the Ritz Brothers, and the animated cartoons in which mayhem, mutilation and brutality are presented as somehow laughable.

To say that pop horror and pop comedy are especially attractive to children (who will break through the barriers of any "rating" system to attend films they recognize as somehow their own, like *Jaws* or *The Exorcist*) is not to dismiss them as "juvenile" but to recognize them as universal, since many more of us are willing to indulge the child in our adult selves than feel free to give rein to what persists of the other sex in our male or female bodies. Yet terror in literature and the popular arts has, as we have noticed, certain moralistic enemies. Perhaps this is due precisely to its ability to cross all conventional role boundaries: not only generational and sexual, but ethnic and class as well. Certainly, I have seen black and white kids, along with adults of all hues and both genders, equally enthralled by the latest version of *Dracula,* of which in fact there have been hundreds on stage, screen and television ever since Bram Stoker's original novel appeared in 1897.

If that late Victorian fantasy has become the favorite pop work of the late twentieth century, that is because like all horror porn (but somehow preeminently so) it stirs in us involuntary physiological responses which, existing prior to acculturation, can only be tempered but never quite controlled by consciously acquired codes of behavior. But so do the three other subgenres of popular porn. And so also does any art which lasts long and pleases many—from the tragedy of Periclean Athens, which so disturbed Plato, to the Elizabethan and Jacobean drama, against which the Puritans relentlessly campaigned, to modernist novels by Joyce and Lawrence, which the courts once forbade good Americans to import into the Land of the Free. In a sense, which we are now in a position to understand, all of those censors were *right.* It is indeed an essential function of literature to release in us unnatural impulses—including the need from time to time to go out of our heads—which we otherwise repress or sublimate for the sake of law and order, civlization, sweet reason itself.

To defend against its enemies the popular drama which he loved, as I love soap operas, cop shows and fright-night films, Aristotle found it strategic to pretend that the dionysiac release afforded the audience by plays, performed in honor of that god of inebriation, was *rationally* explicable in terms of mimesis, instruction and delight. If such works teach us anything, however, it is how *not* to be rational. And if they provide us with pleasure by making us blush, shiver or sustain an erection, it is a strange kind of pleasure on the very verge of pain. The reactions they prompt in us are, moreover, uncontrollable, which is to say, once we have yielded to laughter, it is not always possible to stop at will. We laugh, as we say, "until we cry," i.e., until that laughter has become unendurable.

Similarly, once we begin to sob, we pass out of the control of our conscious minds and our adult notions of how one should behave in public. Once again common parlance gives us the clue. "We cry," we say, "like a baby." Likewise, when we scream in terror at a horror film or grow sexually excited at an X-rated movie, there is no way of staying the process. Yet it is not the actual suffering of relatives or friends which has made us weep; not the allure of living flesh and blood which has stirred us to tumescence; not a ridiculous occurrence in the real world that has set us laughing; not a true threat to life and limb that has made our flesh crawl and our hair stand on end.

What moves us is an illusion, a fiction, a hallucination not even our own, but someone else's imposed on us via words on a page, images flickering on a screen, sounds in the air. But is it not crazy—or the opposite of prudent, at any rate —to go out of control over what we really know is not there, has never happened? "Privileged insanity" would be perhaps the most honest name for what we seek in mythic art: a way of suspending rationality, which, though presumably framed and limited, involves always the minimal risk of no return, a permanent confusion of reality and illusion, as in the famous case of Don Quixote. In any case, continual exposure to the pleasures of pop trains us to indulge impulses which morality and mental hygiene warn us are dangerous. Moreover, as contemporary parents, trying vainly to detach their children from the TV set, are wont to cry out, archetypal pop *is* habit-forming—especially, perhaps, in its post-Gutenberg forms.

But it has always been easy to acquire a taste for, and hard to kick ever since the invention of movable type. I can remember my own parents trying to pull me away from the schlock novels with which I drugged myself in late childhood and early adolescence, whenever, that is, my junk literature was different from that which they preferred. But presumably something new and worse has been added since the electronic revolution: stories on TV do not even have to be "read," which is to say, assimilated with the Gutenberg skills learned in required courses in school. Created by hacks, more likely to be stupid than intelligent but with easy access to their own unconscious where it impinges on the collective unconscious of their time, such "trash" is available to almost anyone, requiring neither subtlety of perception, "education" nor anything resembling good old true-blue Protestant Hard Work.

This is not, however, a characteristic only of what the pious call "trash." All art, high, low or middling, of wide mythic appeal provides on the first encounter (whatever other rewards it may or may not have for the devoted and diligent) *unearned instant gratification:* a gratification necessary to our psychic well-being, for which I once presumed "catharsis" to be a satisfactory name. But whatever may have satisfied anal Aristotle, the metaphor of the child on the potty-chair no longer does me, and so I have been shopping around. Perhaps the most common term used these days for what we seek in the popular arts is "escape," a word ordinarily implying condescension or contempt. Yet, though C. S. Lewis was once moved to observe that the only people to whom the word "escape" is a pejorative are jailers, it is hard to use it as an honorific.

Better surely is Thoreau's observation that what he calls "perennial literature" enables us to be "in dreams awake," and I have actually made that phrase the title of a collection of science fiction. Even more attractive in some ways is Freud's description of our response to such literature as "regression in service of the ego," which I have therefore quoted in earlier apologies for the majority arts. But I find both finally too bland, particularly the latter with its clinical assurance that "privileged insanity" is finally therapeutic and therefore okay.

Yet there is an implicit metaphor in the term "regression" which intrigues me: a suggestion of a return not just to juvenile psychic levels, but of a descent into, a harrowing of Hell, since for Freud the depths of the unconscious were associated with the infernal regions of ancient mythology. He makes this quite explicit in the epigraph to *The Interpretation of Dreams,* an early work which begins as an analysis of jokes but ends as an exploratory trip into his own deep unconscious. *"Flectere si nequeo superos, Acheronta movebo,"* he quotes from Vergil's *Aeneid.* "If I cannot sway the high gods, I will move the power of Hades."

In light of this, it is possible to think of the release of the repressed, which is the function not only of the sort of jokes

Freud analyzed but of all popular literature, as a way of "giving the Devil his due," or even, in the words of the title of a Rolling Stones song, as expressing "sympathy with the Devil." But the point is not evil worship for its own sake à la Mick Jagger, but a recourse to the dark powers in quest of salvation: a way out of the secular limbo we inhabit —the world of getting and spending, and of a least-common-denominator consensus reality enforced in the name of sanity and virtue.

The laureates of majority art seem to know instinctively what the mystical rabbis of the Chasidic movement taught: that we must also serve God with the *yetzer ha ra,* the Evil Impulse. And though they do not always realize it (William Blake, who did, remarked of Milton that he was of the Devil's party without knowing it), neither, as Blake's comment suggests, do the apostles of High Art. In any case, to do justice to that transcendence of good and evil, that marriage of Heaven and Hell, once acted out in ritual orgies and human sacrifices but now entrusted to the humblest arts, we must seek metaphor on the border between mysticism and passion. But we do not have to seek far; such a metaphor is to be found in a long cultural essay, whose title has been traditionally mistranslated as "On the Sublime," written by a writer we call "Longinus," though that was clearly not his name.

· That perhaps Christian critic spoke of the ultimate excellence of literature, which transcended all the rules of the rhetoricians, as *ekstasis,* meaning ecstasy or rapture or transport, a profound alteration of consciousness in which the normal limits of flesh and spirit seem to dissolve. It is an effect, he realized, not necessarily achieved by works highly regarded by critics, or necessarily excluded from the most debased popular art. It appears mysteriously, he taught, in both; present, for instance, in the tag "Let there be light and there was light" from the humble scriptures of the barbarous Hebrews just as in the most precious poetry of the enlightened Greeks. And what is incumbent on us now, it seems to me as I reach the end of definition and move on to advocacy, is to take a cue from Longinus and create an approach to literature in which we will, if not quite abandon, at least drastically downgrade both ethics and aesthetics in favor of "ecstatics."

●

Once we have made *ekstasis* rather than instruction and delight our chief evaluative criterion, we will be well on the way to abandoning all formalist, elitist, methodological criticism, and will have started to invent an eclectic, amateur, neo-Romantic, populist one that will enable us to read what was once popular literature not as popular but as literature, even as it enables us to read what was once High Literature not as high but as literature. By the same token, we will find ourselves speaking less of theme and purport, structure and texture, signified and signifier, metaphor and metonymy, and more of myth, fable, archetype, fantasy, magic and wonder. Even more important, we will be speaking for ourselves, *as* ourselves, rather than *ex cathedra* in the name of some impersonal "tradition." And finally, we will be speaking to, rather than at or over the heads of (it was our eavesdropping colleagues we were really addressing), the mass audience, especially as they are represented by their children, the students they hopefully send to the institutions which support us.

To confess openly the passionate interest in pop which I have long shared with those students, but have lied about to myself as well as to them, would not just ease a classroom situation which I have come to feel intolerable, but help join together the sundered larger community, by making the university a place where we are not further separated from each other. Like all else entertained on the level of full consciousness, religion, for instance, and political ideology, what used to be "literature" divides us against ourselves; while what used to be called "trash," rooted like our dreams and nightmares in shared myth and fantasy, touches us all at a place where we have never been psychically sundered each from each.

Learning to honor the latter as much as the former would for me mean not just reuniting what have become in our culture two literatures and the two audiences, but joining together my two selves, past and present. Surely, one of the motives of the long quest which has brought my aging "me" to this point is a desire to be one again with the "me" my schooling taught me to disavow: the kid who read with all the other kids on the block *Captain Blood, King Solomon's Mines* and *Tom Swift's Giant Cannon,* as well as *Fanny Hill, The Rajah's Ram* and travesties of *Tillie the Toiler* and *Moon Mullins* in the so-called "eight-page bibles."

It was not long, however, before I had learned in classes in "literature" to despise the easy pleasures of high adventure and hard-core porn or even the western and detective stories which my father and I used to share as we shared almost nothing else. I can see him still, sitting by my side, our elbows resting on the kitchen table under the shaded electric light; I without glasses still, but he with thick lenses and a magnifying glass in his hand as he made his half-blind way through the latest Carter Dixon or Max Brand, which he then passed on to me. How quickly we turned the pages in our breathless desire to be done before his bedtime or mine: the way, I cannot help thinking, Richardson's original readers, or Dickens' or Mark Twain's, had flipped through their newest novel—faster and faster and faster before the fading of the light.

If I am concluding on a note of truly Dickensian sentimentality, that is first of all because it is to such an ending that the approach I am taking leads; and I am, as Huck Finn would have said, "rotten glad of it." But it is also because I would in any case have chosen, do at this moment choose, to try to become in full awareness that to which I have all along inadvertently tended: a pop critic, learning (how slowly and painfully, this very sentence reveals) to speak the language of popular literature, the language of Richardson and Dickens, of Harriet Beecher Stowe and Mark Twain, of Edgar Rice Burroughs and Sir Arthur Conan Doyle. Of that language my formal education sought to deprive me, even as it taught me to despise many of the books written in it and the emotions to which they appealed.

I grew up in the age of modernism, of what was then referred to as the "New Poetry" and the "New Criticism," and was taught to eschew not just the sort of sentimentality I have risked in evoking my lost father and the comrades of my childhood, but those commonplaces into which the defense of that sentimentality has betrayed me. If I reject the latter half of the modernists' credo as well as the first, I am impelled to do so not out of some perverse love of the platitude for its own sake. I am, to tell the truth, more than a little tired of the by now elderly Cult of the New, but I have not completely shaken off vestiges of the horror I used to feel whenever I found written in red ink in the margins of my freshman compositions: CLICHÉ! I have nonetheless come to understand that in every stereotype, no matter how weary, there sleeps a true archetype, waiting to be awak-

PART TWO

Opening Up the Canon

Home as Heaven, Home as Hell

In 1960 I published *Love and Death in the American Novel,* a thick, ambitious work in which I tried to come to terms with the myths embodied in what I still referred to as "our great books," the "canon" of American fiction. I had excluded, I assured my readers, no writer "of first rank," nor had I "deliberately sacrificed considerations of value to the pursuit of my themes." It did not occur to me then that the terms "great," "canon," "of first rank" and "value" were themselves problematical. What books were distinguished enough to be properly discussable seemed to me self-evident. The only question was how to read them, and I knew the answer to that: cryptanalytically, contextually, irreverently. Moreover, when in 1967 I prepared a new edition, I decided to add nothing, alter nothing; only slimmed down the unconscionable bulk of the text a little by excising redundancies I had come to find embarrassing.

Yet even at that point I was beginning to be aware of how dubious were the elitist assumptions that had led me to neglect or condescend to certain long-lived best sellers containing myths quite different from those which informed the books I took to be canonical. At the root of my problem, I think, was my accepting as eternally valid a canon of American novels which had, in fact, been established only a few decades before, chiefly by two critical works of high modernism, D. H. Lawrence's *Studies in Classic American Literature* and F. O. Matthiessen's *The*

American Renaissance. That the very notion of a "canon" had been called into question by the rise of mass culture I was not yet prepared to grant. Nor did it occur to me that the near future might demand changes in the modernists' definition of the "great tradition" as profound as those they had worked in the Victorian definition they inherited.

To be sure, I was already growing impatient with what I considered the too rigid elitism of F. R. Leavis and Martin Turnell. Not only was I especially fond of certain novelists they excluded, like Dickens and Balzac, but I was already aware that the explicit politics of their hierarchal criticism was anti-egalitarian, anti-populist, anti-democratic (after all, many modernists were right-wingers, some indeed outright fascists); but I did not condemn it out of hand. For many years I had sought to reconcile in myself the contradictory ideals of a classless society and a hierarchal culture. I was able therefore to regard the indurated snobbism of Leavis, Turnell and company as a regrettable excess of zeal in behalf of "standards" essentially valuable, even *necessary* in a time when notions of excellence were everywhere under attack.

Finally (I was still convinced), it was not the overzealous "highbrows" who were the real enemies of "culture," but the "lowbrows," who despised all standards, and even more perhaps the "middlebrows," who pretended to honor them but wound up praising such pretentious kitsch as Herman Wouk's *Marjorie Morningstar*. "Kitsch," "middlebrow," "highbrow," "lowbrow": it is as hard for me now to remember that I once used such terms in deadly earnest as it was for me then to remember that I was not Matthew Arnold nor was meant to be, but only a culture-climbing Jewish boy from Newark, New Jersey, lost in the mountain West of America, where almost nobody was familiar with such words, or had read any of the art novels in my canon.

Marjorie Morningstar, despite its Eastern setting and largely Jewish cast of characters, was quite another matter, which perhaps explains the rage with which I attacked that poor, inept, pious tract; though maybe it was, rather, my unconfessed suspicion that I who had come to convert the barbarians to the religion of High Art was turning in to a crypto-populist with a Ph.D. I *needed* to believe that thought. I had become a husband and a father, a householder and an academic (my radical politics long since dissolved into nostalgia for a lost revolution and my own lost youth), but I had not become a Babbitt, like some of my colleagues, who, I discovered, went regularly to Kiwanis luncheons but never entered the university library. No, I assured myself, I was still a member in good standing of the intelligentsia, and to prove it I wrote about books which most of my fellow Montanans never read, in a jargon they could not understand. I published, moreover, chiefly in the *Partisan Review*, a journal founded by former Communists, who continued to think of themselves as anti-Stalinist radicals, but had managed, like me, to espouse the revised literary canon of the age of Eliot and Pound, Proust and Mann, Kafka and Joyce.

Their preferred texts were by and large European, but in Lawrence and Mattheissen I found a corresponding list of okay American novels, which they had managed to smuggle into the canon without either diluting "standards" or compromising their own status as free intellectuals. Lawrence, indeed, remained all his life an extra-academic wanderer, a peripatetic disturber of the peace; while Matthiessen, though he had entered the university, functioned there as a kind of dissident-in-residence, "boring from within"—thus providing me with a viable model for my own career. I scarcely noticed, and would not, I suspect, have been dismayed if anyone had brought it to my attention, that somehow all the novelists they praised turned out to be WASP males, and that Lawrence in fact sought to define "the spirit of the place" in which he had briefly sojourned and I had been born without mentioning a single book by a woman or with a black person as a major character.

I did not, in any case, deliberately try to open up their extended canon any further. Yet, without being quite conscious of what I was doing, I subverted it a little by treating in *Love and Death in the American Novel* several all-time best sellers by women writers whom Lawrence and Matthiessen had both ignored. There seemed to me no way of passing over in silence Harriet Beecher Stowe's *Uncle Tom's Cabin*, since it was at least marginally respectable. And having started, I found myself unable to stop until I had also mentioned in passing Maria Cummins' *The Lamplighter* (remarking that thirty years after its appearance, James Joyce's Gerty MacDowell was still echoing her erotic rhetoric), and despite my snide references to the heroine of Susan Warner's *The Wide, Wide World* as "rabbity and inoffensive," I returned to that favorite novel of mid-nineteenth-century females over and over in my text. Finally, however, I lumped Mrs. Stowe with the other two as a "genteel sentimentalist" and, though I sought valiantly to give her her due, ended by faulting her for having failed to achieve "tragic ambivalence or radical protest."

"Tragic," it must be understood, like "ambivalence," was an honorific in the New Critics' cant of the time, along with "serious wit," "irony" and "symbolism." Moreover, I had just been reading James Baldwin's anti-Tom essay, "Everybody's Protest Novel," in which he had condemned *Uncle Tom's Cabin* from the point of view of avant-garde aesthetics and anti-racist politics. In light of the first, he called it "a very bad novel, having in its self-righteous, virtuous sentimentality much in common with *Little Women.*" Fascinatingly, he assumed that for any reader of taste merely to identify Mrs. Stowe's novel with Louisa May Alcott's "girls' books" was enough to damn it. But he felt obliged to make a fully explicit case against "sentimentality," defining it as "the ostentatious parading of excessive and spurious emotion"; then went on to argue that it is "the mark of dishonesty, the inability to feel . . . and it is always, therefore, the signal of secret and violent inhumanity, the mask of cruelty." Finally he added in a cry of masculine protest, made all the more poignant perhaps by the fact that he himself was both a Negro and a homosexual (the terms "black" and "gay" had not yet become fashionable), "Tom has been . . . divested of his sex."

Yet elsewhere Baldwin has confessed that Mrs. Stowe's novel was one of his favorite boyhood books, even as it was one of my own. As a matter of fact, his mother, troubled by what must have seemed to her his unnatural addiction to that white woman's book, kept snatching it away from him and hiding it. But he always managed to find it again, not merely rereading it in privacy (for reasons which we can only surmise) but sharing it with his younger brothers and sisters, with whom he was required to play a quasi-maternal role. "As they were born," he tells us, "I took them over with one hand and held a book in the other . . . and in this way I read *Uncle Tom's Cabin* . . . over and over and over again." But that early passion he later denied, and his total recantation helped persuade me to make my own partial one.

Even the qualified praise I gave Mrs. Stowe in *Love and Death in the American Novel* began after a while to appear to me if not downright perverse, at least rather eccentric, since later classroom handbooks, though they have at least acknowledged her existence, have tended to apologize for doing so. *The Literary History of the United States,* for instance, concludes ruefully that "Harriet Beecher Stowe was neither a great personality nor a great artist," while the aging "New Critics" responsible for a recent college anthology preface their selection from Mrs. Stowe's masterpiece by asking, "How good is *Uncle Tom's Cabin* as a novel?" and answering, "Not very good if we judge it by the highest fictional standards." To be sure, it has had its defenders, from Tolstoi and William Dean Howells to V. L. Parrington and Van Wyck Brooks, and from Kenneth Lynn to Ellen Moers to Anthony Burgess. But most of them have felt obliged to confess its inadequacy as art, Parrington, for instance, writing, "Despite its obvious blemishes of structure and sentimentalism . . . it was noble propaganda." Propaganda, yes, even "noble" propaganda; but "literature"— not quite. Kenneth Lynn has dissented from this majority opinion, protesting, "Those critics who label *Uncle Tom's Cabin* good propaganda but bad art cannot have given sufficient time to the novel. . . . If they should ever linger over it long enough . . . they would surely cease to perpetuate one of the most unjust clichés in all of American criticism."

But Lynn's credentials are those of a literary historian rather than a critic, and I remain, therefore, still convinced of what Howells, who both deeply loved and clearly understood the book, expressed so well: "But really, is it a novel, in the sense that *War and Peace* is a novel, or *Madame Bovary,* or *L'Assommoir . . .* or *Esther Waters . . .* or *The Return of the Native,* or *Virgin Soil . . .* ? In a certain way it is greater than any of these except the first; but its chief virtue, or its prime virtue, is in the address to the conscience, and not its address to the taste; to the ethical sense, not the aesthetical sense." So long as I distrusted the "ethical" and depended on "aesthetical" criteria as defined by modernism, I could find no way to rank *Uncle Tom's Cabin* with the "classics" of our tradition like *Moby Dick, The Scarlet Letter, Huckleberry Finn* or even *The Leatherstocking Tales.*

It seems to me in retrospect, however, that I was already being a bit disingenuous, since by 1960 I had admitted in print that Cooper too lacked "tragic ambivalence" and "radical protest," and was beginning to suspect that he was blatantly "sentimental" as well. Certainly, the scene in which Natty Bumppo and Chingachgook, the childless white warrior and the bereaved red one, sit side by side at the campfire in wordless mourning for Uncas, the son of Chingachgook and symbol for the doomed Indian people, not merely extorts our tears as shamelessly as the flogging to death of Uncle Tom, but also signals a "secret and violent inhumanity," erotic and racist.

We have clinical proof of this in the case of *Uncle Tom's Cabin*, which Sigmund Freud reports in his classic study of sado-masochism, "A Child Is Being Beaten," was used by certain of his patients to cue fantasies that brought them to masturbatory orgasm. The evidence against *The Last of the Mohicans* is more circumstantial but, I think, equally convincing, since in his *Table Talk* Adolf Hitler confesses that this was his favorite novel. Why, then, did I in 1960 describe the one as "genteel," "sentimental" and "melodramatic," reserving for the other the more honorific labels of "mythic" and "archetypal"?

It was in part, I suppose, simple *machismo*, as deep and instinctive as my sense of self, that made Cooper's sympathetic "masculine" sentimentality unobtrusive enough not to conceal from me the myth which motivated it. Mrs. Stowe's "feminine" pathos, on the other hand, was uncongenial enough to prevent my perceiving the equally valid archetype which underlay it. But more than this, I was influenced by the fact that the anti-domestic myth of *The Last of the Mohicans*, which imagines true love and liberty as possible only far from the world of women, is central also to canonical books like *Moby Dick* and *Huckleberry Finn*; though, to be sure, it reappears too in what has been traditionally considered "trash," on stage, screen and television, as well as in print.

The myth which informs *Uncle Tom's Cabin*, however, in which home, marriage and mother are postulated as the greatest goods, belongs *only* to what I had been taught to regard as "subliterature"; so that indeed I may have failed to do it justice less because of male chauvinism than elitist snobbery. It is true, in any event, that I gave even scanter consideration than I had to Mrs. Stowe and her sisters to male writers of great mythopoeic powers whose fantasies were based on macho myths that similarly found no echo in High Literature. In my compendious study of American fiction from 1789 to 1959, I ignored completely, for instance, the two greatest exploiters of the Darwinian *mythos* of survival of the fittest, both proud of being "manly" men. I did not even mention the name of either the resolutely "lowbrow" Edgar Rice Burroughs (who wanted to call himself "Normal Bean" on the title page of his first novel) or that marginal "middlebrow" Jack London.

I have begun recently to try to come to terms with the first, and I keep promising myself that someday I will deal at length with the second, to whom I still do not quite understand my response. Yet, though *Tarzan of the Apes* and *The Call of the Wild* titillated my deep fantasy as a boy, and I can return to them still with a pleasure more than merely nostalgic, the archetypes they embody threaten always to turn into stereotypes, and they seem to me in any case unreliable clues to the nature of the deep American psyche. Certainly they are less central, less illuminating, than the myth of interethnic male bonding, which I have been exploring with almost monomaniacal exclusivity for all of my critical career.

There is, however, a second myth of equal importance, to which I regret having paid so little attention for so long; because without fully understanding it, I have come to realize, it is impossible fully to understand the first, with which it exists in dialectical tension. What I am talking about is the myth classically formulated in *Uncle Tom's Cabin* (let us call it the myth of Home as Heaven), which— without at first being aware of what I was up to—I have been learning to take seriously for the last fifteen or more years. *Re*-learning to take it seriously, I suppose I should say, as I had been able to do as a child, but could not do as an adult until I had unlearned literary "standards," by measuring them against Mrs. Stowe's novel rather than it against them.

Once I had begun to do so, it became clear that the American books which, according to those standards, were clearly superior to hers were not only more elegantly structured and textured, more ideologically dense, more overtly subversive—more difficult and challenging, in short—but they almost invariably celebrated the flight from civilization and the settlement, church and school, from everything which had survived (under female auspices) of Christian humanism in the New World—thus reinforcing the myth of Home as Hell.

The uniquely American hero/anti-hero of such books rescues no maiden, like Perseus, kills no dragon, like St. George, discovers no treasure, like Beowulf or Siegfried; he does not even manage at long last to get back to his wife, like Odysseus. He is, in fact, an anti-Odysseus, who finds his identity by *running away from home*. This may seem a boyish notion of heroism; yet it is first embodied in Rip Van Winkle, who enters the scene already mature and leaves it a grizzled old man, while Rip's immediate successor, Natty Bumppo, makes his central appearance even older. But he grows younger and younger, as his author dreams a dream in which time runs backward from civilization to virgin wilderness. Here the new Eve, the WASP wife, has not yet been created, and the new Adam lives in an innocent anti-marriage with a Noble Red Man, called Chingachgook or the Great Serpent, quite like Satan, the primordial enemy of Woman.

It was Cooper who first realized that the anti-wife must be nonwhite as well as nonfemale, and mythically it seems scarcely to matter what hue of nonwhite. He can be brown like Melville's Queequeg or black like Twain's Nigger Jim; but at the moment he becomes a Negro, his runaway mate turns into the boy who will not grow up, which is to say, Huck Finn, and the myth achieves its final form. Later, the wilderness lovers undergo even stranger transmogrifications, but two essential elements of the myth never change: the nightmare of misogyny and the dream of racial reconciliation.

It is, however, misogyny in a peculiarly American form: a view of women which identifies them with everything that must be escaped in order to be free. Even in the dying twentieth century such latter-day avatars of the "runaway boy" as R. P. McMurphy in Ken Kesey's *One Flew Over the Cuckoo's Nest* continue to repeat in their own words the cry of Huckleberry Finn, "Aunt Sally, she wants to adopt me and civilize me . . . but I been there before." Actually, Twain had first written, "*They* want to adopt me and civilize me," but his sure instinct led him to revise it to "Aunt Sally, *she* . . ."

All Americans, therefore (including girls and women,

who also grew up reading Mark Twain), at levels deeper than ideology perceive white women as the enemy, which may explain why even the most enlightened of us, male and female alike, end up cheering McMurphy's attempted rape-murder of Big Nurse at the movies, and why, after all, ERA may never become part of the Constitution. How can it be, we ask ourselves, between waking and sleeping, that our mythical oppressors now consider themselves, claim to have considered themselves all along, the oppressed? But, of course, the myth of the wilderness companions represents also the male ex-European's dream of effecting —behind the backs of white women, as it were—a reconciliation with those fellow males we know we have really, *really* oppressed.

That reconciliation does not, however, envisage a marriage in the flesh. Only in the spirit can white and non-white become one. Our anti-heroes do not flee white women to beget on red/brown/black/yellow ones children neither white nor nonwhite. *The Leatherstocking Tales* are haunted by a horror of miscegenation; so that just as white girls flee the threat of Indian rape, Natty recoils in dismay when asked to mate with a "squaw." "There's no cross in my blood," he cries, and he prefers to die without issue rather than father an heir unable to make the same boast.

In later versions of the myth, like *Moby Dick* and *Huckleberry Finn,* the threat of miscegenation is scarcely permitted to cross the threshold of consciousness. Yet we know from Melville's *Typee* and Twain's *Pudd'nhead Wilson* that their authors too were possessed by a fear of "blood pollution," which, indeed, it may be a covert function of the myth of male bonding to exorcise. But in the favorite books of the wives and mothers left behind by Rip, Natty, Ishmael and Huck, that nightmare horror is openly exploited. It represents, in fact, the dark underside of their counter-myth, in which home is portrayed as the earthly paradise, and marriage and integration into the family not as a fate to be fled for the sake of freedom, but as one to be sought in quest of maturity, responsibility and Christian salvation.

Precisely for this reason, perhaps, the pop novels which exploit this counter-myth have been able to deal, in a way in which the "classics" of male bonding have not, with traumatic historical events climaxing in the Civil War and its tragic aftermath. Surrendering these events, along with the nightmare images of black-white rape and flogging, which are their mythic context, to the domestic romancers, our "classic" male novelists have ended by substituting nostalgia for history. Mark Twain, for instance, retreating to his own antebellum boyhood, makes of slavery an occasion for paeans to transcendent homoerotic love, when he does not travesty it in heartless burlesque. And Walt Whitman converts the War Between the States into a backdrop for the masochistic adventures of a wound-dresser among beautiful, maimed young men.

Only William Faulkner, last heir to the tradition of misogyny and male bonding, confronts head-on the nightmare terror of miscegenation. But this is because, straddling the line between High Literature and pop, he draws also on the tradition which begins with Harriet Beecher Stowe. Certain lines, for instance, spoken by Dilsey in *The Sound and the Fury* could be transferred, without jarring the reader, to Uncle Tom. But the stylistic context in which they appear, modeled on elitist European novels like Joyce's *Ulysses*, has alienated the majority audience that responded passionately to a series of truly popular works, which begins with Mrs. Stowe's book and the "Tom plays" into which it was almost immediately translated, and is continued in Thomas Dixon, Jr.'s *The Leopard's Spots* and *The Clansman* (along with *The Birth of a Nation,* a film derived from them by D. W. Griffith), Margaret Mitchell's *Gone With the Wind* (both as a novel and a movie) and Alex Haley's *Roots* (in all of its pop versions, from the predigested book selection to what threatened for a while to become an endlessly continued TV series).

Read as a single work composed over more than a century, in many media and by many hands, these constitute a hitherto unperceived "epic," embodying a myth of our history unequaled in scope and resonance by any work of High Art. No epic, however, was ever created so inadvertently, so improbably, arising out of a tradition at once disreputable and genteel, which seemed destined forever to produce not literature of high seriousness, "doctrinal to a nation," but only ephemeral best sellers. Yet precisely for this reason they have been loved by the majority audience, which considers them not epical at all (the very word turns them off) but "good reads." And indeed they are, singly and compositely, a "good read": not merely celebrating domesticity, but moving inexorably to their expected "happy endings," permitting easy identification with their sympathetic protagonists, and providing along the way opportunities for shudders and thrills, laughter and tears.

The archetypal ancestry of this fictional mode goes back as far as the fairy tale—"Cinderella," in particular—and in other cultures it has been adopted by writers as distinguished as Samuel Richardson and Charles Dickens. But in America it was from the start the almost exclusive province of the unpretentious authors of "best sellers," particularly women writing for women. Beginning with Susanna Rowson, whose *Charlotte Temple* appeared before the end of the eighteenth century, their line continued with what Hawthorne in the mid-nineteenth (envious of their sales, perhaps, as well as contemptuous of their values) called the "horde of damned female scribblers." And they have, in fact, kept "scribbling" down to our own time, including in their numbers Susan Warner, Mrs. E. D. E. N. Southworth, Louisa May Alcott, Helen Hunt Jackson, Alice Hegan Rice, Edna Ferber, Fannie Hurst, Taylor Caldwell, etc., etc.

In the post-print media, the laureates of the domestic myth have fared even better, winning equal time with the makers of the wilderness myth. Until very recently, however, they were kept separate and distinct, programs of the first kind being shown on television only during the hours when men were traditionally in the office and the shop rather than at home. But with the shift in gender roles begotten by the latest wave of the women's movement, they have begun to invade the evening hours. Yet by and large, each day until dusk our TV screens are still possessed by the daytime serials, the so-called soap operas, whose family crises are typically acted out in enclosed spaces: living rooms, bedrooms, kitchens or offices, from which the characters, usually related by blood or marriage, escape occasionally to hospital rooms, psychiatric wards, prison cells or courtrooms—sometimes even to exotic resorts in Jamaica or Bermuda.

More often than not, in any case, the action is framed by three walls of a set (whose closure is completed by the fourth wall behind our heads), not so much a home away from home as a home continuous with the one in which we watch. Seldom does anyone ride a horse, a car, a plane on screen, and no one ever floats down the Mississippi on a raft or sails off on a whaling ship. Nor is anyone ever alone willingly or for long, for all aspire to heterosexual bonding, marriage, children, integration into the family. To be sure, no marriage lasts long; not because the wedded state is despised, but precisely because it is the sole conceivable Happy Ending, and the soap opera can never end. Only begin again, which is to say, move toward another marriage, and another, and another . . . doomed sometimes, quasi-incestuous always, but never, never joining together the races, never breaching the miscegenation taboo.

Once night falls, however (and amidst the encroaching after-dark soaps and soft-porn sitcoms), the westerns, the cop shows, the s.f. spectaculars reassert their dominance and we head out for the Territory once more—riding the range, prowling the streets of the urban jungle, penetrating outer space. And wherever long-term bonding occurs it is likely to involve a pair of ethnically disparate bachelors: the Jew Starsky and the Gentile Hutch, the black Tenspeed and the white Brownshoe, the earthling Captain Kirk and the Vulcan Mr. Spock. But they are being driven from the air these days, these descendants of Natty Bumppo and Chingachgook—attacked from all sides, presumably because of the ambience of violence in which alone their love can flourish. One suspects that on a deeper level the hostility to them is rooted in a distrust of interethnic male bonding itself.

If, however, as TV programming suggests, the American mind is possessed by a pair of antithetical myths, split down the middle in a kind of institutionalized ambivalence (since, of course, men watch soaps and women cop shows), we would never guess it when we leave television for the classroom—and begin the required reading of the "masterworks of our tradition," as defined by the Guardians of High Culture. These guardians have traditionally been white Anglo-Saxon Protestants, more often than not genteel, almost invariably straight males or closet gays. Even when vulgarians of lesser breeds or women have more recently begun to make it into the Old Boys Club, they have done so by introjecting the values of their predecessors, proving, therefore, quite as incapable of judging fairly works produced by and for culturally marginal groups in our society, including those to which they themselves belong.

Only *Uncle Tom's Cabin* among the books best loved by such groups has seemed at least *problematical* to those guardians—much abused, but a contender still for inclusion in a misogynist canon, which extends from Washington Irving to Saul Bellow ("What do they want?" he asks about women through the protagonist of *Herzog*. "They eat green salad and they drink blood"). It is, therefore, with that book that any attempt to redeem the feminine pop tradition and its essential archetype must begin.

It is scarcely surprising that *Uncle Tom's Cabin, or Life Among the Lowly* should contain the most compendious gallery of homes in all American literature, ranging from the humble Kentucky habitation which gives the novel its name ("In one corner of it stood a bed, covered neatly with a snowy spread.... The wall over the fireplace was adorned with some very brilliant scriptural prints, and a portrait of General Washington") to the elegant New Orleans summer villa of the St. Clares ("The common sitting room opened on to a large garden, fragrant with every picturesque plant and flower of the tropics"), and from the prim New England farmhouse of Miss Ophelia's family ("Within . . . wide clean rooms, where nothing seems to be doing or going to be done, where everything is once and forever rigidly in place") to the squalid and decayed mansion of Simon Legree ("The wallpaper was defaced in spots with slops of beer and wine or garnished with . . . long sums footed up, as if somebody had been practicing arithmetic there").

After all, Harriet Beecher Stowe had been a lifelong homemaker, who was to publish in 1865 a kind of domestic guidebook called *House and Home Papers* and to co-author four years later with her sister Catherine *American Woman's Home*, dedicated to "THE WOMEN OF AMERICA, in whose hands rest the real destinies of the Republic, as moulded by early training and preserved amid the maturer influences of home." It seems inevitable, then, that even in a novel dealing with the larger problems of slavery and states' rights (but also addressed to women) the myth of the Utopian Household appears—receiving, indeed, its classic formulation.

The earthly paradise which Mrs. Stowe describes is presumably an ordinary Quaker household, maternal, nurturing, almost edible, and—be it noted—*all white* except for the temporary residents, Eliza, a black mother fleeing to save her child, and George, her bitter and troubled husband, who rejoins her there by happy chance. The names of the inhabitants, however, are allegorical (the presiding matriarch is called, for instance, Rachel Halliday, in memory of the Old Testament mother forever weeping for her children and refusing to be comforted), and the archetypal implications of the scene are reinforced by references to an unfallen Eden in which an aging and chaste Venus peacefully reigns.

> . . . all moved obediently to Rachel's gentle "Hadn't thee better?" on the work of getting breakfast; for a breakfast in the luxurious valleys of Indiana is a thing complicated and multi-form, and like picking up the rose-leaves . . . in Paradise, asking other hands than those of the original mother. . . . Bards have written of the cestus of Venus, that turned the heads of all the world in successive generations. We had rather, for our part, have the cestus of Rachel Halliday, that kept heads from being turned, and made everything go on harmoniously. We think it is more suited to our modern days, decidedly.

More resonant mythologically than the classical or biblical names, however, are the words "mother" and "home" which echo and re-echo through the passage:

> Rachel never looked so truly and benignly happy as at the head of her table. There was so much motherliness and full-heartedness even in the way she passed a plate of cakes or poured a cup of coffee, that it seemed to put a spirit into the food and drink she offered. . . . This, indeed, was a home—*home* . . .

It was the assimilation of the slavery issue into so homely a scene which won the hearts of the readers of "female" best sellers, ordinarily indifferent to the world of "male" politics, persuading them that the "patriarchal institution," as Mrs. Stowe called slavery—not quite aware, I think, of the full implications of the metaphor—was a threat to Home and Mother and Family. Once freed, she suggested, black Americans would aspire to the kind of "happy ending" which she and her genteel audience demanded of their favorite novels: the reunion of parents and children, husbands and wives, in monogamous Christian households.

Just such a household she describes at the Dickens-like tearful-cheerful conclusion of her book, when George and Eliza, safe across the Canadian border, gather together with their son and daughter, plus a miraculously preserved and rediscovered mother and sister, in a truly Pickwickian love feast.

> The scene now changes to a small, neat tenement, in the outskirts of Montreal; the time, evening. A cheerful fire blazes on the hearth; a tea-table, covered with a snowy cloth, stands prepared for the evening meal. . . . But to return to our friends, whom we left wiping their eyes, and recovering from too great and sudden a joy. They are now seated around the social board, and are getting decidely companionable.

If George, the new head of his own house, dreams of a further emigration to Africa, it is not in order to "light out for the territory ahead of the rest," like Huckleberry Finn, to whom domestic "civilization" seems the end rather than the beginning of freedom; much less is it to search for his "roots," like some late twentieth-century black nationalist. Far from desiring to find an alternative to the Christian culture which has enslaved and unmanned him, a way of life based on polytheism, tribalism, polygamy or free sexuality, he plans to spread the Christian gospel to his unredeemed brethren on the Dark Continent: "As a Christian patriot, a teacher of Christianity, I go to *my country*," he writes to a friend; and doubtless Mrs. Stowe's first fans dreamed of his bringing to the benighted not just literacy and "the sublime doctrine of love and forgiveness," but "small, neat tenements" and "snowy tablecloths" as well.

Not even those mothers, however, whom Mrs. Stowe continually addresses in asides ("If it were *your* Harry, mother, or your Will, that were going to be torn from you . . . tomorrow morning . . .") seem to have been much moved by the evocation of the servantless Quaker household, in which order is so effortlessly preserved and even the furniture is motherly; nor have the loving but desexed characters who inhabit it lived on among their dearest memories. What has continued to survive in the imagination not just of mothers but the whole world is what is truly mythic in *Uncle Tom's Cabin.*

In the Quaker household, we are dealing not with myth but mythology—contrived, self-conscious, verging on allegory—a fantasy arising not out of the public nightmares of race and sex which Mrs. Stowe shared with her contemporaries in a nation moving toward total war, but out of her personal insecurities: her fear of growing old, her conviction that she was not beautiful, her inability to control her children (a favorite son would become an alcoholic and drift from sight) or to keep her house in order, though she in fact always had servants, some of them black and all apparently as inefficient as she. Writing of a typical day in her own nonutopian household, Mrs. Stowe walks the thin line between hilarity and despair:

> This meal being cleared away, Mr. Stowe dispatched to market with various memoranda of provisions, etc., and baby being washed and dressed, I begin to think what next must be done. I start to cut out some little dresses . . . when Master Henry makes a doleful lip and falls to crying with might and main. I catch him up, and, turning round, see one of his sisters flourishing the things out of my workbox in fine style. Moving it away and looking the other side, I see the second little mischief seated by the hearth chewing coals and scraping up ashes with great apparent relish. Grandmother lays hold upon her and charitably offers to endeavor to quiet baby while I go on with my work. I set at it again . . . measure them once more to see which is the right one, and proceed . . . when I see the twins on the point of quarreling with each other. Number one pushes number two over. Number two screams: that frightens the baby, and he joins in. I call number one a naughty girl, take the persecuted one in my arms, and endeavor to comfort her . . .

How different the Hallidays—Rachel, her impotent and scarcely visible husband, her incredibly cheerful and cooperative children—are not just from Mrs. Stowe, her husband and their children, but even more from others of her characters, mysteriously known even to those who have never read Mrs. Stowe's novel: Uncle Tom, Eliza, Topsy,

Little Eva and Simon Legree. Primordial images rather than living persons, they emerge mysteriously from the collective unconscious and pass, scarcely mediated by her almost transparent text, into the public domain, to which, like all authentic popular literature, they properly belong.

Similarly, the scenes which stay with us forever seem as archetypal and oneiric as those protagonists: Eliza leaping from ice floe to ice floe in pursuit of freedom, or Eva, on the verge of maturity, dying a death lingering enough not just to convert her demure black anti-type, Topsy, and her Byronic father, but to extort tears from generations of readers. Eliza's scene is shorter than we can believe—like a fragmentary dream dreamed in the moment before waking —while Eva's is described in considerable detail; but both have the realer-than-real vividness of hallucinations:

There was a sound in that chamber, first of one who stepped quickly. It was Miss Ophelia, who had resolved to sit up all night with her little charge, and who, at the turn of the night, had discerned what experienced nurses significantly call "a change." The outer door was quickly opened, and Tom, who was watching outside, was on the alert, in a moment.

"Go for the doctor, Tom! lose not a moment," said Miss Ophelia; and, stepping across the room, she rapped at St. Clare's door.

"Cousin," she said, "I wish you would come."

Those words fell on his heart like clods upon a coffin. Why did they? He was up and in the room in an instant, and bending over Eva, who still slept.

What was it he saw that made his heart stand still? Why was no word spoken between the two? Thou canst say, who hast seen that same expression on the face dearest to thee;—that look indescribable, hopeless, unmistakable, that says to thee that thy beloved is no longer thine.

On the face of the child, however, there was no ghastly imprint—only a high and almost sublime expression—the over-shadowing presence of spiritual natures, the dawning of immortal life in that childish soul . . .

. . . The child lay panting on her pillows, as one exhausted—the large clear eyes rolled up and fixed. Ah, what said those eyes, that spoke so much of heaven? Earth was past, and earthly pain; but so solemn, so mysterious, was the triumphant brightness of that face, that it checked even the sobs of sorrow. They pressed around her, in breathless stillness.

"Eva," said St. Clare, gently.

She did not hear.

"O, Eva, tell us what you see? What is it?" said her father.

A bright, a glorious smile passed over her face, and she said, brokenly—"O! love—joy—peace!" gave one sigh, and passed from death unto life!

"Farewell, beloved child! the bright, eternal doors have closed after thee; we shall see thy sweet face no more. O, woe for them who watched thy entrance into heaven, when they shall wake and find only the cold gray sky of daily life, and thou gone forever."

What haunts us most deeply, however, is the scene of Uncle Tom being beaten to death by Simon Legree, flanked by his black henchmen Sambo and Quimbo. Rooted in history, as Mrs. Stowe understands it, they seem less historical figures than projections of a misandry otherwise difficult for a dutiful wife, sister and daughter of strong pious males to confess. Yet the white Vermonter Legree embodies the kind of macho Yankee inflexibility she must have known from earliest childhood, while the other two, with "their coarse, heavy features; their great eyes, rolling enviously . . . their barbarous, guttural, half-brute intonation," seem figments of the fear of black phallic power which Mrs. Stowe took such pains elsewhere to euphemize or deny. It is the first, the New Englander, however, who performs the deed of darkness, while his dusky overseers merely stand by—yet are party to the total horror all the same:

> Legree drew in a long breath; and, suppressing his rage, took Tom by the arm, and, approaching his face almost to his, said, in a terrible voice, "Hark 'e, Tom! —ye think, 'cause I've let you off before, I don't mean what I say; but this time, I've *made up my mind* and counted the cost. You've always stood it out agin' me: now, I'll *conquer ye, or kill ye!*—one or t'other. I'll count every drop of blood there is in you, and take 'em, one by one, till ye give up!"

It is an encounter which lives on in the depths of my own mind with hallucinatory vividness, as seems appropriate

enough in light of the fact that it originally came to Mrs.
Stowe as a hallucination. To me, moreover, as to her and
her readers, early and late, both that event and the gothic
swampland plantation on which it occurs represent (whatever demurrers the conscious mind may make) the quintes-
sential, the archetypal Deep South. Yet, of course, she had
never known that region at first hand, so that it remains as
imaginary and symbolic as the "Europe" of Poe's tales of
terror. "Dark Places," she calls the chapter in which Uncle
Tom first sees the infernal landscape of "Down the River,"
adding the epigraph: "The dark places of the earth are full
of the habitations of cruelty"; then describes for us the
"dreary pine barrens, where the wind whispered mournfully . . . the doleful trees rising out of the slimy, spongy
ground, hung with long wreaths of funereal black moss,
while ever and anon the loathsome form of the moccasin
snake might be seen sliding among broken stumps."

Oddly enough, her vision of Tom's death in the bayous
of Louisiana came to her in polar New England, rather than
when she was as close to the real South as she ever got,
which is to say, in Cincinnati, just across the river from
slaveholding Kentucky. She had, in fact, just moved to
snowbound Bowdoin, Maine, where her husband had been
appointed professor of theology at the local college, when
her imagination began to be possessed of images of black
field hands toiling and suffering in cotton fields under a
sweltering sun. At first, as December storms shook the
house around her and she lay sleepless beside her half-
frozen babies, she thought only of the blizzards of her Connecticut childhood, her parents struggling homeward
through mounting drifts. But seated at a communion service in the college church in February 1852, she saw before
her, lit by a meridional glare brighter than the dim northern
light at the windows, the bloody and broken body of an old
black man beaten to death by his white master. And barely
repressing her tears, she rushed home to write down (the
words are her son's, remembering, echoing hers years afterward) "the vision which had been blown into her mind
as by a mighty wind."

Then, the ink scarcely dry, she read the first installment
of what was to become *Uncle Tom's Cabin* aloud to her
children, who "broke into convulsions of weeping," and
only when they were asleep did she permit herself to give
way to tears. "I remember," she wrote to one of her sons a

quarter of a century later, ". . . weeping over you as you lay sleeping beside me, and I thought of the slave mothers whose babies were torn from them." But surely she was thinking too of the child she had lost before leaving Cincinnati, the son she always referred to as "the most beautiful and beloved" of all her brood, since elsewhere—indeed, more than once—she noted for posterity that "it was at his dying bed that I learned what a poor slave mother may feel when her child is torn away from her." And she added, "I felt that I could never be consoled for it, unless this crushing of my own heart might enable me to work out some great good to others."

That "great good" turned out to be, of course, *Uncle Tom's Cabin,* whose serial publication she began almost immediately, not quite knowing at first where she was going or how long it would take her—but sustained, it would appear, by other hallucinations as vivid as the first. Moreover, as she sought to make of these images a popular fiction (her family was financially dependent at this point on her earnings as a writer), it occurred to her that it would not be sufficient merely to portray the suffering of a black male under the lash. To move as well as convince American mothers, and through them their husbands and sons, it was necessary also to portray slavery as an offense against the Family, the Utopian Household, Motherhood itself.

Contemporary accounts written by fugitive male slaves often tell of their being driven to resistance and flight by separation from their male buddies, but such stories had, for Mrs. Stowe, no mythic resonance. Or perhaps she was dimly aware that to have portrayed slavery as an offense against male bonding rather than marriage and parenthood would have meant falling out of the myth she shared with her female audience. She actually made one small concession to her masculine readers by introducing a minor subplot involving the tender relationship between Tom and young "Marse George," the son of his original master. But though that white boy pledges eternal love to the old black slave and keeps the faith, he finds him again too late to save him from the fury of Simon Legree and has to content himself (how reading the book at the age of seven or eight, I thrilled to that scene) with knocking Legree to the ground.

It was a compromise with her own pacifist principles that Mrs. Stowe was willing to make, knowing that some of her readers, especially the boys and men among them, would not be content with Tom's passive Christian "victory" over his oppressor, for whom he prays with his dying breath. She was, however, unwilling (and for this the small boy in me has never quite forgiven her) to let any love but that of Christ triumph over oppression and death. She never managed to describe the horror she saw at the communion rail as well as she did George's punching-out of Legree. But it survives in our memories, all the same, like the other key scenes of the book, as image or icon rather than text.

The words ,she finds or does not find simply do not matter, since even when she does find them (as in the description of Eva's death), they are woefully inadequate by conventional literary "standards." Her most mythically resonant tableaus are in fact usually the "worst" written: shrill to the point of hysteria, sickly-sweet to the verge of nausea, yet somehow so magically moving that they transcend not just the criteria of taste but credibility itself. It must be remembered, moreover, that the text we read has already been much edited, indeed almost rewritten. Like Emily Dickinson, Mrs. Stowe used in place of most other marks of punctuation an all-purpose dash: a characteristic, it would seem, of mid-nineteenth-century ladies' epistolary style. But her editors not only repunctuated her manuscripts, they "corrected" them.

William Dean Howells, who worked with her when she was already a practiced old hand at her craft, was moved to comment in this regard: "As for the author of *Uncle Tom's Cabin* her syntax was such a snare to her that it sometimes needed the combined skill of all the proof-readers and the assistant editor to extricate her." Then he added, to make clear the limits of editorial revision: "Of course, nothing was ever written into her work, but in changes of diction, in correction of solecisms, in transposition of phrases, the text was largely rewritten on the margin of her proofs. The soul of her art was present, but the form was so often absent, that when it was clothed on anew, it would have been hard to say whose cut the garment was of in many places."

It is pointless, then, to treat her as if she were *mutatis mutandis* another Flaubert, and misleading to insist on her radical difference from the hacks who translated her works to the stage. It was not they who invented the character whom a squeamish latter-day admirer of the "true" Mrs.

Stowe, Ellen Moers, refers to as "tractly Little Eva." Consequently, it is impossible after the fact to edit out of her text Eva's embarrassing "Christian" defense of slavery: "It makes for so many more around to love." Like the equally soupy pious last words which Uncle Tom breathes into the ear of the boy who arrives just too late to save him ("I love every creatur', every whar!—it's nothing *but* love! O Mas'r George! what a thing 'tis to be a Christian!"), it belongs to the "soul" of her art, however great a stumbling block it may be to modernist critics.

Even harder for them to accept are certain of Mrs. Stowe's assumptions about the nature and destiny of black Americans, since she was what we call nowadays a "racist," which is to say, one who believes that whites and blacks are intrinsically different. Yet three of the enduring archetypal characters in her novel are Afro-Americans, as seems only fair in light of the fact that, for better or worse, it was she who invented American blacks for the imagination of the whole world, converting them from facts of history, demography and economics to avatars and archetypes.

She was not the first American author to have created Negro characters. They had appeared earlier in novels and stories by such eminent writers as James Fenimore Cooper, Edgar Allan Poe and Herman Melville, but somehow they had remained archetypally inert, refusing to leap from the printed page to the public domain. And though the long-lived minstrel show had begun to invent its pervasive stereotypes of plantation life before Mrs. Stowe ever set pen to paper, they too failed to kindle the imagination of the world. To be sure, Mrs. Stowe herself was influenced by them, so that before we learn the real name of George and Eliza Harris' small son, Harry, we hear him hailed as "Jim Crow." Moreover, many of the minor blacks who surround her serious protagonists are modeled on the clowns in blackface who cracked jokes with a white interlocutor.

But clearly, images of black Americans could not stir an emotional response adequate to the horrors of slavery so long as they remained merely comic. Small wonder, then, that Mr. Bones retreated to the wings once Topsy had revealed the pathos beneath the burlesque, once Eliza had fled the bloodhounds on the ice (though only in the dramatic version) and Uncle Tom had been beaten to death in full view of a weeping household. Nor is it surprising that the figure of the martyred black slave under the lash, too old to be a sexual threat, too pious to evoke fears of violent revenge, captured the deep fantasy of a white world, haunted (since the Haitian revolt at least) with nightmares of black insurrection, and needing therefore to be assured that tears rather than blood would be sufficient to erase their guilt.

There are, to be sure, standard minstrel-show types among the astonishing array of Afro-American characters who move through the crowded pages of *Uncle Tom's Cabin*, comic darkies brought on for comic relief. Others represent stereotypes of other kinds, ranging from the faithful servant to the naked victim on the slave block, while a few, like Augustine St. Clare's spoiled and vain Creole valet, "Mr. Adolph," are rendered with the objective "realism" of a social observer. But only Eliza, Topsy and Tom, pressing on toward their foreknown endings—a bittersweet martyrdom, a breathless escape to freedom, an improbable conversion to a lifetime of Christian service—mysteriously survive outside the fiction in which they were born.

It is they alone who have become models, archetypal grids through which we have for so long perceived the Negroes around us and they themselves that, desiring to change the relationship of blacks and whites in the "real" world, we discover that we must deal with those deep images as well as laws and social custom. But, of course, most potent of the three in this regard is Uncle Tom. Indeed, among the "good niggers" of our literature, only Mark Twain's Jim has achieved a comparable mythological status, the wilderness companion of the white runaway from civilization, originally conceived as a red man but transformed in *Huckleberry Finn* into a black man.

T HE MANY MOTHERS
OF UNCLE TOM'S CABIN

There has come into existence in the years since Mrs.
Stowe first burst on an adoring world a mythological "bad
nigger" as compelling and memorable as Mrs. Stowe's
"good nigger" or Mark Twain's Jim. This shadow figure of
the black rapist I cannot help suspecting already lurked in
her own unconscious, as it lurked in the collective unconscious of the American people—erupting even before the
Civil War in rumors of the violation of white women by
black males and consequent riots in the streets, like one
that had occurred in Cincinnati while Mrs. Stowe was living there and learning the few facts she knew at first hand
about white-black relations in the South. But committed to
making a case for abolition, she left the evocation of that
nightmare archetype to later writers, both white and black,
to whom Jim seemed irrelevant and Uncle Tom an abomi-
nable lie: to Thomas Dixon, Jr., for instance, on the one
side, and Richard Wright and Eldridge Cleaver, on the
other.
   She was not, let it be understood, however genteel,
squeamish about alluding to sexual relations between
blacks and whites. Interethnic rape is, in fact, a major
theme in her sado-masochistic masterpiece—as central as
interethnic flagellation, which she eroticized to the point
where it seems merely another version of sexual violation.
But strategic considerations impelled her to deal exclusively with the rape or attempted rape of black girls by

white men, servants by masters. Toward the novel's conclusion, for instance, there is a long section which alternates descriptions of Tom's brutalization and death under the lash of Simon Legree with scenes in which the same Legree pursues through a decaying plantation house his former slave mistress, the aging and half-mad Cassy, and Emmeline, a beautiful young quadroon, whom he hopes to make her successor.

Before that double climax, Cassy has managed to tell to Tom her earlier erotic misadventures with white lovers and masters, a melodramatic tale which begins like an idyllic romance and ends in betrayal, insanity and murder. It constitutes, in fact, a sketch for a whole other novel, which Mrs. Stowe never wrote; though it has been attempted scores of times since, the last time perhaps as recently as 1955 in Robert Penn Warren's *Band of Angels*. In any case, both Cassy's story and Emmeline's have disappeared from the memory of the common reader as totally as has the Quaker household. In these instances, however, selective amnesia sets in not because they are too "allegorical," but because they are too "novelistic," i.e., dependent for their credibility on psychological "realism" rather than hallucinatory vividness.

It is, I suppose, for similar reasons that Little Eva's Bad Mother, Marie St. Clare (she is called in deliberate irony by the name of the mother of Christ), self-pitying, hypochondriacal, destructive to all around her, has also been forgotten by the popular audience. Her husband, Augustine, more "womanly" than she, which is to say, more sensitive and loving, but impotent and doomed, has fared a little better. He is remembered, however, not as the center of the "novelistic" scenes which he shares with his wife, but on the periphery of more mythic ones dominated by his dying daughter, in her relationship with those other archetypal personae, Topsy and Tom.

Inevitable as it is, I must confess I regret the disappearance of Mrs. St. Clare from collective memory, for in some sense she is worthy to stand with such other avatars of the neurotic Southern Lady as Faulkner's Mrs. Compson or even Margaret Mitchell's Scarlett O'Hara. Returning to the book, I sometimes find myself in fact flipping to the pages in which Mrs. Stowe, after having pinned her down in a twice-repeated phrase ("she consisted of a fine figure, a pair of splendid eyes and a hundred thousand dollars"), proceeds to show Marie St. Clare's failure as a wife, a mother and a mistress of black servants, and her total lack of sympathy for others compounded by monumental self-pity. Of all the voices in the book, it is her self-justifying whine that I find it hardest to exorcise, shuddering at the cruelty it barely conceals as I never shudder at the naked histrionics of Legree: "So you just see . . . what you've got to manage. A household without any rule; where servants have it all their own way, do what they please, and have what they please, except so far as I, with my feeble health, have kept up governments. I keep my cowhide about, and sometimes I do lay it on; but the exertion is always too much for me."

Yet I know that however successful "novelistically," this portrait of the Bad Mother fails to become mythic like that of the Wicked Slave Driver. It arises not out of the part of Mrs. Stowe's unconscious continuous with the collective unconscious, but out of repressed resentments, very private and personal, a clash of domestic life-styles. The vicious precision of the portrayal betrays its motivation: the need of a brilliant, homely, harried Northern housewife to take revenge on her spoiled, indolent and, alas, beautiful sisters of the South. Nonetheless, in this book addressed primarily to the Good Mothers of America, there is no sketch of a Good Mother, either white or black, equal in intensity and resonance to this portrait of a Bad one.

The book's chief white Good Mother, Rachel Halliday, whatever her symbolic importance, stands outside the main action, like those other kindly maternal WASPs whom Eliza encounters on her flight. And Eliza herself, part white, part black—but certainly not black enough to make it as a real "mammy"—dominates only what becomes as the novel progresses a subplot, a digression from the main story of martyrdom and redemption. Even in her archetypal scene, she functions primarily not as a Mother but as the Maiden in Flight. Had she been captured by the slave trader, Haley (we clearly perceive), that would have meant not merely her separation from her little son, so sketchily rendered that it seems hard to believe the bundle of rags she clutches to her beautiful bosom contains a living child, but her own sexual degradation. She seems, in that scene, even less wife than mother, although Mrs. Stowe had earlier insisted on the pathos of her parting from her husband, George Harris, who is absent as she crosses the ice, i.e., absent from the

mythic center of her plight; and he has therefore faded from
the collective memory as completely as his son.

There are other adequately black "mammies" in great
numbers, however (usually as fat as they are ebon), and we
see them either jolly and nurturing in the midst of children,
black and white, or bereft of them and in tears. But all the
way from Uncle Tom's wife, Aunt Chloe, to Little Eva's
mammy, they tend to be stereotypes, pathetic when they
are not comic. In any case, even the latter, "a middle-aged
mulatto woman of very respectable appearance," whose
unselfish love for Eva is contrasted with that of her white
mother ("This woman did not tell her that she made her
head ache, but on the contrary, she hugged her, and
laughed, and cried, till her sanity was a thing to be doubted
of"), is kept off scene at the mythological moment when
the beloved child is about to die, so that Uncle Tom can
move front and center to assume his archetypal role.

More central than these Good Black Mothers, though finally not of true mythic resonance either, are certain Good
White Mothers dead before the main action of the novel
begins. Returning as ghosts or God's messengers, sometimes, it would seem, as the Christian God Him/Herself
(when Augustine St. Clare says of his mother "*she* was *divine!*" he intends no hyperbole), they save their erring
sons, if they repent in time—as does St. Clare, who calls
her holy name with his last breath. Or if they do not, they
damn them for all eternity, as in the case of Simon Legree.

There is something about the mysterious connection of
damnation and motherly love which titillates as well as
troubles Mrs. Stowe. She attempts, therefore, to explain in
theological terms why the letter from his abused and rejected mother, telling him that on her deathbed she had
blessed and forgiven him, instead of consoling Legree,
"wrought in that demoniac heart of sin only as a damning
sentence, bringing with it a fearful looking for of judgment
and fiery indignation." "Ye who have wondered to hear, in
the same evangel, that God is love, and that God is a con-
suming fire," she admonishes her readers, "see ye not how,
to the soul resolved in evil, perfect love is the most fearful
torture . . . ?"

Uncle Tom is the one character in her book who would
save even Simon Legree, and seems therefore to represent
all in the author which, in spite of the patriarchal doctrine

of predestination, yearns toward "womanly" forgiveness, conceives love as endlessly salvational and Hell therefore as eternally empty. "He ain't done me no real harm," the dying Tom says of the man who has struck him down, foaming in dark passion, "only opened the gates of the kingdom for me; that's all." Thus he proves himself once more, as he had already demonstrated at the bedside of martyred Little Eva, the book's ultimate and absolute Good Mother. That Uncle Tom is in some sense a white mother like his author, despite his blackface and drag, other critics than I have perceived, Helen Papashvily and William R. Taylor most recently. Indeed, it is hard to miss the equation in the text and texture of Mrs. Stowe's novel: Woman = Mother = Slave = Black; or simplifying, Woman = Black, Black = Woman. The final formulation represents most accurately perhaps her perception of the relationship between race and gender, since, unlike the hard-core feminists of her time and ours, she did not believe that women played the role vis-à-vis men of "niggers." Yet Charlotte Brontë appears to have thought so, or at least this is what Ellen Moers would have us believe she meant by her well-known comment that "Mrs. Stowe had felt the iron of slavery enter into her heart, from childhood upwards."

To me, however, it all seems a little more complicated than that, and I would like to think that Charlotte Brontë was sensitive enough to have been aware of it. If as a female Harriet Beecher Stowe found it possible from childhood on to identify with persecuted slaves, she could scarcely have avoided identifying with their persecutors as well. After all, her Grandmother Foote, with whom she sometimes spent summers, had two indentured black servants, who, though they could look forward to eventual freedom, were obliged to call their mistress's granddaughter "Miss Harriet," while to her they were simply Harry and Dinah. That the experience stayed with her we know from the fact that the first black character in her most famous book to be called by name, the threatened black child of Eliza, is "Harry," and the St. Clares' cook is called "Dinah." The latter resembles physically, however, the woman who helped out in Mrs. Stowe's own kitchen in Cincinnati (almost always her servants were black), "a regular epitome of slave life in herself; fat, gentle, easy, loving and loveable," who, to complicate matters even further, bore the name Eliza.

As the description of this Eliza suggests, Mrs. Stowe was (in the contemporary sense of the word) at once "sexist" and "racist," believing that just as whites and blacks are intrinsically different, so, alas, are males and females. She thought, moreover, that their differences corresponded exactly, i.e., that "the Anglo-Saxon race" possessed preeminently those qualities Mrs. Stowe's age considered "masculine," being "stern, inflexible, energetic . . . dominant and commanding" and, at their worst, "hot and hasty." "Africans," on the other hand, were, as women were then presumed to be, "naturally patient, timid and unenterprising, not naturally daring . . . but home-loving and affectionate." And Tom, being the most African of all (as opposed, say, to George Harris, a mulatto with certain macho traits inherited from his white father), is the most womanly, most motherly, possessing "to the full, the gentle domestic heart which, woe for them! has been a peculiar characteristic of his unhappy race."

Once we realize the degree to which, metaphorically, mythically, Tom is female and white, we will be able to understand the sense in which Mrs. Stowe's novel, though she rejected radical feminism even as she rejected radical abolitionism, is a protest in behalf of bourgeois white womanhood as well as of black slaves. In it images bred by female paranoia, itself bred by male oppression, have been transferred to those stigmatized not for their sex but the color of their skin. Unlike her half-sister, Isabella, Harriet did not dream of "being called to the presidency of a matriarchal government" of the United States, which would eventually be "merged with the kingdom of Christ in a great millennial period." Nor did she, like her sister's mentor, Victoria Woodhull, advocate women's claiming for themselves all the traditional privileges of men, including erotic freedom.

Pacific rather than militant and domestic rather than "liberated," she dreamed only of being able to die well under the extremest persecution, forgiving her persecutors and, by God's grace, converting them to a redeemed life, in which they would disavow not only violence and slavery but sexual promiscuity, whiskey, tobacco and cussing. All of this she projects onto Tom, who as her surrogate and that of her sisters in Christ does not reflect invidiously on Afro-American masculinity. Rather, his character suggests that the salvation of the world depends on men as well as women being willing to practice the virtues that her time had come to call "feminine," though their more proper name is "Christian." Nor does Mrs. Stowe insist that all men should or can achieve so pure an *imitatio Christi* in their lives, George Harris, for instance, representing an alternative possibility. And if contemporary black males perceived this, perhaps they would not feel quite so free (or is it *driven?*) to use "Tom" as a term of contempt.

Yet Mrs. Stowe's suffering hero is a woman only in spirit, a maternal animal in a male body, which turns out to be, alas (in this respect, James Baldwin is right), a castrated one. In the novel's opening pages, to be sure, we meet Tom as a father of young children, but by the time he has encountered Little Eva it is hard to remember this, or remembering, to believe it, since in shifting sex roles he has become not merely maternal and old (*how* old we never quite know) but neutered.

Only thus in fact could his author evoke images of him holding in his muscular black arms the frail, pale body of a beautiful white girl without calling up nightmare fears of interethnic rape. Iconographically, certain of Tom's scenes with Little Eva are not very different from later ones portraying the black rapist carrying his unconscious pale victim toward defloration and death. Only the tone is altered and the symbolic role of the Negro, so that the resonances it stirs are not those associated with the primordial images of Kore, the Eternal Daughter, ravished by her Dark Father, the King of Hell. It seems, rather, one more version of what has been called the "Protestant Pietà," reminding us of Cordelia dead in the arms of Lear, or Little Nell in those of her grandfather. Neither Shakespeare, however, nor Dickens (as Dostoievski perceived and made manifest in *The Possessed*) quite managed to avoid overtones of incestuous passion debouching in murder. But these seem quite absent from Mrs. Stowe's recension of the myth, in which Tom represents not the impotent and resentful father but the Blessed Male Mother of a virgin Female Christ.

All feelings associated with rape have been transferred to the final archetypal scene in which Tom has become the passive victim, and his ravisher, in a strategic mythological inversion, the book's most macho, Anglo-Saxon and lustful character, Legree. He is assisted, to be sure, by Sambo and Quimbo, representing everything in white nightmares of black sexuality and aggression which Uncle Tom denies: "The two gigantic negroes that now laid hold of Tom . . . might have formed no unapt personification of the powers of darkness." The vision with which it all began, though it came to Mrs. Stowe in church, becomes here truly obscene as Legree, "foaming with rage" and determined to assert his ultimate power as absolute master ("And isn't he MINE? Can't I do what I like with him?" he cries over Tom's fallen body), consummates what it is tempting to think of as connubial murder and rape. Meanwhile, Tom, like some dutiful middle-class white Christian wife of the time, can only answer male brutality with submissive prayer: "Mas'r, if you was sick, or in trouble, or dying, I'd *give* ye my heart's blood."

Being a good Christian lady, Mrs. Stowe refuses to describe that scene in detail, leaving it to our pornographic imaginations. "What man has nerve to do," she explains piously, "man has not nerve to hear." But, of course, it is all the more effective for that very reason: not just satisfying the mass audience's need for righteous indignation and sado-masochistic titillation, but establishing that identification of "nigger" with woman, woman with "nigger," which made the progress from abolitionism to feminism inevitable for certain of Mrs. Stowe's readers.

It is harder to believe that Mrs. Stowe's great potboiler was responsible for the outbreak of the Civil War, though Abraham Lincoln thought so, or at least was moved to say so in her presence. For a while, readers on both sides of the Mason-Dixon line seem to have read it with equal pleasure; it began to divide North from South (after all, Mrs. Stowe had deliberately made her most arrant villain a New Englander by birth) only when it was taken up by apologists for and against slavery. To be sure, there are political implications everywhere in Mrs. Stowe's dream book, but like all dreams it told its dreamers only what they already knew, thus leading not to a change of heart and mind but greater self-awareness. The outcome of such dreams in the waking world is therefore not action but literature: precisely such a work as *Uncle Tom's Cabin*, which may have helped Americans, Northern and Southern, *perceive* differently the war they were bound in any case to fight, but cannot have hastened its coming.

On its conscious level, Mrs. Stowe's novel neither

preached nor foresaw a war between the states. What she hoped for was the voluntary freeing of slaves by individual owners, the spread of education among those thus freed and their consequent emigration to Africa, where they would take over the Christianizing of that continent which white missionaries had begun. What she feared was a general slave uprising, like that in Haiti. After all, Mrs. Stowe was not only a chiliastic Christian but the child of a revolutionary age, in which the oppressed everywhere were turning against their masters. That movement, which peaked in 1848, inspired almost simultaneously two literary responses, one profoundly European, the other peculiarly American: Marx and Engels' *Communist Manifesto* and her *Uncle Tom's Cabin.* If, according to the first, the specter haunting Europe was Communism, according to the second, the specter haunting America was black revolt. None of the characters in *Uncle Tom's Cabin,* however, really embody this threat, certainly not Tom. Even George Harris, her single Negro militant, is not permitted to fire the gun he raises against his white pursuers, and when the diabolical Sambo and Quimbo turn against their brutal master it is to espouse Christianity rather than bloodshed, arson, murder and rape. In her second novel, *Dred: A Tale of the Great Dismal Swamp,* Mrs. Stowe attempted to tell a story of slave rebellion, but the result was a failure—mythologically inert, structurally confused, moving to no one.

In fact, Mrs. Stowe never again created a fiction which touched the popular imagination. Scholars and critics, uneasy with *Uncle Tom's Cabin,* like to pretend that toward the end of her writing career she succeeded in producing "better" books, *Old Town Folks,* for instance. But it is hard to believe that any ordinary reader has ever loved such bloodless evocations of New England life, much less shuddered or wept over them, shamelessly out of control. Only once (by God's grace, she would have said) was she permitted to peer into the darkness of the American unconscious and to redeem for daylight the phantasms, black and white, who inhabit it: phantasms to whom she gave the local habitation and the names by which we have identified them ever since.

For the rest of her life, she lived the life of a celebrity, a little pompous and something of a fool, as in her self-styled defense of Lady Byron which was really an attack on the incestuous Lord Byron, whom she extravagantly admired and passionately despised; and in the end, she went out of her mind. Meanwhile, her reputation kept increasing, her single great work amended, continued, in some sense completed, by anonymous or forgotten hacks.

Even before her death, the deathless characters she had first imagined, Tom, Eliza, Topsy, Eva, had ceased to belong to her, entering the world not of High Literature but of popular entertainment, in which all goods are held in common. During her last years, her story may have been known to everyone, but fewer and fewer knew it from having read her book rather than having seen "Tom plays," which proliferated throughout the world. Moved by curiosity, she herself once attended a performance, peering through the closed curtains of a private box, though she had condemned theater and opera, along with swearing, gambling, smoking, slavery and hard drink, in the pages of *Uncle Tom's Cabin* itself.

Henry James, remembering her tale in *A Small Boy and Others*, which he published in 1913, recalls it more vividly as theater than as printed text, evoking with the name of Mrs. Stowe those of actresses who had played Eliza, Cassy, Topsy and Eva, as well as that of P. T. Barnum, at whose American Museum he had first watched it side by side with midgets, giants, a counterfeit mermaid and a black ex-slave who claimed to be the world's oldest woman. He ends his account by assuring us that he enjoyed the play only as "camp": "However, the point exactly was that we attended this spectacle just in order *not* to be beguiled, just in order to enjoy with ironic detachment and, at the very most, to be amused ourselves at our sensibility should it prove to have been trapped and caught."

It is clear, despite his retrospective irony, that his sensibility had been "trapped and caught," and in speculating on the story's insidious appeal, he notes—for perhaps the first time in critical discourse—a quality which distinguishes all popular art from High Art, namely, its ability to move from one medium to another without loss of intensity or alteration of meaning, its independence, in short, of the form in which it is first rendered. "Letters," James wrote, "here, languished unconscious, and Uncle Tom, instead of making even one of the cheap short cuts through the medium in which books breathe, even as fishes in water, went gaily roundabout it altogether, as if a fish, a wonderful 'leaping fish,' had simply flown through the air. This feat accomplished, the surprising creature could naturally fly anywhere, and one of the first things it did was thus to flutter down on every stage, literally without exception, in America and Europe."

Like many popular genres, however, the popular theater of the nineteenth century in which Mrs. Stowe's "wonderful 'leaping fish' " had fluttered down proved a transitory rather than a final form—giving way to movies, radio and TV, which more quickly reached an even larger audience. I was born just too late ever to have seen a "Tom play," and I know them only as they are preserved in films: performed, for instance, before Yul Brynner as King of Siam in *The King and I,* or glimpsed over the shoulder of Shirley Temple, in a moving picture whose name I have forgotten, though not the scene in which the ingenue, as Little Eva, wins over her beloved's mother, hitherto as hostile to theater and actresses as Mrs. Stowe herself.

I am more directly familiar with the fictional spin-offs from *Uncle Tom's Cabin,* which began to appear side by side with the dramatic versions, responses in novel form by various hands. Such unauthorized sequels to her best seller may have seemed to Mrs. Stowe an infringement of copyright and a threat to her livelihood. But like Cervantes and Dickens before her, she had to endure them as a consequence of her kind of success, learning the hard way that in the realm of popular art, books are as independent of their authors as of their medium.

In any case, anti-Tom books like *Aunt Phillis's Cabin; or Southern Life As It Is, Uncle Tom's Cabin As It Is, Uncle Tom in England; or, Proof That White's Black* never attracted a large audience—not so much because their authors were untalented (a couple were, in fact, already immensely popular) as because they failed to understand that the book they sought to "answer" was a dream-fantasy even more concerned with death, sexual purity and the bourgeois home than with the Fugitive Slave Law.

T HE ANTI-TOM NOVEL

AND THE COMING

OF THE FIRST GREAT WAR:

FROM THOMAS DIXON, JR.,

TO D. W. GRIFFITH

Only when a writer appeared who was as obsessed and visionary as Mrs. Stowe could her compelling images of race and sex be replaced by others of quite different significance. That writer was Thomas Dixon, Jr., whose name is little known at the moment, though his novels sold millions of copies in the early twentieth century, precisely because they seemed the long-awaited response to Mrs. Stowe. "It is an epoch-making book," one critic wrote of *The Leopard's Spots,* "and a worthy successor to *Uncle Tom's Cabin.* It is superior in power of thought and graphic description." Others, however, appalled at Dixon's vilification of black men and his defense of the Ku Klux Klan, attacked him with a fury equal to that earlier turned against Mrs. Stowe. Accusing him of being "the high priest of lawlessness, the prophet of anarchy" and a stirrer-up of "enmity between race and race," they called in righteous indignation for the censorship of his books.

To Dixon, however, his detractors seemed of little importance, since he had taken on the dead and sanctified patron saint of them all. Mrs. Stowe had had the first word in the great debate, a word that had captured the heart of the world; but he was determined to have the last, and to couch it in the fictional form, melodramatic and sentimental, that he had learned from her. It seems doubtful, indeed, that he would ever have become a novelist at all without her example and provocation. Though not yet forty when he

began to write *The Leopard's Spots,* he had already been a
farmer, a scholarship student at Johns Hopkins University,
a dropout vainly trying to make it on the New York stage, a
lawyer, a legislator, a minister of the gospel, a pamphleteer
attacking strong drink and "infidels" like Robert Ingersoll
and, finally, a popular lecturer.

It was in fact "during one of his lecturing tours," his
biographer, Raymond A. Cook, tells us, that "Dixon attended a dramatization of Harriet Beecher Stowe's *Uncle
Tom's Cabin.* Angered by what seemed to him a great injustice to the South, he could hardly keep from leaping to
his feet and denouncing the drama as false. Finally, when
the performance was over, he rose with tears in his eyes
and vowed bitterly that he would someday tell the 'true
story' of the South." That "true story" became a trilogy of
novels, *The Leopard's Spots* (1902), *The Clansman* (1905)
and *The Traitor* (1907), after which, though the threat of
"racial mongrelization" continued to obsess him, Dixon directed his fictional fire chiefly against his other favorite
bugaboos: socialism, pacifism, feminism, monarchism and
booze.

Never, in any case, did he write except in behalf of what
seemed to him a worthy cause. "I have made no effort to
write literature," he declared. "I have no ambition to shine
as a literary gymnast. . . . My sole purpose in writing was to
reach and influence the minds of millions. I had a message
and I wrote it as vividly and simply as I knew how." It is
an anti-aesthetic credo not unlike that of Mrs. Stowe, who
once said of *Uncle Tom's Cabin* that she "no more thought
of style or literary excellence than the mother who rushes
into the street and cries for help to save her children from
a burning house, thinks of the teachings of the rhetorician
or the elocutionist." To be sure, Dixon's controlling metaphor is more pastoral than matriarchal, but like Mrs. Stowe,
he understood that to win the mass audience one had to
project their irrational wishes and fears in "pictures" or
"visions," detachable from the words in which they were
transmitted.

What made his task easier was the fact that, also like her,
he prized female virginity and the integrity of the home,
embodying the one in the image of the Spotless Maiden
and the other in that of the Holy Mother. "Every woman,"
he has one of his more sympathetic characters declare, "is

something divine to me. I think of God as a woman, not a man—a great loving Mother of all life." For him, however, the supreme threat to these avatars of the feminine is not, as for Mrs. Stowe, the slave trader and slave driver, but the half-bestial black man released from white patriarchal restraints.

Dixon is finally no defender of slavery, granting that Emancipation was necessary for the development of a united nation. But it was unforgivable for the North, he argues, in the name of "Reconstruction," to make black ex-slaves into the masters of their former owners—rather than persuading them to leave en masse for Africa, or to live in segregated communities as eternal inferiors. He is fond of quoting Lincoln as having said, "I believe there is a physical difference between the white and black races which will forever forbid their living together on terms of political and social equality." He admired Lincoln without reservation, claiming that he was not just a "Friend of the South," as he described him in the dramatis personae of *The Clansman,* but a "Southerner," by which he meant just such a descendant of Scotch-Irish peasants as himself and the organizers of the Klan, one of whom was, in fact, Dixon's uncle.

Dixon sometimes refers to those original Klansmen, the heroes of his books, as "Anglo-Saxons," though the Anglo-Saxon aristocracy of the Old South would have spurned such ethnic confusion. Even as Mrs. Stowe pleaded the cause of women in the guise of attacking slavery, Dixon pleaded the cause of the Scotch-Irish in the name of white supremacy. And like Mrs. Stowe, he managed to translate his peculiar plight into universal images; so that his "redneck" fantasies of nigger-hating and lynch law appealed not only to his redneck brethren but to declassed WASP plantation owners fighting to establish a New South, and even to recent immigrants from eastern or southern Europe confronting free Negroes in the cities of the Midwest and Northeast.

He did not, however, really know what he was doing at first, beyond burlesquing Mrs. Stowe's masterpiece. The working title of *The Leopard's Spots* was "The Rise of Simon Legree"; though the name of the book was changed, Legree remains of considerable importance even in the revised version. We learn, for instance, how he survived the

Civil War: "He shaved clean, and . . . wore dresses for two years, did housework"; and how, afterward, he prepared for his new career as a capitalist and sexual exploiter of factory girls: "He wore a silk hat and a new suit of clothes made by a fashionable tailor. . . . His teeth that once were pointed like the fangs of a wolf had been filed by a dentist."

Other characters out of *Uncle Tom's Cabin* are similarly travestied, especially the now grown-up son of Eliza, renamed "George" by Dixon, though Mrs. Stowe had called him "Harry." Handsome and almost white, George Harris enters the scene as a Harvard graduate, scholar, poet and protégé of the champion of black liberation, the Honorable Everett Lowell, with whose daughter he falls in love. When he asks for her hand, however, his liberal New England sponsor turns cold and hostile, initiating a dialogue in which the deep fears that obsessed Dixon and the mass audience of the early twentieth century find their classic expression:

> Harris winced and sprang to his feet, trembling with passion. "I see," he sneered; "the soul of Simon Legree has at last become the soul of the nation. The South expresses the same luminous truth with a little more clumsy brutality. But their way is after all more merciful. The human body becomes unconscious at the touch of an oil-fed flame in sixty seconds. Your methods are more refined and more hellish in cruelty. You have trained my ears to hear, eyes to see, hands to touch and heart to feel, that you might torture with the denial of every cry of body and soul and roast me in the flames of impossible desires for time and eternity!"
>
> "That will do now. There's the door!" thundered Lowell, with a gesture of stern emphasis. "I happen to know the important fact that a man or woman of Negro ancestry, though a century removed, will suddenly breed back to a pure Negro child, thick-lipped, kinky-headed, flat-nosed, black-skinned. One drop of your blood in my family could push it backward three thousand years in history. If you were able to win her consent, a thing unthinkable, I would do what old Virginius did in the Roman Forum—kill her with my own hand, rather than see her sink in your arms into the black waters of Negroid life! Now go!"

It is not, of course, with "fact" that we are dealing here (though many reputable anthropologists of that time would have insisted that Everett Lowell spoke "scientific truth") but fantasy: a fantasy based on fear of "racial mongreli- zation" resulting from Emancipation, which presumably freed black males not just from slavery but from restraints on their lust for white women. Though Mrs. Stowe refuses to confess the existence of that lust (much less a corre- sponding yearning on the part of white women for black males), the popular mind had long been haunted by a sus- picion of both. Yet not until fifty years after the Civil War did a new myth of miscegenation replace the older one of black females sexually exploited by their white masters, who then had the mulatto offspring whipped or sold away from their mothers.

In *Uncle Tom's Cabin* there is, as we have noticed, an equivocal icon, transmitted by the "Tom plays" to every stage of the world, portraying frail white female flesh en- folded in the brawny arms of a black male. But since the flesh belongs to the eternally virginal Little Eva and the arms to a castrated "motherly" Tom, it all seems safe enough. "It was Tom's greatest delight," Mrs. Stowe tells us, "to carry her frail form in his arms . . . now up and down her room, now out into the veranda." And when her weaker white father protests that this is his obligation and privi- lege, Eva answers, "Oh, Papa, let Tom take me . . . He car- ries me so strong."

If there are erotic overtones in that final phrase "He car- ries me so strong," Mrs. Stowe seems to have been unaware of them. Yet she registers through Miss Ophelia, an old- maid New England cousin of Augustine St. Clare, the Northerner's horror of any physical contact between the races. "Well," that spinster declares, after she has watched Little Eva warmly embracing slaves of both sexes, "I want to be kind to everybody, and I wouldn't have anything hurt; but as to kissing—" She cannot manage to say the final word, so that her cousin St. Clare has to finish for her, "Niggers." The explicit horror as well as the implicit eros of "kissing niggers," Dixon, moved by his own covert lust and fear, raises to an ultimate pitch of intensity in *The Leopard's Spots* and *The Clansman,* thus converting Mrs. Stowe's innocent idyll into a tableau of murderous lust.

Rape or the threat of rape has always been a staple of American popular fiction: essential not only to hard-core pornography for "men only" and women's gothic romances (called in the trade, for this very reason, "bodice-rippers"), but in comic books, western pulp stories, fright films, cop shows and even TV "documentaries" about little girls lost in the big city. Nor did it wait to enter literature until the invention of the modern novel. Shakespeare was, especially early in his career, obsessed by it, making it the central subject of one of his most ambitious poems, *The Rape of Lucrece,* and the most shameless of his crowd-pleasing plays, *Titus Andronicus.* Long before the Renaissance, moreover, sexual violation had played a key role in classical mythology, in which new gods and heroes are begotten by Olympians on mortal women, possessed by force or deceit. Zeus, the chief of the gods, is also the most active violator of female humans, ravishing Europa in the form of a bull, Leda in the guise of a swan, and Danaë as a shower of gold.

Such ancient prototypes, however, are all examples of "rape from above," exercises of the *droit du seigneur;* felt as disturbing, perhaps, but not morally reprehensible until the growth of secularism and democracy had challenged the notion that high social status carried with it power over the bodies of inferiors. Even the mythological snatching away of Proserpine by the King of the Underworld (in what surely must be a vestigial matriarchal myth), though it grieved her mother, Ceres, and brought temporary infertility to the earth, eventuates in what we must assume to be a reasonably happy "arranged" marriage.

But for generations, millennia, all marriages were "arranged," which is to say, occurred without the prior consent of the female partner, either through negotiations of the concerned parents or by "capture." Marriage by capture or, indeed, casual rape and abandonment have throughout most of human history been the expected-accepted (though not, to be sure, welcomed) fate of the womenfolk of the defeated in war. I can remember, for instance, being asked during World War II by an old Japanese woman, a civilian internee on the island of Tinian (we had just finished an improvised tea ceremony, she, I and an aged Shinto priest, squatting among rusted tin cans), "And how many women have you raped in the Great War?" There was no irony intended; she assumed that prerogative to be an appropriate tribute to the Navy uniform I wore.

By Shakespeare's time, the violation of upper-class women by men of their own caste, which is to say, "peer rape," had come to be regarded as a heinous crime. But not until a couple of centuries later was the forcing of any female, high or low, Christian or pagan, considered the ultimate outrage—particularly by the bourgeoisie, just then rising from a position of relative impotence to one of real power. In fact, one of the major themes of the novel, the preferred genre of that class, was a protest (think of Samuel Richardson's *Pamela*) against the sexual exploitation of their daughters by the "libertine" aristocracy.

Before seduction and rape could be mythicized as absolute evils, however, the codes of "courtly love," which justified adulterous leisure-class dalliance, had to be transformed into the bourgeois myth of romantic love eventuating in marriage. But once marriage is regarded as the institutionalization of mutual affection, rather than a socio-economic arrangement or a necessary evil required for the continuation of the species, courtship becomes necessary: "the wooing and winning" of a girl, who has the power to accept her suitor, give herself freely, or *not*. We are talking, after all, about the period of the Enlightenment, when movements for the rights of children and of women first began, and the daughters of bourgeois families, who read books, were well aware of both.

Though marriage still demanded of them the surrender of those rights after the ceremony, they jealously guarded them before, protesting "arranged" matches, on the one hand, and "seduction" or "rape," on the other. Unlike the first, the latter two involve not just a loss of freedom but of "honor"—more specifically that female "honor" which depends on the maintenance of sexual purity. Formerly associated only with "ladies," a privileged aristocratic few, it too had been fought for as a right. Once attained, however, it proved a trap, the very opposite of liberation, since for the bourgeoisie the abstract notion of "honor" was oddly *literalized*, i.e., totally identified with the physical "maidenhead," the hymen.

Any rupture of that membrane, therefore, indeed any genital penetration, even one visited on an unwilling or unconscious victim, was considered an eternal "pollution," a "stain" removable only by death. Though suicide was in the victim's power, the murder of her rapist was not. This was considered the privilege of her father, brothers, other male kinsmen and friends, whose masculine "honor" in fact demanded they exact such revenge. This mythological syndrome possessed the imagination of European readers and writers from the moment the Richardsonian novel came into existence, so that seduction, rape and revenge for rape became a staple of the novel on the Continent and in England down to the time of Thomas Hardy.

Such scenes are, however, entirely absent from American "classics" of male bonding like *Moby Dick* and *Huckleberry Finn*, much as, and for the same reasons that, wooing and marriage are absent. Such books, therefore, are "pure," as the moralists of their age defined purity, and so, despite their subversion of home and marriage, were considered "safe" reading for children, as, ironically enough, many contemporary domestic best sellers were not. Or maybe the distinction is fair enough, since there is indeed something lubricious and voyeuristic in the latter kind of novel's oblique references to the "fate worse than death"—a crypto-pornographic appeal only made worse by its ostensible piety.

Such a show of piety is missing from the pages of Cooper's *Leatherstocking Tales*, though in *The Last of the Mohicans* there is a similar lubricious appeal to the Peeping Tom in us all. It is not to be found, to be sure, in the central story of Uncas, Chingachgook and Natty Bumppo, which celebrates an utterly sublimated homoerotic passion joining white and red. But it is present in the all-white boy-gets-girl romance which Cooper introduced, I cannot help suspecting, to win the largest possible share of the mass audience (he was, after all, as much entrepreneur as artist) by appealing to believers in the myth of Home as Heaven as well as those convinced that Home is Hell. In that frame story, a standard upper-class juvenile and ingenue make it through great perils to the happy ending of married bliss forever after, and chief among those perils is the threat to the virginity of the pearl-pale maiden by an Ignoble Savage, Magua. But this constitutes a uniquely American version of female violation, "rape from below": in which the representative of an oppressed race seeks revenge against his oppressors by subjecting their daughters to miscegenous deflowering.

Cooper in *The Last of the Mohicans* portrays the offense against the Pure Maiden not as outright ravishment but only the threat of "forced marriage," since he was aware that in Indian culture it was permitted to inflict on a prisoner of war any indignity *except* rape. Moreover, the girl for whom Magua really lusts, though the offspring of a British officer, is not quite white, having a Creole mother, which is to say, a touch of the black, a race lower on Cooper's mythological scale than the red. At any rate, her deflowering, though it seems always on the verge of occurring, is never consummated.

Cooper seems to have learned this strategy from Sir Walter Scott, the European inventor of the historical romance, in particular from *Ivanhoe*, in which two heroines, the fair Rowena and the dark Rebecca, are continually menaced by Norman would-be rapists, from whom, however, they escape intact. Yet, though their not-quite violation contains overtones of not-quite miscegenation (Rowena being a Saxon and Rebecca a "Jewess"), there is no real threat of racial degradation, since the would-be violators are of cognate ethnic origin and, indeed, of a higher social class than the girls they try to violate.

What they contemplate is still the *droit du seigneur*, which their victims, Jewish and Christian, reject in the name of a higher religious law, and which nineteenth-century readers spurned out of a belief in "true love." Finally, whatever old-fashioned reservations Scott may have had about permitting a union between Jew and Saxon (his more up-to-date fans pleaded with him to let Rebecca and Ivanhoe marry, but he remained adamant), he believed passionately in intermarriage between Saxon and Norman, granting always that it be consummated lovingly and freely rather than in response to *force majeur*. Only thus, he argued, long after the historical fact, could a united and triumphant England be created.

Not, however, until rape was reimagined as a threat from a hopelessly inferior and utterly rejected Other could the sinister subtheme of the American domestic novel achieve its final form; and Cooper's Bad Indian failed to fill the bill. It was the Afro-American who was destined to become the archetypal subhuman rapist, once Emancipation had released him to the swarming streets of our post–Civil War cities. He enters literature, however, under male auspices, since by the mid-nineteenth century women writing for women had grown so genteel that even offstage seductions were beginning to disappear from their chaste pages. The black rapist makes his debut not in "serious" novels for men but in best sellers, like the melodramatic, soft-porn "mysteries" of Eugène Sue, George Reynolds and, in this country, George Lippard.

Interethnic rape and revenge for rape are themes which continue to haunt pop books intended primarily for males, climaxing in the most popular of all, Edgar Rice Burroughs' Tarzan series. Throughout its many volumes, Tarzan's wife, Jane, is assaulted over and over (along with any other nubile white female who wanders into their jungle territory) by members of lesser breeds, ranging from gorillas and great apes to black Africans, Arabs and "Huns." She is, however, invariably rescued before the worst has happened by her mate, who, though he is overtaken by a conveniently recurring amnesia and forgets her for long stretches, always recovers and arrives in the nick of time. Such attempts on his mythologically inviolable best-loved serve to give the Lord of the Jungle an excuse for enforcing vigilante justice: knifing, strangling or hanging from trees the subhuman assailants who threaten not just Jane but, archetypally understood, all white womanhood.

He is particularly vicious in lynching presumptuous members of the black "savage" tribe which killed his "mother," i.e., the female great ape who suckled and protected him in his infancy. It is hard to remain unaware of analogies with the myth which sustained the Ku Klux Klan, and surely Burroughs must have had some dim sense that he was writing about the American racial situation in encoded form. But he portrays Tarzan as being really Lord Greystoke, an English aristocrat, and though he occasionally sets a scene in America (Jane is, after all, an American girl), his preferred arena of action is a more than half-imaginary Africa, an absolute Someplace Else.

His literary models were such pop laureates of "taking up the White Man's Burden" as Rider Haggard and Rudyard Kipling, without whose apologies for British imperialism, *She* and *The Jungle Book*, the Tarzan series might never have been conceived. Despite its evocation of ethnic conflict and lynch law, therefore, Burroughs' pop saga offered American readers in the era from just before World War I until just after World War II not so much an opportunity to confront and exorcise the social problems they actually faced in an urbanized United States as a way of escaping their own history, indeed history itself.

Thomas Dixon, Jr., on the other hand, had already begun to create, more than a decade before the appearance of *Tarzan of the Apes,* a version of the myth of rape, miscegenation and heroism available to the female audience nurtured on domestic best sellers as well as the readers of super-macho pop to whom Burroughs was chiefly to appeal. In addition, Dixon's books were unequivocally American, rooted in our political past and speaking to our problematic present—though there are echoes of Kipling in the subtitle of his first book, "A Romance of the White Man's Burden." But this scarcely compromises his nativism, any more than does his dependence on Sir Walter Scott. Not only had Cooper turned to that source before him, and for that matter, Mrs. Stowe herself, but so also had the Ku Klux Klan, as the last word of its very name indicates.

Of this fact Dixon constantly reminds us, speaking, for instance, in the preface of his second novel, *The Clansman,* of how "the young South" in its effort to save the life of "the Aryan race" had been "led by the reincarnated souls of the Clansmen of Old Scotland." Clearly, Dixon's "Old Scotland" comes not out of documented history but out of the Scottish author whom Mark Twain in *Life on the Mississippi* had already accused, more than twenty years before, of having "run the people mad, a couple of generations ago, with his medieval romances. The South has not yet recovered from the debilitating influence of his books. Admiration of his fantastic heroes and their grotesque 'chivalry' doings and romantic juvenilities still survives here."

That ersatz version of chivalry still possesses Dixon, who proves, however, considerably less genteel than the author of *Ivanhoe.* He is, that is to say, enough of a "vulgar" American to make rape, black-white rape, his explicit theme; though he has a hard time describing it in detail or at first hand. In *The Leopard's Spots,* he compromises by keeping the archetypal scene offstage. We hear the nigger-hating father of little Flora, the fated white victim, warn her, "But, baby, don't you dare go nigh er nigger . . . no more'n you would a rattlesnake." Then the author intervenes to inform us, "She believed with her child's simple faith that all nature was as innocent as her own heart," at which point she disappears to return as a corpse, "her clothes torn to shreds and stained with blood." "It was too plain, the terrible crime that had been committed," Dixon adds, lest we have missed the point; but, of course, we have not.

Later, in *The Clansman*, Dixon is more circumstantial, though even this time he renders the scene at second hand, as its black villain, Gus, under hypnotism, reenacts the crime, whose "sullied" victim has at that point committed suicide, jumping from a cliff hand in hand with her approving mother. "His thick lips were drawn upward in an ugly leer and his sinister bead-eye gleamed like a gorilla's. A single fierce leap and the black claws clutched the air slowly as if sinking into the soft white throat." Gus's execution by the listening jury of Clansmen follows immediately, but is not described; as if one image of ultimate violence were enough to satisfy the self-righteous sadism of the audience: rape *or* lynching, but not both.

In *The Leopard's Spots*, in which the rape was merely suggested, the lynching had been recounted at some length: "They reached the spot where the child's body had been found. They tied the screaming, praying Negro to a live pine and piled around his body a great heap of dead wood and saturated it with oil. And then they poured oil on his clothes." Such "insane brutality" is apparently too much for ambivalent Dixon, who had witnessed a similar lynching as a child. Though he cannot forbear recounting it with evident relish, he expresses moral reservations about it through a Klan leader unable to stop the mob he had begun by inciting. Nonetheless, it is scenes like these which have remained in the memory of a mass audience which soon forgot his travesties of characters from *Uncle Tom's Cabin*, his evocation of historical figures like Lincoln and Thaddeus Stevens, and his editorial asides about states' rights. No more did they remember for very long the single love story he told over and over, in which some clean-cut, clean-limbed son of the Old South not only rises to leadership in the Klan but delivers from her father's tyranny some incredibly beautiful beloved.

But the mythology of rape and lynching on a border where alien cultures meet evokes images which haunt us still in a world vexed by even more exacerbated conflicts of white and black, white and brown, white and yellow, white and red, yellow and black, black and red, brown and yellow. Like *Uncle Tom's Cabin*, therefore, his novels become occasions, on the one hand, for translations into other media (by which, unlike Mrs. Stowe, he profited immensely) and, on the other, for fictional rebuttals, many of them written by blacks. It was not, however, until the appearance of Alex Haley's *Roots* in 1976 that any of the latter reached the popular audience he had touched.

Earlier anti-anti-Tom books by Negro authors have fared less well, so that even the titles of Sutton E. Gregg's *The Hindered Hand,* published in 1905, and J. W. Grant's *Out of the Darkness; or Diabolism and Destiny,* which appeared in 1909, are known now only to specialists in early black American literature. Parochial attempts to present the case for racial intermarriage and social equality or to set straight the record on Reconstruction, they failed not only because they lack literary skill and mythic resonance, but also because the backlash of white guilt and self-hatred, on which Haley would later capitalize, still lay far in the future.

A work which did move the majority audience in the ten years between the publication of *The Clansman* and the beginning of World War I was the play which Dixon himself made of that book, and which he marketed by soliciting pre-production plaudits from the then Secretary of State, John Hay, and Albert Bigelow Paine, the future biographer of Mark Twain. When it finally was produced, however, even in the South more sober-minded critics condemned it as "a riot breeder . . . designed to excite rage and race hatred"; and in some Northern cities, there were indeed riots. But on the whole, the box-office response was tumultuously favorable, leading Dixon to speculate that it might ultimately be seen by ten million spectators. Sitting in the theater, moreover, he was thrilled as no novelist in his lonely study ever can be. "There," he wrote later, "I saw, felt and heard, and touched the hands of my readers and their united heart beat lifted me to the heights."

In some ways, however, the stage was too limited for the epic effects he dreamed. How could four horsemen galloping on a treadmill before a flimsy backdrop represent the glory and terror of the assembled Klan riding to the rescue of white womanhood? But there was a new medium through which he could reach an even larger audience, achieve even greater fame and fortune. He set to work almost immediately, therefore, on a movie scenario; but when, in 1911, he began his search for a producer, he found at first only timid entrepreneurs scared to attempt so ambitious and controversial a project.

Fortunately, his script fell into the hands of D. W. Griffith, a young director with ambitions as boundless as his own, and ready, at precisely that point, to try his hand at a major work. Griffith, the son of a Confederate officer, and an unreconstructed Southerner, was possessed by the same myth of the South that cued Dixon's deepest fantasy. Moreover, he was equally responsive to popular taste. "The peanuts-and-popcorn audience controlled Griffith," writes Karl Brown, a cameraman, who watched the shooting of the film, "and as long as he lived, thought and had his being with the strictest compliance with their unspoken wishes, he could do no wrong."

Brown had already read, and hated, Dixon's novel. "It wasn't much of a story," he comments. "Terribly biased, utterly unfair, the usual diatribe of a fire-eating Southerner, reverend or no reverend." Moreover, Griffith exaggerated in the filming everything which had offended Brown to begin with, making the black villains more villainous, the white heroes more unbelievably noble, the even whiter heroines more passive, fluttering and ethereal. "There was nothing high-flown or arty about *The Clansman* as Griffith shot it," Brown concludes: "Everything was of the earth, earthy." But, of course, it *worked*, whipping its first audience into a frenzy, and making millionaires of both Griffith and Dixon.

Ironically, Dixon was to disappear in the shadow of Griffith, who proved to be a natural genius, and thenceforward came to be thought of as America's greatest moviemaker. The classic tribute to him and his film, ultimately called *The Birth of a Nation*, was written by James Agee in 1948, when the film was seldom shown for fear of boycotts and picket lines, and therefore took considerable chutzpah to present. Agee is aware not only of the magnificence of the film, but of its status as anti-High Art, referring to Griffith as a "primitive" capable as "only great and primitive artists can be, of . . . perceiving and perfecting the tremendous magical images that underlie the memory and imagination of entire peoples."

When Agee comes to specifying Griffith's tremendous "magical images," however, two of them turn out to have been borrowed from Dixon: "the ride of the Clansmen; the rapist and his victim among the dark leaves." Yet he seems unaware of Dixon's existence and fails, therefore, to understand why Griffith for all his talent never again was able to project archetypes that have refused to fade from the mind of the world. It is not surprising that other critics, unsympathetic from the start, have persisted in ignoring that novelist. Yet on the morning after the opening of *The Birth of a Nation,* it was Dixon's intermission speech rather than Griffith's which the newspapers reported at length, since the aging novelist was better known than the young director, and the story still associated chiefly with him.

Dixon had in fact helped produce an earlier version, shot though never cut; and this time too he was involved from the start, holing up in New York with Griffith for many weeks of consultation, then shipping him off to Hollywood loaded down with his original screenplay plus the historical documents he had used in researching it. It was Dixon, too, who persuaded Griffith to change the name of the film to *The Birth of a Nation,* shouting across the cheers of the first-night audience that *The Clansman* was "too tame a title for so powerful a story."

Griffith has left an account of the "vision" which came to him as he first read Dixon's novel: at the center of which shone the "flashing sword" of his father, old "Thunder Jake" Griffith, with which as a boy he had watched him threaten, half in jest, a cowering Negro. And he tells us further that he read it aloud to his company before shooting began. Certainly, anyone familiar with Dixon's novels can recognize in the finished film specific borrowings from *The Leopard's Spots* as well as *The Clansman,* however altered on the set (Griffith worked from no fixed script) or in the cutting room.

What chiefly survives in the new medium are Dixon's mythic versions of North and South, male and female, black and white, and especially his vision of Reconstruction as an orgy of looting and rape, loosed in a world of gallantry and grace by greedy invaders and bewildered ex-slaves: a saturnalia subdued only by the Christian Knights of the Klan, whose fiery crosses betoken the end of nightmare and the dawn of a new day. No one who has seen the ride of the Klan in *The Birth of a Nation* can ever forget it: those silent hooves pounding as if forever through a dream landscape, the camera returning again and again to the hushed riders bent over the sweating backs of their horses, then cutting to their wives, mothers and daughters trapped in a house around which a horde of black devils swirls, banging against wall and door with rapacious hands.

There is no doubt in the mind of any viewer about why the few old men trapped with them hold cocked pistols to the heads of their women. We have already seen the fate of white innocence, called this time "Little Sister," and this time driven over the edge of a cliff by the black rapist, Gus. Lifted from Dixon's novel, Gus becomes a more ultimate horror when played by a white man in blackface, dosed with hydrogen peroxide until he foams at the mouth, like Legree at the point of smiting Uncle Tom.

Karl Brown has described the reaction of the first-night audience to that charge of the Klan: "The cheers began to arise from all over the packed house." Though more high-minded film critics have ever since tended to deplore it ("Here was the pattern for the cheapest and most hollow film sensations," Jay Leyda writes, "the ornament of every film that hoped to stamp out all intellectual stimulus with a brutal physical impact"), it has provided the model for a million B-movie rides to the rescue, in which, no matter how stereotyped, it never quite loses its primordial power. But no one has ever done it better than Griffith in *The Birth of a Nation*, at the climax of which audiences still go out of control.

I myself once saw, for example, the members of a left-wing ciné club in Athens, believers all in the equality of the races and the unmitigated evil of the Klan, rise to their feet at ten o'clock in the morning (the year was 1960, two wars and innumerable revolutions after the making of the film) to scream with bloodlust and approval equal to that of the racist first-nighters of 1915 as white womanhood was once more delivered from the threat of black rape. It was not merely the magic of Griffith, that old "master of motion," which plunged them open-eyed first into, then out of a nightmare, in which God knows what ultimate enemies of their own were threatening what prized and virginal darlings. Also at work were the myths which Griffith had inherited from Dixon, and which Dixon had somehow derived from Harriet Beecher Stowe, whose work, it should be added, the entire crew of the film knew even better than

they did Dixon's. In fact, Karl Brown tells us, the exterior
set of the small Southern town, in which the action of *The
Birth of a Nation* begins, was modeled on shared memories
of the "Tom plays," a mythological setting in which Dixon's characters proved no less at home than Mrs. Stowe's.

There is something profoundly disturbing about the
power of vulgar works like Dixon's and Griffith's to move
us at a level beneath that of our conscious allegiances, religious or political. I can understand, therefore, why groups
used in such works to symbolize "evil" should protest their
showing, and why organizations espousing doctrines which
those works subvert should join in trying to ban them. Despite my distrust of all who believe themselves absolutely
right and my unqualified opposition to censorship in any
form, I can sympathize with the attempt of the NAACP to
suppress *The Birth of a Nation* for its "loathsome misrepre-
sentations of colored people and the glorification of the
hideous and murderous band of Ku Klux Klan." But as a
writer often considered controversial in my own time, I
identify more with Griffith's rage at what he calls the
"drooling travesty of sense" perpetrated "by ill minded
censors and politicians . . . playing for the Negro vote."

In any case, such attempts at suppression did not, could
not, cannot work. There is no way to censor troubled
dreams, in which our otherwise unconfessed ambivalence
about, say, the emancipation of black slaves finds symbolic
expression, since such dreams are in the unconscious of all
Americans, including white politicians and the black voters
for whom they claim to speak. It seems to me instructive
that the NAACP, which harried Dixon and Griffith in 1915,
three decades later bestowed a special award on Butterfly
McQueen for acting out in the film version of *Gone With
the Wind* a condescending stereotype of the "good nigger"
quite compatible with the mythology of *The Clansman* and
The Birth of a Nation.

G ONE WITH THE WIND:

THE FEMINIZATION OF

THE ANTI-TOM NOVEL

Dixon, who lived to 1946, recognized Margaret Mitchell as his literary heir, sending her a letter immediately after the publication of *Gone With the Wind* in 1936 to tell her how much it had moved him, and to assure her that he intended writing a book-length study of her work. In quick response, she acknowledged her indebtedness to him, explaining, "I was practically raised on your books and love them very much. . . . When I was eleven years old I decided I would dramatize your book 'The Traitor'—and dramatize it I did in six acts." It is curious that the novel she chose was the last and least admired of his trilogy in praise of the Klan rather than either of the two which Griffith had transformed into *The Birth of a Nation;* but, of course, the ideology and mythology are the same, and, with certain modifications due to her sex and generation, they became hers forever.

Unfortunately, we have neither Miss Mitchell's play nor Dixon's critical essay on her. The first has disappeared, and the second never came into existence, since Dixon died of a cerebral hemorrhage before he got around to writing it. I can, however, imagine how sympathetically he would have responded to her view of Reconstruction as a total disaster, and of the Klan as its somewhat equivocal but necessary and—until it had outlived its usefulness—salutary consequence. I presume that he would have approved also of her portrayal of black American slaves as childlike, docile and, unless subverted by outside instigators, utterly faithful to their masters. Finally, perhaps (or at least so I would like to believe), he might have acknowledged that with her book the South's long quarrel with Harriet Beecher Stowe had at last eventuated in a fiction as moving and memorable as *Uncle Tom's Cabin* itself.

He is unlikely, however, to have suspected that by the last decades of the twentieth century *Gone With the Wind,* in print and on the screen, would have replaced that mid-nineteenth-century pop classic as the most widely circulated and best loved of all American fictions, not merely in the United States but throughout the world. More people, of course, than have ever read the book have seen the movie, which I myself once watched in a fishing village in Yugoslavia, dubbed into French and subtitled in Croatian —but so immediately apprehensible in terms of its images that no one seemed dismayed even when, from time to time, the sound track sputtered and died. I was, consequently, scarcely surprised when in 1980 it was voted by a sampling of representative Americans as one of the ten best American films of all time.

Yet I was, I must confess, a little startled to learn that at almost the same moment it was being requested by the Communist regime of North Vietnam as one of the two first films (the other, confusingly enough, was Hitler's favorite movie, *King Kong*) in a program of cultural exchange, on the basis of which, presumably, mutual affection and esteem would be reestablished between our recently hostile countries. This odd selection is partly explicable in terms of the immunity of popular taste to ideology, though there may have been an ideological base as well, if the commissars of culture in Hanoi were aware, as I have recently become, of Mme. Chiang Ching's unpredictably high opinion of Margaret Mitchell's elegy for the Old South.

In the course of the trial against the so-called Gang of Four it was revealed that she had apparently proposed at the height of the Chinese "Cultural Revolution" that instead of "classics," Western or Eastern, students in the People's Universities be taught what she considered true models for people's literature: *Gone With the Wind* and *Little Women,* the book James Baldwin had lumped with *Uncle Tom's Cabin* as a particularly repellent example of sado-sentimentality. The latter novel had in fact at an earlier stage of the Chinese Revolution been translated and played everywhere as an example of popular theater; but things were changing in China as in the West in the late sixties, and moving in directions which Sun Yat-sen could not have surmised.

Nor could Dixon, I suspect, in the late forties have foreseen Mitchell's triumph over Stowe. He might, however, have had some sense (in which case, his generous response is all the more impressive) that his own trilogy would eventually disappear in the shadow of *Gone With the Wind*. Maybe it was inevitable that in a subgenre which women had long made their own, it would take another woman to create a counter-myth as compelling as Mrs. Stowe's. Or maybe it is merely that mythopoeically Miss Mitchell was more gifted than Dixon. Certainly no character from any of his novels has entered the communal dreams of the mass audience, in which Scarlett, Melanie, Rhett Butler, Ashley Wilkes and Mammy live on as vividly as Uncle Tom, Eliza, Topsy, Simon Legree and Little Eva.

All but one of Miss Mitchell's mythic characters, however, are—despite the number of blacks who populate her pages—white. Moreover, though the black rapist, the archetypal "bad nigger," foreshadowed in Dixon and Griffith's Gus, haunts the imaginations of her heroine, her family and friends, and even makes a brief appearance on the scene, he has proved less memorable than relatively minor "good niggers," like Big Sam, Dilsey, Polk, and Uncle Peter, who, more or less efficiently, serve, protect and, as Faulkner liked to put it, "endure." One especially survives, as indestructible as Scarlett herself. Indeed, when all else of traditional Southern culture is gone with the wind—the armies of the Confederacy defeated, the great houses pillaged and burned, the courtly lovers, whether impotent cavaliers like Ashley Wilkes or sexy scoundrels like Rhett Butler, departed—her "good nigger"-in-chief, Mammy, remains to preside over the book's bittersweet ending.

Like all protagonists of the domestic tradition in American letters who do not die for our sins, Scarlett O'Hara must end by "going home" rather than fleeing to the "territory ahead," like some anti-domestic Huck Finn. But home means people as well as a place, and there is almost no one left at Tara to welcome her back. Her always shadowy aristocratic mother has long since disappeared, followed by her

Irish immigrant father, driven to death by drink and madness; and her children, in whom the childless Margaret Mitchell never is able to make us quite believe, have died melodramatically or mysteriously vanished from the action.

The point is, I think (though I must admit it has taken me a long time to understand this), that Miss Mitchell's book, unlike Mrs. Stowe's, is addressed not to the Mothers of America but to the Daughters, and her heroine must therefore remain a daughter to its final page. In a real sense Scarlett, though she grows older and richer, refuses to grow up; even after war and starvation, multiple marriage and bereavement, pregnancy and miscarriage, assuring herself that "tomorrow is another day"—like an adolescent who does not believe that she will ever die. To be an unchanging mythic daughter, however, she needs an unchanging mythic mother, not (as her actual white mama aspires to be) a viable role model whom she will by emulating eventually replace. And just such an alternative "mother" was available to more privileged whites in the Old South: a figure too alien to be emulated, but undemanding and nurturing, warm, buxom and *black;* one for whom her charge remains eternally a child, to be scolded in jest and spoiled in full earnest.

If the "home" to which Scarlett yearns to return is in part Tara, the land itself, which her Irish father taught her outlasts everything, it is also, as he could not know, her quasi-immortal Mammy. "Suddenly she wanted Mammy desperately, as she had wanted her when she was a little girl, wanted the broad bosom, on which to lay her head, the gnarled black hand on her hair. Mammy, the last link with the old days." But Mammy, we realize, whom no betrayal can alienate, no Emancipation Proclamation deliver from the eternal bondage of love, is really Uncle Tom, the Great Black Mother of us all—with whom Mrs. Stowe identifies, being herself the mother of many, but to whom the childless Margaret Mitchell could only dream of returning.

Miss Mitchell was not, however, the first to reveal the secret of Tom's gender. Long before *Gone With the Wind,* his/her true sex had become evident: in Faulkner's Dilsey, for instance, whose epitaph (in the androgynous plural) closes *The Sound and the Fury,* "DILSEY. They endured"; and in Aunt Jemima, whose turbaned head has grinned at three generations of Americans from the pancake box that has become her final home. But it took Margaret Mitchell, that 1920s flapper and newspaper sob-sister turned laureate to a nation by the Great Depression, to fix her new image in popular literature once and for all. The other women we chiefly remember out of this essentially feminine fantasy, from honey-dripping, doomed Melanie (who accepts the old-fashioned maternal role Scarlett rejects, living for service and self-sacrifice) to mindless, heartless, indomitable and desirable Scarlett herself, are splittings of Mitchell's ambivalent self, like our surrogates in REM sleep. Or else they are stock figures, like Belle Watling, the Whore with a Heart of Gold, or Prissy, the sniveling comic black servant.

But Mammy she inherits from the book she thought she despised, the Yankee abolitionist's dream of a love transcending the ambiguity of gender as well as the horrors of slavery. Not just Mammy, but indeed many of Mitchell's more benign "darkies" (it was her preferred name for them), seem spin-offs of Mrs. Stowe's faithful, pious but childishly naïve hero/heroine, since she perceives them all through the same screen of pity and condescension. "Negroes," Margaret Mitchell explains to the reader at one point, speaking for herself as well as Scarlett, "had to be handled gently, as though they were children, directed, praised, petted, scolded." And, she would further have us believe, they were so treated in the antebellum South, whatever readers of *Uncle Tom's Cabin* may have been misled into thinking was the case.

It is, in fact, with Mrs. Stowe's uncritical fans that she is quarreling, rather than with the book itself (which, indeed, she may never have read), in the single passage in which she mentions it by name. "Accepting *Uncle Tom's Cabin* as revelation," she writes, "second only to the Bible, the Yankee women all wanted to know about the bloodhounds which every Southerner kept to track down runaway slaves. . . . They wanted to know about the dreadful branding irons which the planters used to mark the faces of their slaves and the cat-o'-nine-tails with which they beat them to death and they evidenced what Scarlett felt was a very nasty and ill-bred interest in slave concubinage."

She seems never quite to have realized how much the fate of her own book was to be like that of Mrs. Stowe's, its acceptance by the majority audience as a new, revised secular scripture leading to its rejection by literary critics.

From the moment of publication, it was faulted, especially in quarters where a taste for High Literature was combined with leftist politics, for its exploitation of "false sentiment and heady goo" and its promulgation of the presumably defunct "plantation legend." To such attacks, Miss Mitchell purported to be indifferent. "I'd have to do so much explaining to family and friends," she wrote, "if the aesthetes and radicals of literature liked it." Then she adds, in an apology which seems to echo those of Mrs. Stowe and Thomas Dixon: "I'm not a stylist, God knows, and couldn't be if I tried." Yet something in her seems to have yearned for critical acclaim, for she responded immediately and gratefully to what favorable notices appeared.

For a little while, in fact, the issue seemed in doubt, but once a blockbuster movie had been made of *Gone With the Wind*, she was doomed to critical oblivion, a fate confirmed when the film proved to be as aesthetically undistinguished as her prose. Though credited to a single director and scriptwriter, it was actually directed by two and written by eleven or twelve, a patchwork job with no controlling intelligence behind it, except her own. The millions who first read, then saw *Gone With the Wind* responded to it not as literature but as myth, remembering not even the original author, much less those responsible for adapting her novel to the screen, but the actors who embodied her personae: Clark Gable, already mythic before he was cast as Rhett, Vivien Leigh, who became mythic from the moment she became Scarlett, and to a lesser degree, Leslie Howard and Olivia de Havilland, who played Ashley and Melanie Wilkes.

To most of those millions, ignorant of or indifferent to history, the retreat of the Confederate Army, Sherman's March to the Sea and the Burning of Atlanta represented a legend not of the antebellum past but of the mid-Depression present, dressed, to be sure, in the trappings of High Romance. Though she had begun her novel in the early twenties, Miss Mitchell finished it under the shadow of the great collapse of 1929, and as she revised it for publication, unemployment, strikes and the threat of violence possessed the streets of our desolate cities, into which free blacks, sons and daughters of those she had portrayed, had been pouring since the end of World War I. Meanwhile, overseas, Nazis and Communists goose-stepped and chanted, evoking the menace of revolution and the threat of World War II, which had already begun by 1939, when the movie version was released. Small wonder, then, that *GWTW* (after a while just its initials were enough to identify it), with its odd blending of "realism" and escapism, became the most popular work of the age, rivaled by nothing in the bookstores, and challenged at the box office only by *The Wizard of Oz*, which appeared in the same year.

Yet no history of our literature in the thirties, written then or afterward, has considered it worthy of mention side by side with either the books that decade itself prized, like the novels of James T. Farrell, John Dos Passos and John Steinbeck, or those by authors we have recently come to prefer, like Nathanael West, Henry Roth or Daniel Fuchs. Even the so-called proletarian novelists, touted by the Communist press of the time but read even then by no more than a thousand or two of the faithful and ever since by almost no one, are dutifully recorded (Jack Conroy's *The Disinherited*, for instance, or Robert Cantwell's *Land of Plenty*) by cultural historians and recalled respectfully on memorial occasions.

I can remember one such occasion, a retrospective symposium on the thirties, held at Stanford University in the early sixties, at which Farrell and Nelson Algren were present to reminisce and be honored. For some reason, which escaped me at the time, I had been invited too. When, however, I chose to speak not of their work or that of contemporaries they admired, but about *Gone With the Wind* (though I had secretly enjoyed both book and film for a long while, it was the first time I had come out of the closet), I was greeted with skepticism and disbelief, as if I were up to my tedious *enfant terrible* tricks once more.

It is true that even before then, *Gone With the Wind* had been cited occasionally as evidence of the decline of taste in an age of mass culture, most memorably perhaps in Gershom Legman's frenetic attack on comic books and best sellers, *Love and Death* (1948). He links it with such forgettable potboilers by women writers of the period as *Forever Amber* and *Duchess Hotspur,* which he describes as pathological celebrations of the "Bitch Heroine"; then he asks (and answers himself immediately):

What was the message of the most phenomenally successful best-seller of the first half of the twentieth century—a book that sold fifty thousand copies on its first day of sale, millions since? Literary history will ask us. Why have we not yet set down the answer? The message of Margaret Mitchell's *Gone With the Wind* was hate. Nothing more. Hate, and war between the sexes from beginning to end, set—symbolically enough— against the background of another great civil war. Miss Mitchell's heroine ruins every man's life she touches, and that is what makes her a heroine. Utterly brainless, utterly shallow, vain, and useless—particularly in bed —Miss Mitchell's Venus Dominatrix wields the whip with a strong hand, figuratively over the back of every man who wants her sexually, and every woman who stands in her way; physically and in fact on a mere "nigger" to the tune of *That's Why the Ku Klux Was Born.*

There is a sense, however, in which Legman is, though wrong in details (in the novel, Scarlett actually beats no one), right in general. *Gone With the Wind* is essentially sado-masochistic, though less in the tradition of *Forever Amber* than of *Uncle Tom's Cabin, The Clansman, The Birth of a Nation* and *Roots.* Like the latter, it is based on a fantasy of interethnic rape as the supreme expression of the violence between sexes and races which underlies much of our history. In the continuing underground epic of which it is a part, only such rape (along with interracial flagellation, which is symbolically equivalent) is an archetypal constant. Nor does it matter whether white men are shown sexually exploiting black girls, or black men brutally assaulting white ones, but only that the male rapist be portrayed as an evil aggressor, successful or frustrated, and his female victim as passive and innocent. Always, moreover, in the pattern story, the "pollution" of female innocence is avenged: whether, as in *Uncle Tom's Cabin,* by God working on the conscience of the white perpetrator of evil or, as in *The Clansman,* by righteous white men banded together in God's name to lynch the black aggressor.

Rape and vengeance for rape are frequently alluded to in *Gone With the Wind* and even more often present in the minds of its female characters. Sometimes, indeed, especially on the periphery of the main plot, they conform to the Dixonian stereotype, as, for instance, when Captain Rhett Butler confesses to Scarlett O'Hara, "I'm as guilty as Cain. I did kill the nigger. He was uppity to a lady, and what else could a Southern gentleman do?" But the three attempted rapes (only one of them consummated) of Scarlett herself do not fit the formula at all. In fact, her first assailant is not black but white, though clearly lower class, a Union soldier, described as "a thick, rough-looking man with an unkempt black beard straggling over his unbuttoned blue jacket. Little close-set eyes, squinting in the sun glare."

Scarlett confronts him in her ravaged family house, all effective males long since gone; and, though she is scared for a moment, executes him on the spot:

> Like lightning, she shoved her weapon over the bannisters and into the startled bearded face. Before he could even fumble at his belt, she pulled the trigger. . . . The man crashed backwards to the floor. . . . Hardly aware that she was moving, Scarlett ran down the stairs and stood over him, gazing down into what was left of the face above the beard, a bloody pit where the nose had been, glazing eyes burned with powder.

It is not guilt she feels at having committed murder, or even joy at having preserved her "honor," but a strange exultation and renewed vitality: "She was vitally alive again, vitally glad with a cool tigerish joy. She could have ground her heel into the gaping wound which had been his nose and taken sweet pleasure in the feel of his warm blood on her bare feet."

The scene was so well rendered in the movie version that, we are told, the first-night spectators in Miss Mitchell's native Atlanta rose to their feet and cheered. Though the surrender at Appomattox lay seventy years in the past, for one moment they could forget the defeat of the Old Cause, as a Daughter of the Confederacy triumphed over a Son of the North, revenging what Southerners always thought of in their deep imaginations as the "rape of the South." But surely the women in that audience in Atlanta (like their sisters in New York and Chicago, Omaha and Los Angeles) applauded also Scarlett's lonely triumph—uncompromised by male intervention—over the more ancient enemy, men: all of whom, kindly husbands, loving fathers, dutiful sons, ardent lovers, blur into the figure of the Rapist in the nightmares even of those who in waking hours do not consider themselves ravished or oppressed.

At any rate, it is death we are cheering if, Northerners or Southerners, male or female, we cheer with them: the death of some absolutely villainous Other, however we identify it/him/her in our unconscious. Death is also the outcome of the second assault on Scarlett's "honor." But this time it is more equivocal, stirring no cheers in any audience in which I have ever sat. Once more, she is armed and, when confronted by a would-be rapist, shoots. She fires "point-blank" at "the squat black negro with a chest like a gorilla," who (egged on by a white-trash accomplice) lunges lubriciously at her as she drives her buggy past a shantytown "which had the worst reputation of any spot in or near Atlanta. . . . Men went by with their pistols loosened in their holsters and nice women never willingly passed it."

Her head is already full of nightmare images of Negro rapists, for at this point Reconstruction has destroyed the traditional "law and order" of the slaveholders and "the negroes were completely out of hand." Indeed, the barely anthropoid assailant who threatens her seems such an image made living flesh, though, as in a nightmare, he seems invulnerable. At any rate, "whether or not she hit him," the "black ape" does not stop until he has begun to reenact just such a standard dream scenario of "rape from below" as Dixon might have imagined:

> The negro was beside her, so close that she could smell the rank odor of him as he tried to drag her over the buggy side. With her one free hand she fought madly, clawing at his face, and then she felt his big hand at her throat and, with a ripping noise, her basque was torn open from neck to waist. Then the black hand fumbled between her breasts, and terror and repulsion such as she had never known came over her and she screamed like an insane woman.

Just short of violation, however, she is rescued by Big Sam, a plantation slave from the old days at Tara, on the run from Federal justice. Even he with his giant's strength, however, cannot destroy the spectral ravisher, whom he pursues into the dark. "Ah hope Ah done kill dat black baboon," he tells her on his return. "But Ah din wait ter fine out." We do learn that he has knocked down the white accomplice in the road, and Scarlett then runs over him with the buggy; but apparently, he miraculously survives too. Vengeance is therefore left for the Klan (again we seem to be slipping back into the tried-and-true Dixonian formula), who raid the shantytown the next night, leaving behind two corpses, one black, one white. Whether they were the actual perpetrators of Scarlett's not-quite-rape is never made clear. Nor does it seem to matter, since the restitution which is demanded is symbolic, not against an individual, but a race and a class whose members no longer "know their place."

The scenario is totally disrupted, however, when United States troops surround the would-be avengers in white and kill two of the Klansmen. All of the masked riders are revealed at that point as Scarlett's family and friends, though she has until then been kept in ignorance of the fact because of her business and social relations with the Yankee occupation forces. Indeed, not only is her hitherto despised husband, Frank Kennedy, one of the dead, but her beloved Ashley is badly wounded. For a while, in fact, it looks as if almost every male with whom she is closely associated (except for Rhett Butler, who, like her, plays a double game for fun and profit) will be jailed or driven into exile in Texas. Finally, though, they are all saved by a stratagem of Rhett's which turns the high melodrama of Southern chivalry into low comedy.

At this point it becomes clear that Margaret Mitchell has relentlessly, albeit regretfully and tenderly, been undercutting the Dixonian formula from the start. It is, after all, not innocent "Little Sister" who has been "polluted" by the touch of what she, like Dixon, describes as "Simian" black hands, but a selfish, driving, conniving woman—who has provoked violation and invoked thereby the knee-jerk response of Southern gentlemen. She has, moreover, acted out of pride, stubbornness and the desire to get rich quick. Everyone of her own caste and color (except, of course, eternally tolerant and loving Melanie) acknowledges this, some to her face. And finally, in maudlin drunkenness, she ends by reproaching herself: "She had killed Frank . . . just as surely as if it had been her finger that pulled the trigger. He had begged her not to go about alone but she had not listened to him."

Her guilt is compounded by the fact that she is really relieved to be rid of a man she has never loved but was

willing to marry for his store and his mill—warranties that
she would never again go hungry. Never has she seemed
so utterly despicable as at this moment. Yet when, sniveling, whining and reeling from too much brandy, she cries
out to Rhett Butler, like some frightened child, "I'm afraid
I'll die and go to hell," he first laughs, then takes her into
his arms.

> She felt again the rush of helplessness, the sinking
> yielding, the surging tide of warmth that left her limp.
> . . . He bent her head across his arm and kissed her,
> softly at first, and then with a swift gradation of inten-
> sity that made her cling to him as the only solid thing
> in a dizzy swaying world. His insistent mouth was part-
> ing her shaking lips, sending wild tremors along her
> nerves. . . . And before a swimming giddiness spun her
> round and round, she knew she was kissing him back.

Though the scene ends with his proposing marriage to
her (since, after all, she is now *free*), and she accepts, the
groundwork has been laid not for the conventional "happily ever after" of the domestic romance, but for a third and
even more ambiguous rape. It is not "rape from below"
which is threatened (and accomplished) this last time
around, but "peer rape," marital rape, as Scarlett is forced
by Rhett, whom she has banned from her bed lest she bear
another child and lose forever her girlish eighteen-and-
one-half-inch waist. Though she has not yet realized that
the man she accepted as her last husband is her one true
love (still dreaming in his arms of unattainable, eunuchoid
Ashley), she has long suspected that he is the only peer,
male or female, she has ever encountered.

He is her equal not just in erotic power and a talent for
survival, but in arrogance, cunning and contempt for
"honor" in all of its meanings. "We are not gentlemen and
we have no honor," he has told her. "That is why we flourish like green bay trees." He is, indeed, intellectually superior to her, for she is barely literate and, though skillful
in manipulating men and money, inept when it comes to
language or ideas. Nonetheless, he loves her desperately,
and is aware of it long before she recognizes her own answering passion. When he forces her, therefore, it is not
merely out of drunken rage and jealousy of his rival, but in

genuine desire. At first, she feels only panic fear as he pursues her, with clear intent to take her to bed:

> Rhett, running lightly as an Indian, was beside her in
> the dark. His breath was hot on her face and his hands
> went round her roughly, under the wrapper, against
> her bare skin. . . .
> He swung her off her feet into his arms and started
> up the stairs. . . . He hurt her and she cried out, muf-
> fled, frightened. Up the stairs, he went in the utter ˙
> darkness, up, up, and she was wild with fear.

"Dark," "darkness": this becomes the leitmotif, as the
swarthy husband she thought she knew becomes a Black
Stranger, fading first into the image of the Negro rapist and
finally into that of the archetypal King of the Underworld:
Pluto snatching Proserpine from the daylight world to his
eternally sunless realm.

> He was a mad stranger and this was a black darkness
> she did not know, darker than death. He was like
> death, carrying her away in arms that hurt . . . he
> stopped suddenly on the landing and, turning her
> swiftly in his arms, bent over her and kissed her with a
> savagery and completeness that wiped out everything
> from her mind but the dark into which she was sinking.
> . . . She was darkness and he was darkness and there
> had never been anything before this time, only dark-
> ness and his lips upon her . . .

Finally, however, she *likes* it (as perhaps only a female
writer would dare to confess, though there are echoes of
D. H. Lawrence in the passage), likes being mastered by
the dark power of the male, likes being raped:

> Suddenly she had a wild thrill such as she had never
> known; joy, fear, madness, excitement, surrender to
> arms that were too strong, lips too bruising. . . . For the
> first time in her life she had met something stronger
> than she, someone she could neither bully nor break,
> someone who was bullying and breaking her . . .

She has also had, one suspects, for the first time in her life
an orgasm; though Miss Mitchell does not quite say this,
telling us instead that when Scarlett wakes the next morn-

ing the only feeling she can recall which matched in intensity the one she experienced in her rapist's arms was the ecstasy she had attained after murdering her Yankee assailant: "For the first time in her life she had felt . . . passion as sweeping and primitive . . . as dizzy sweet as the cold hate when she had shot the Yankee."

Rhett, however, has left before Scarlett awakens, and returns briefly only to apologize—unaware of her pleasure and unwilling to listen; then leaves again for three months. By the time he comes back, she knows she is pregnant, but her attempt to share her new joy is similarly ill-fated. They end in a bitter quarrel, in the course of which, trying to repay his indifference with pain, she cries, "Oh God, I wish it was anybody's baby but yours." And he answers in cold irony, "Cheer up . . . maybe you'll have a miscarriage." She lunges at him then in fury, "to claw him," to draw blood, but misses and falls down the same steps on which he had initiated her rape—losing the child. Once more rape ends in death, this time extorting from the reader tears rather than cheers.

It is an effective scene in the book and even more so in the film, which has fixed that mythological staircase in the mind of the mass audience forever. But the critical establishment has almost universally scorned its obvious irony, raw melodrama and shameless sado-masochistic appeal. Not that even the most elite critics are dismayed by violence per se—finding it quite tolerable in Faulkner, for instance, or Hemingway, the latter of whom Miss Mitchell considered too brutal to bear. What in Gone With the Wind appalls even the most reactionary among them, who share its politics and racism, is the sentimentalism beneath the horror, the myth of Home as Heaven at the novel's heart, and even more, perhaps, Miss Mitchell's failure to redeem that horror with high style or lofty ideas.

It is, however, this very unpretentiousness, which they take as a sign that she is one of them, which disarms the millions of watchers, many of whom deplore cop shows and westerns as being "too violent" but make of each new TV showing of Gone With the Wind a family ritual. They do not acknowledge even to themselves that what moves them most deeply about it is the nightmare of black insurrection and white violation. Instead, they typically allude to the heroism and independence of Scarlett and the high romance of her troubled relationship with Rhett Butler, who some of them doubtless believe will someday return to her arms, though the single line they are likely to be able to quote from the book is the one Rhett speaks as he leaves her, presumably forever, "Frankly, my dear, I don't give a damn."

To the guardians of literary "standards," however, Miss Mitchell's low piety and high romance are as unspeakable as the soft-core porn they disguise; further clues to the dirty little secret that her continuing popularity in spite of their contempt threatens to give away: that much, if not indeed all, story which long endures and pleases many does so in large part by providing the "vulgar" satisfactions of terror, sexual titillation and the release of tears. That is why *The Literary History of the United States,* for example, devotes not a single line of all its fourteen hundred-odd pages to a discussion of *Gone With the Wind* as literature, merely reporting the statistics of its sales at home and abroad (3.5 million copies sold in 1936–37, etc.) as if it were an event in the marketplace and not the Republic of Letters. Inevitably, in the same paragraph, it mentions that other marketplace success of the thirties, Hervey Allen's *Anthony Adverse,* but its editors do not pause to speculate why the latter had dropped from public memory a decade after publication, while images, scenes, characters, even names from the former have continued to live on in the deep imagination of readers all over the world—including, of course, me.

Yet for many years, despite this fact and my populist politics, I kept secret my affection for that book, which I alluded to in *Love and Death in the American Novel,* for instance, with phrases like "popular literature . . . far traditional book . . . stereotypes . . . sentimentality . . . best seller . . . ready-made masturbatory fantasies." Even my remarks to the Stanford symposium on the thirties, where I had insisted on talking about Margaret Mitchell, were (as I recall) ambivalent, ambiguous—and, in any case, I never committed them to print. Indeed, her disconcertingly "immortal" book remains for me even now a test case, harder to come to terms with by far—for reasons I do not quite understand—than *Uncle Tom's Cabin* or *The Birth of a Nation* or *The Clansman* itself. The first two are, after all, however inadvertently, borderline "works of art," even judged by traditional elitist standards; while the last, since it is recognized by everyone at this point as unmitigated junk, can be condescended to in "camp" style as Peter Bog-danovich did in *Nickelodeon*.

But *Gone With the Wind* divides the audience, being still thought of by many as a "great book," real literature. I was therefore not surprised when quite recently a woman grad-uate student in English, committed now exclusively to the exegesis of Virginia Woolf and Emily Dickinson, confessed to me that as an undergraduate she had proudly displayed it on her dormitory bookshelves, until the scorn of her more sophisticated classmates drove her to keep it out of sight. In any case, I am still a little defensive about my own ad-miration for it, as I was reminded some three or four years ago when a letter arrived on my desk, which I have still not answered (though I make a point of responding to *all* mail), except insofar as this book is an answer. Addressed to "Dr. Lesley Fielder," that letter managed by spelling both my names wrong to set in operation habits of condescension, which at that point I had learned to be ashamed of, though not quite to repress.

"It is my understanding," it began, "and that of my A.P. class at Sacred Heart Academy that you feel there are no great female characters in American Literature. I feel, how-ever, that Scarlett O'Hara of Margaret Mitchell's *Gone With the Wind* should be considered for the following rea-sons. . . ." It concluded, "I am writing to you because of your literary background and I would like to know your opinion of my opinion." When I still had proper literary opinions, still thought I knew what "literature" was, I would have written (in fact, found myself on the point of writing): "My dear So-and-So, My generalization about there being no great female characters in American Litera-ture still stands, since *Gone With the Wind* is not part of American Literature proper, but only of sub- or para-litera-ture."

In the twenty years since, I have come to realize that I had not then told the whole truth about my response to Miss Mitchell's novel, since, after all, I had devoted to it only two pages out of the six hundred I had allowed myself to cover the whole span of our fiction. Furthermore, I have since become a defender of majority literature, have I not, of which *Gone With the Wind* is a chief glory? Nonetheless, I found myself confronting that letter—and, candor compels me to admit, find myself still—not entirely free of ambivalence: an ambivalence reflected in the vestigial scorn I cannot quite repress for the girl from Sacred Heart Academy who *begins* with a high regard for *Gone With the Wind* rather than ends with it (like me) after having passed through an initiation into the world of elitist standards. Precisely because of that initiation, perhaps, there persists in me a sneaky inclination to believe that Scarlett O'Hara, despite her mythic dimensions, does not deserve to be ranked with such "truly" archetypal figures out of our own literature as Natty Bumppo, Captain Ahab, Daisy Miller or Hester Prynne, much less with their European prototypes, Odysseus, Aeneas, Hamlet, Don Quixote, Medea, Jocasta or Emma Bovary.

Yet I would be hard pressed to defend such a hierarchal distinction, which depends on what I have come to believe is a definition of literature no longer appropriate to a mass society. I am, moreover, willing to follow the logic of my anti-elitist position even if it leads to the redemption not just of good-bad works I have always secretly loved, like *Gone With the Wind, The Birth of a Nation* and *Uncle Tom's Cabin,* but also such a prefabricated piece of commodity schlock as Alex Haley's *Roots,* which, subsidized by the *Reader's Digest* and blessed by the PTA, evokes in me an initial distrust I find it hard to overcome.

ALEX HALEY'S ROOTS:
UNCLE TOM REWRITES

UNCLE TOM'S CABIN

Alex Haley's *Roots* is an equivocal book, its authorship problematical and its genre uncertain. How much of it was actually written by Haley remains unclear, since, confronted by a suit for plagiarism, he settled out of court—dismayed, it would appear, that the ghostwriter to whom he seems to have entrusted the section in question had without his knowledge lifted pieces out of someone else's previously published novel. That those pieces were already clichés, stereotypes about slavery and Africa long in the public domain, would have meant nothing in court, any more than the fact that Haley's book was the work of many hands.

Plagiarism is in law a punishable offense, and in the mind of the popular audience a betrayal of trust. But "ghostwriting," whether acknowledged or not, is in both tribunals considered an acceptable practice; and editorial "revision," no matter how drastic, ignored by tacit consent. It seems to me, however, that if we are to understand the kind of book *Roots* is, we must begin by realizing how great a role was played in its production by heavy editing, and how typical this is of most books by popular novelists, writing under pressure of time and for a living. Sometimes, indeed, the work of such writers, who are more often than not weak in execution skills and uninterested in style, is virtually rewritten by anonymous employees of their publishers.

If the names of such quasi-collaborators do not appear on the title page, no subterfuge is involved, since neither they nor the person whose name does appear there doubts for one moment who is, as the *cinéastes* put it, the true *auteur* of the work. Moreover, in the case of books, unlike that of movies, there is no convention of listing "credits" for all who have contributed to their final form. Yet ever since the invention of the Gutenberg process, the production of novels has been, like film though to a lesser degree, a communal, cooperative process, involving artists and technicians of various kinds: researchers, copy editors, layout people, compositors, printers, binders, jacket designers and, most notably, for a long while at least, illustrators.

Since the advent of modernism, "serious" fiction has tended not to be illustrated, and as our century has worn on, almost all "adult" books, no matter how popular their appeal, have followed suit. But before the age of Proust, Mann and Joyce, pictures played a part nearly equal to words in establishing the "images" so essential to popular fiction. George Cruikshank, for instance, always argued that he rather than Dickens had fixed the icon of Fagin in *Oliver Twist*. And there is little doubt that Sidney Paget created in his illustrations an image of Sherlock Holmes more like his own brother than the sleuth described in Conan Doyle's text. The importance of such collaborators had been recognized from the start, since their names appeared not merely under each picture but on the title page itself, right below that of the author.

Always unacknowledged, however, though indeed his/her role was (and remains) even more important, is the editor—or, as writers are accustomed to say, "my editor." With that penultimate authority (the final word, the writers are assured, is their own), who presides over all subordinate amenders of their manuscripts from typed copy to galleys to page proofs to bound volumes, writers enter into a relationship for which they are in the beginning quite unprepared: this total stranger claims the right, as even their mates and best friends scarcely dare do, to correct errors they have made, challenge assumptions they have failed to examine, lay profane hands on favorite phrases and tricks of punctuation, even urge excision of what they consider essential to their vision or suggest additions to what they believe fully and elegantly expressed.

It is hard, not just at first but always, to accept advice from one to whom no blame will accrue for the final result (and no credit either, to be sure)—especially hard, perhaps, for the heirs of modernism who believe in the uniqueness of their perceptions and the integrity of their text. But it helps a little to realize that not merely hacks and neophytes have profited by that relationship, but even the most ambitious and distinguished authors; indeed (if we are to believe William Dean Howells, who functioned both as author and as editor) the latter more than the former. "It would not do to say," he writes—thinking, we must assume, of Henry James and Mark Twain as well as Harriet Beecher Stowe—"how many of the first writers owed their correctness to the zeal of our proofreading, but I may say there were very few who did not owe something. The wisest and ablest were the most patient and grateful . . . under correction; it was only the beginning and the more ignorant who were angry."

Nor is it always just a matter of schoolmarmish "correction," as Howells rather disingenuously suggests. Sometimes, indeed, editorial revision goes far bayond catching "solecisms" and transposing phrases, but ends in total restructuring, as in the famous case of Thomas Wolfe and Maxwell Perkins. Perkins was also the editor of writers as different from each other as Scott Fitzgerald and Taylor Caldwell, but is best known for having given to *Look Homeward, Angel* and *Of Time and the River* whatever shape and coherence they have. To be sure, he downplays his role as co-creator of those novels in an essay on which he was still working when he died in 1947—in an attempt, as his words make clear, to deliver Wolfe from critical scorn. "He dedicated the book to me," Perkins observed of *Of Time and the River,* "in most extravagant terms. . . . It gave shallow people the impression that Wolfe could not function as a writer without collaboration, and one critic even used some such phrases as 'Wolfe and Perkins—Perkins and Wolfe, what way is that to write a novel . . .' No writer could possibly tolerate the assumption, which perhaps Tom almost himself did, that he was dependent as a writer upon anyone else."

Nonetheless, Perkins' essay constitutes the closest thing we have to a candid account of how a talented editor can help make an untidy manuscript into a well-shaped book without betraying its original inspiration. We can only wish there were others of a similar kind, dealing with novelists more highly regarded by the critical establishment: an account, for instance, of the relationship between William Faulkner and those editors at Random House who protected his privacy, kept him sober and working, and made suggestions for revising what seemed to them, according to their lights, commercially or aesthetically unviable.

But this seems unlikely, since the whole matter is regarded these days as a dirty little secret, like the relationship of literature and lucre, and therefore to be kept at all costs both from lowbrow readers, whom it would presumably just confuse, and highbrow critics, whom clearly it would embarrass. Indeed, some unreconstructed apostles of modernism refuse to confess it even to themselves, greeting any mention of it with lofty indignation. Nonetheless, I attempted recently, at a symposium on the state of letters in a technological age, to open the subject, by confessing publicly my indebtedness to certain of my own editors (particularly Catherine Carver, who had long worked with Leon Edel and Saul Bellow as well as me), expressing my gratitude to them for having urged on me changes in my books which would never have occurred to me without them, and which my wounded vanity resisted for a long time.

But one of my fellow panelists, an indurated Francophile elitist of the old school, responded huffily that *she* at least (like Flaubert before her, she implied) had never permitted any editor to tamper with her *mots justes*, and *I*, who had, must by that very token have "sold out." Like Alex Haley, she probably would have specified, had she deigned to recognize his humble existence. But I found myself thinking of Wolfe and Faulkner, Dickens and Twain and Harriet Beecher Stowe; though Haley's *Roots* must indeed also be taken into account, since it represents the ultimate *reductio* of editing: the mass-produced, almost authorless novel. To confuse matters even further, though peddled as fiction, *Roots* purports to be autobiographical and historical, which is to say, nonfiction with fictional trimmings.

Indeed, the sole indisputable thing about it is its astonishing popularity: 1.5 million copies sold in the original hardback edition, even more in paperback versions, the audience for the TV series peaking at 30 million, translations almost immediately into twenty-four languages, etc., etc. What such statistics indicate is more than a personal success story. They make clear that with *Roots,* a black American (never mind his white editors, ghost- and script-writers) succeeded for the first time in modifying the mythology of black-white relations in the United States for the *majority audience.* The only black author before Haley to have touched the hearts and opened the purse strings of that audience is Frank Yerby, who (though he does occasionally deal with miscegenation in his historical "bodice-rippers") is not thought of, nor, I suspect, does he think of himself, as black at all.

Other Afro-American writers of considerable talent have attempted to re-mythologize themselves and their people, from the time of Jean Toomer to that of Ishmael Reed. They have moved, however, not the masses, black or white, but an elite minority of professional readers, chiefly white, on whose guilt, self-hatred and self-righteousness they have battered. Even Richard Wright, whose *Native Son* became a play and a movie, never managed to capture the great audience; the name of his protagonist, Bigger Thomas, remains unknown to the millions of television viewers to whom Margaret Mitchell's Mammy and Alex Haley's Kunta Kinte were, at least for a while, household words.

When such a truly popular black writer did appear, it was predictable that it would be not with an alienated "art novel," like Wright's, but with a pop romance celebrating Home as Heaven. Only in that familiar form, aesthetically naïve, marginally literate but of great mythopoeic power, could he/she create a rival myth of his/her own people and their history as potent as those of Stowe, Dixon and Mitchell. Less predictable, though comprehensible enough, was the fact that when that long-awaited book did appear in Haley's *Roots,* it would be condensed by the *Reader's Digest,* that secular bible of white Middle America; assigned by white teachers as well as black in every classroom in the land; and bought by those earnest souls, chiefly white, who read only what they believe to be "good for them." Indeed, this almost universal acclaim makes *Roots* different from earlier contributions to our inadvertent epic.

Even *Uncle Tom's Cabin,* despite its accessibility to all generations and classes, divided its readers politically, geographically and ethnically: first setting pro-slavery

Southerners against Northern abolitionists, and after Emancipation, resentful blacks against self-congratulatory "liberal" whites. As late as 1976, Ishmael Reed, favorite "post-modernist" black novelist of the white critics, was still bitterly attacking Mrs. Stowe as a snob who had condescended to Lincoln and as a plagiarist who had tried to pass off as her own a slave narrative by the "original Uncle Tom":

> Old Harriet. Naughty Harriet. Accusing Lord Byron of pornography. She couldn't take to Lincoln. She liked Nobility. Curious. The woman who was credited with ruining the Planters was a toady to Nobility, just as they were. Strange, history. Complicated, too. It will always be a mystery, history. New disclosures are as bizarre as the most bizarre fantasy.
>
> Harriet caught some of it. She popularized the American novel and introduced it to Europe. *Uncle Tom's Cabin.* Writing is strange, though. That story caught up with her. The story she "borrowed" from Josiah Henson. Harriet only wanted enough money to buy a silk dress. The paper mills ground day and night. She'd read Josiah Henson's book. That Harriet was alert. *The Life of Josiah Henson, Formerly a Slave.* Seventy-seven pages long. It was short, but it was his. It was all he had. His story.

The anti-Tom books which responded to Mrs. Stowe's proved equally controversial, since they too subverted, if not the actual values of many "opinion makers" of their time, at least their notions of decorum. Dixon was labeled by some a rabid racist even then, and nowadays no voice is raised in his defense, since the latter-day Klansmen now futilely demonstrating in our streets are likely never to have heard of him. Even Griffith's *Birth of a Nation,* despite its high praise by more recent darlings of the *cinéastes* like Pudovkin and Eisenstein, is—at the moment I write this—being picketed yet again on the campus of Harvard University. And Margaret Mitchell, scorned by the left-wing intellectuals of her own time, was still being evoked as the ultimate enemy of the black nationalists of the sixties. Malcolm X, for instance, recalling his youth, writes: "I remember one thing that marred this time for me: the movie 'Gone With the Wind.' When it played in Mason, I was the only Negro in the theater, and when Butterfly

McQueen went into her act, I felt like crawling under the rug."

But the only voices raised against *Roots* were those of a very few hysterical rightists, discredited in the eyes of establishment liberals and conservatives alike even before the appearance of their scarcely literate Letters to the Editor. At least this was true in the United States, where even the handful of black writers with elitist pretensions who found *Roots* absurd—its Negro dialect a throwback to "Amos 'n' Andy," its version of African culture pitifully naïve and its politics timid—sniggered in private. They sought to avoid any public statement that might seem to give aid and comfort to the enemies of black power, or to undercut the growing pride of black people in their race. Only Ishmael Reed, professional dissenter and baiter of the smug, black or white, spoke out. And it was possible to discount his dissenting opinion on the grounds of sheer envy, since Haley's "potboiler" had not merely outsold his competing novel but had obliterated it from the consciousness of the reading public.

In France and Germany, on the other hand, where translations of *Roots* quickly appeared and sold well enough, though not quite as spectacularly as in the United States, the intellectuals were more openly scornful—particularly after the spin-off television series had been dubbed and shown on their own networks. The French typically framed each of the episodes with a *débat* involving critics and social scientists, as a way, I suppose, of justifying such a concession to "mass entertainment." And not surprisingly, most of the panelists, characteristically obsessed with the notion of "authenticity," agreed "that *Roots* was just another commercial enterprise, no more authentic than *Gone With the Wind*."

The Germans proved just as standardly anti-American and even more resolutely elitist. As a matter of fact, the TV station which showed the series (having invested some $800,000 for the privilege) began with an apology: announcing that what its viewers were about to see was "not up to our aesthetic, dramaturgical and technical standards." And the critics, with very few exceptions (one of whom praised the program as "an answer to *Gone With the Wind*"), followed suit, condemning it for its "inverted racism" and its "ultimate prudishness in sexual matters and a related perverse lust in violence." Finally, the majority concurred that it was "shameless . . . serial kitsch," "lowbrow popular culture" no better than *Tarzan* or (a comparison inevitable under the circumstances) the melodramas of Karl May, that still much-read German imitator of James Fenimore Cooper.

Meanwhile in America, even the staunchest erstwhile defenders of High Literature salved their consciences with a few apologetic reservations about a work as awkwardly structured and ineptly written as *The Clansman* itself, or retreated into abashed silence. Some, like James Baldwin, even touted it extravagantly. "An act of faith and courage . . ." he wrote of *Roots*, "an act of love . . . it suggests with great power how each of us . . . can't but be the vehicle of the history which produced us." He had apparently forgotten the lesson taught him by Richard Wright, and recorded in his essay "Alas, Poor Richard": " 'Roots,' Richard would snort, when I had finally worked my way around to this dreary subject, 'what—roots! Next thing you'll be telling me is that all colored folks have rhythm.' "

Nor did he apparently remember that he had condemned Mrs. Stowe for precisely the combination of sentimentality and brutality which constitutes the essential appeal of Haley's novel. A reader unfamiliar with *Gone With the Wind* would have a hard time telling Margaret Mitchell's ironic précis of *Uncle Tom's Cabin* ("the bloodhounds which every Southerner kept to track down runaway slaves . . . the dreadful branding irons which the planters used to mark . . . their slaves and the cat-o'-nine-tails with which they beat them to death . . . slave concubinage") from a plot summary of what happens to Haley's Kunta Kinte after falling into the hands of white slavers.

Yet Mrs. Stowe's name is never mentioned by Alex Haley. Indeed, *Roots* may well be the only notable book written by a black American which contains not a single reference to *Uncle Tom's Cabin*. Even the terms "Tom" and "Uncle Tom" are oddly absent, though Haley's most eminent Afro-American predecessors use those epithets as often and as automatically as black street people, who may not even know the name of Mrs. Stowe. Such writers, moreover, never fail to mention her book, against which they strive to define themselves in desperate ambivalence. That Richard Wright called the anti-Tom hero of *Native Son*

"Bigger Thomas" in due deliberation is attested to by the fact that he entitled his first collection of stories *Uncle Tom's Chillun*, and James Baldwin, his self-declared spiritual "heir," carries on the tradition. Even in the iconoclastic sixties, Malcolm X takes time out from tirades against the white "devils" to inform us, "Of course, I read *Uncle Tom's Cabin*. In fact, I believe that's the only novel I have ever read since I started serious reading." And Eldridge Cleaver interrupts his meditations on black and white sexuality in *Soul on Ice* to observe that "the most alienated view of America was preached by . . . Harriet Beecher Stowe in *Uncle Tom's Cabin*."

All of them, however, end by rejecting her androgynous Christian protagonist as a role model, identifying instead with the prepotent "bad nigger," the rapist of white women, first projected in fear and loathing by Dixon, Griffith and Mitchell, and reembodied in Wright's Bigger. "No American Negro exists," James Baldwin once remarked, "who does not have his private Bigger Thomas living in the skull." But the inarticulate and apolitical Bigger was, we remember, the improbable alter ego of a super-articulate Communist author, married to a white woman and destined to end up as the darling of the French intellectuals. Perhaps for this reason, Wright could not quite manage to make him perform the archetypal act of darkness. It is a black girl whom Bigger actually rapes and murders, after having lusted for but not assaulted, then half-accidentally killed, a white one. To be sure, he hacks off the head of the latter, providing an atrocity bloody enough to satisfy guilty white liberals and angry blacks; but he remains, all the same, a kind of crypto-"good bad nigger."

Not until the slogans of the civil rights movement had been drowned out by ones of "Black Power" was the Dixonian myth of the "bad nigger" fully introjected by Afro-Americans. "Come up, black dada nihilismus," LeRoi Jones chanted in *The Dead Lecturer*. "Rape the white girls. Rape their fathers. Cut the mothers' throats." And Eldridge Cleaver first lived, then translated back into literature in *Soul on Ice*, the nightmare role of the revolutionary black rapist: "I became a rapist . . . I started out by practicing on black girls in the ghetto . . . and when I considered myself smooth enough, I crossed the tracks and sought out white prey. . . . Rape was an insurrectionary act."

The moment which produced such manifestos, however,

is fifteen years past; though the black pride it nurtured survives, it has shed the abrasive militancy and intransigent separatism of the late sixties. It demands, therefore, myths not of black brutalization debouching in murder and rape, but of the persistence in the black community of dignity and heroism, along with such bourgeois virtues as piety, domesticity and sexual fidelity. Descriptions of the "essential blackness" of black life in white America, like the classic passage in Richard Wright's *Black Boy* ("I used to mull over the strange absence of real kindness in Negroes, how unstable was our tenderness, how lacking in genuine passion we are, how void of great hope, how timid our joy, how bare our traditions, how hollow our memories, how lacking we were in those intangible sentiments which bind man to man"), have come to seem irrelevant, offensive, untrue.

In some ways, Mrs. Stowe's idyllic legend of black family life under slavery is more like what our age demands; but to sustain this myth of the black family in the late seventies a new myth of Africa is required, and here she proves of little use. Her genteel, feminist dream of Mother Africa beating the patriarchal swords of Anglo-Saxondom into plowshares has come to seem as quaint as Edgar Rice Burroughs' macho nightmare of a Dark Continent of predators and cannibals tamable only by a white man who combines the ferocity of a savage with the values of a natural aristocrat.

Neither is the Mau Mau model of counter-terror, so dear to the hearts of the early Black Panthers, entirely satisfactory, any more than the dream dreamed by the Harlem Renaissance of Africa as the black man's "unspeakably dark, guilty, erotic past," driven underground by white puritanism. What has been revived in their place is the romantic myth of the Noble Savage, as translated in the Afro-American cultural centers of the United States, where young men and women in quest of a tradition learn Swahili, dress in dashikis and dance to jungle drums.

The image that possesses them is no longer that of the "good good nigger" as projected in Uncle Tom or of the "bad bad nigger" as embodied in Eldridge Cleaver, but of the "good bad nigger" as imagined by Malcolm X *after* his break with Elijah Muhammad. Malcolm X, however, dead at the hands of fellow blacks ("The niggers will kill me," he had prophesied), did not survive to write the scriptures of the new mythology. And, in any case, he was not a writer of books, only a maker of speeches and a scribbler of cryptic notes on crumpled napkins, from which his so-called *Autobiography* was reconstructed by Alex Haley, a writer of fiction, who had to believe for reasons of his own that he was dealing with fact. A regular contributor to the *Reader's Digest,* his model not just for *The Autobiography of Malcolm X* but for *Roots* as well was that standard *Digest* piece, "The Most Unforgettable Character I Have Ever Known."

It is indeed his ability to make it at the heart of the white establishment, for twenty years in the Coast Guard and ten more in the mass media (including *Playboy,* for which he did a series of interviews), that qualified Haley to become the laureate of black-white relations in a time of accommodation. He is, in short, a "good good nigger," an "Uncle Tom," late twentieth-century style. At least that is what he seemed in Malcolm X's eyes—and reflexively in his own— at the moment of their first meeting. In any case, the epithet he avoided in *Roots* appears in Haley's description of that meeting. "We got off to a very poor start," Haley explains. "To use a word he liked, I think both of us were a bit 'spooky' . . . I had heard him bitterly attack other Negro writers as 'Uncle Toms.' . . . My twenty years in the military service and my Christian religious persuasion didn't help either."

Earlier in the book, Haley had reported Malcolm X as saying, "Today's Uncle Tom doesn't wear a handkerchief on his head. . . . He's usually well-dressed and well-educated . . . a professional Negro." And Haley cannot resist reporting the "professional" qualifications of his own family in his book's final Happy Ending. Strategically suppressed by the scriptwriters of the TV version of *Roots,* it is confessed in the back-cover blurb of the paperback edition, which boasts that his saga "ends . . . at the Arkansas funeral of a black professor whose children are a teacher, a Navy architect, an assistant director of the U.S. Information Agency, and an author. The author is Alex Haley."

This seems fair enough in light of the fact that throughout the book Haley strives to portray his forebears even in Africa aspiring to a bourgeois life-style that would have pleased Mrs. Stowe. When Chicken George, for instance, prophesies for the benefit of his wife, Matilda, the domestic utopia which lies ahead for them after freedom, he does so in the following terms: "How you reckon you look settin' in yo' own house, yo' own stuffed furniture, an' all dem knickknacks? How 'bout Miss Tilda axin' de other free nigger womens over for tea in de mornin's, an' y'all jes' settin' 'roun talkin' 'bout 'ranging' y'all's flowers, an' sich as dat?"

It is, however, not that simple, since finally *Roots* is not really a Tom book, any more than it is an anti-Tom one. Yet, after the fact, Haley was much pleased by the critics who described it as "the most important book in terms of social change since *Uncle Tom's Cabin*." "If that is true," he is reported as saying, "I can only be humbled by that fact." It is an anti-anti-Tom book, and appropriately enough, its most memorable, which is to say, its only even approximately mythic character, Kunta Kinte, is an anti-anti-Tom: a noble African who after a symbolic castration and a happy marriage becomes a "good bad nigger," passing on the hope of freedom, but running away no more. In light of this, it scarcely matters how true to scholarship or the living Africans' perception of their own past Haley's version of Kunta Kinte is. Anthropologists have charged that he was taken in by a notably unreliable *griot*, or oral historian; and the Gambian government two years after he had released his first findings barred all Afro-Americans from becoming permanent residents in their country. But the book continued to move millions of readers, unaware that Kunta Kinte is less a portrait of Haley's first American ancestor, legendary or real, than of Malcolm X as Haley perceived him in guilt or envy.

Even as the living Haley ghostwrote the *Autobiography*, Malcolm X, from beyond the grave, ghostwrote what is most authentic and moving in *Roots*—the story of Kunta Kinte. Like Malcolm X, the Moslem Kunta Kinte rejects his white Christian name, dreams of a return to Africa not just for himself but for all black Americans, and is an old-fashioned sexist, believing that women should not be taught to read and that their place is in the home. He is, moreover, an inverted racist, convinced not only that all whites invariably do evil to all blacks but that they have an offensive odor and are properly classified not as human but as *toubob*, "devils," who must be resisted unto death. Like the almost-white Black Muslim who possessed him, Haley is driven to euphemize Africa to the same extent he vilifies the American South. Though he perfunctorily admits the existence of slavery on that continent and the complicity of black Africans in the slave trade, he manages to make them seem innocuous, as he does the prevailing violence of African life. If someone is forever beating someone else in Haley's Gambian village, it is *for their own good,* only white men presumably being capable of gratuitous brutality.

It is, however, in the area of sexuality that Haley most flagrantly falsifies the record. Though his Mandinkas are Moslems committed to polygamy, Haley cannot bring himself to portray Kunta Kinte's father as having taken a second wife. And though tribal custom demands that men not marry until they are thirty or thirty-five, he would have us believe that there was no premarital sex among the Mandinkas; and so Kunta Kinte (in the book's most palpable absurdity) remains a virgin until he is thirty-nine! Haley may have been influenced in this by the twelve-year celibacy which Malcolm X imposed on himself from the moment he became a Muslim until the time he discovered that his spiritual leader, Elijah Muhammad, was sexually exploiting his female secretaries. But finally his reticence about sex (like his squeamish insistence that all black slave children wore diapers) tells us more about Haley and his commitment to monogamy and bourgeois values than it does about Malcolm X.

Sexual passion in *Roots* (except for the comic Porgy-and-Bess tomcatting of Chicken George) is portrayed as essentially evil: the final indignity visited by white male masters on black female slaves, like the whipping inflicted by those same masters on black males—often their own bastard children. Scenes of rape and flagellation are as essential to his vision as to that of Mrs. Stowe or Thomas Dixon, Jr., or Margaret Mitchell, though his victims are, of course, always black. Nowhere is there any hint that black men may even desire, much less violate, white women, nor any suggestion that black women may have on occasion invited, welcomed or boasted about being chosen as bed partners of "Old Massa." This is left for highbrow ironists like Ishmael Reed, more interested in subverting the stereotypes of the mass audience, black or white, than in exploiting them pruriently.

Whatever his motives, Haley ends by providing his audience (chiefly white, it would seem, at least as far as print is concerned, since less than one percent of the letters he got in response to the *Reader's Digest* version came from blacks) with the double pleasure of vicariously indulging in and indignantly deploring interethnic rape or flagellation. The purplest passage in *Roots*—rendered in even greater detail than the beatings or brandings—is the description of the rape of Kizzy by Massa Tom Lea: "As she flailed her arms in agony and arched her back to shake him off, he banged her head against the floor, again, again, again, then began slapping her—more and more excitedly —until Kizzy felt her dress being snatched upward, her undergarments being ripped . . . she felt his hands fumbling upward between her thighs, finding, fingering her private parts, squeezing and spreading them. . . . Then came the searing pain as he forced his way into her."

This is, of course, not documented history but, like three-quarters of Haley's book, fiction: based, in this case, on a fantasy as endemic in the collective unconscious of America as the rape and murder of white innocence at the hands of black lust; and, for that matter, already used in earlier fiction by blacks and whites, which Haley and his collaborators may or may not have read. What he was familiar with, and what, indeed, may have planted the seed of this scene in his imagination, was a standard oratorical bit of Malcolm X, recorded in the so-called *Autobiography:*

> During slavery, *think* of it, it was a *rare* one of our black grandmothers, our great-grandmothers and our great-great-grandmothers who escaped the white rapist slavemaster. That rapist slavemaster who emasculated the black man . . . with threats, with fear . . . until even today the black man lives with fear of the white man in his heart! Lives even today still under the heel of the white man!
> *Think* of it—think of that black slave man filled with fear and dread, hearing the screams of his wife, his mother, his daughter being *taken*—in the barn, the kitchen, in the bushes! *Think* of it, my dear brothers and sisters! *Think* of hearing wives, mothers, daughters being *raped!* And you were too filled with *fear* of the rapist to do anything about it!

The opening to this gambit casts light also on Haley's response to the mixed ethnic ancestry which such a long history of white-black rape implies. Malcolm X, auburn-haired and even paler in skin color than brown-skinned Haley, could scarcely stay away from the subject:

> Turn around, *look* at each other! What shade of black African polluted by devil white man are you? You see me—well, in the streets they used to call me Detroit Red. Yes! Yes, that raping, red-headed devil was my *grandfather!* That close, yes! My *mother's* father! She didn't like to speak of it, can you blame her? . . . If I could drain away *his* blood that pollutes *my* body, and pollutes *my* complexion, I'd do it! Because I hate every drop of the rapist's blood that's in me!
> And it's not just me, it's *all* of us!

Blacks possessed by this erotic myth of their history think of themselves archetypally as hybrid Sons—pledged to eternal combat against all that is Euro-American in them, which they identify with the despised Father, for the sake of what is Afro-American, which they identify with the be-loved Mother.

Mrs. Stowe recognized this well over a century before Malcolm X had begun to preach to his Muslim brethren, entrusting similar sentiments to the most militant (though still Christian) of her "good niggers," George Harris. "My sympathies," he declares in a letter sent to a friend just before he sails for Africa, "are not for my father's race, but for my mother's. To him I was no more than a fine dog or horse but to her . . . I was a child . . . I *know* she always loved me dearly, I know it by my own heart." Conse-quently, even the pious nationalism betrays beneath its ideological surface an Oedipal rage which transcends eth-nicity; and perhaps explains the mother-centered nature of the black family, which recent liberal revisionist historians have sought—vainly, I think—to deny. Released in full in-tensity by Malcolm X, the hatred of the Father persists even in the blander Alex Haley, whose search for "roots" not merely excludes—consciously and on principle—the white masters who are also his ancestors but—in total unaware-ness—his whole paternal line of descent, black or white.

But, of course, it matters little how selective and skewed is Haley's version of his pedigree, since it was not primarily for its genealogy that readers turned to *Roots*. Part of what made it especially attractive at the moment of its appearance may have been its expression of the revulsion from the Melting Pot Americanism of the last decades, which has eventuated in a plague of bumper stickers, lapel buttons and T-shirts announcing "I'm proud to be Irish," or "Polish," or "Italian," or whatever. Moreover, there is no doubt that *Roots* helped to encourage among descendants of immigrants to the United States, most of whom had little stake in and less love for the cultures they fled, the purchase (whatever is demanded in our America, someone will sell) of genealogical charts, as suspect as Haley's own.

But all this was secondary, as was also its inversion of black stereotypes. Though the TV version did win thirty-seven Emmy nominations and the largest share of the viewing audience of any program ever, this was not because it told at long last the "truth" about slavery and Reconstruction. The second largest viewership, which surely included in its numbers many of the same people who thrilled to *Roots,* had sat entranced not many months earlier before a showing of *Gone With the Wind.* They neither believed nor disbelieved, merely suspended disbelief, when confronted with a totally contradictory version of those events, since what was important was that both shows provided images of black-white atrocities, which is to say, similar opportunities to "release the repressed." How pointless, then, the debate about the historical veracity of Haley's book, except insofar as it reminds us that *all* contributions to our inadvertent prose epic have claimed to be more truth than fantasy—and were in that sense "hoaxes." Not just the works of Mrs. Stowe and Dixon, D. W. Griffith and Margaret Mitchell, but the slave narratives and white histories of Reconstruction on which they drew were, to one degree or another, fictional constructs.

The relation of *Uncle Tom's Cabin* to the slave narrative of Josiah Henson is especially interesting in this regard. Ishmael Reed is wrong. Only after she wrote her best seller did Mrs. Stowe discover it, citing it to prove to her proslavery opponents that "good good niggers" did in fact exist. But Henson, it turns out, was not that good after all; and in any case his "true" account had been ghostwritten by a white journalist, who was not above amending it in later editions to make it conform even more closely to Mrs. Stowe's novel. Henson himself, though cagey at first, ended by claiming, perhaps even believing, that he was the original, authentic Uncle Tom. And Mrs. Stowe came to believe it too, collaborating with Henson in inventing a meeting between them which seems never to have occurred. The meta-myth which they thus created has ever since been exploited for the benefit of American tourists by the Chamber of Commerce of the small Ontario town in which Henson died, even as the airline which organizes tours to Gambia exploits Haley's mytho-history of his family; which is to say, it has become a fact of socio-economic life.

Even so, the pop-epical books which derive from Mrs. Stowe, whether or not they *tell* the truth, *become* the truth, being, once read or watched on stage or screen, experiences quite as real as any other. It is only when we begin to check their correspondence to life lived outside their fictional frame that we ask whether or not they are consistent with each other, or with something we have decided to call the "truth." Elite critics do not ordinarily demand of what they regard as High Literature, even when its subject is "history," that it be in this sense "true." They are not a bit upset, for instance, when Shakespeare in *Henry VI* vilifies Joan of Arc as a transvestite whore, even if they themselves think of her as a heroine and a saint. Yet they feel free to denounce Dixon for his "misrepresentation" of slavery and the Negro, or to scold Margaret Mitchell for the "falsity" of her account of the rise of the Klan.

But this seems inevitable in light of the fact that their books raise questions which continue to divide us in black and white America. We are all possessed by rival myths of slavery and its aftermath, so that what is involved when we quarrel with Dixon or Mitchell is not a conflict of myth and history, but of myth and myth: *our* myth, which we call the truth, versus *their* myth, which we consider a damned lie. Ever since its wholesale conversion to a "liberal," abolitionist mythology, the critical establishment has tended to question the historicity of books written by white supremacists like Dixon and Mitchell, while accepting the views of Mrs. Stowe and Haley not as gospel, perhaps, but near enough—i.e., if skewed, skewed in the "right direction."

Yet the question of historical truth cannot be avoided altogether, since there are some admirers of Haley for whom *Roots* does not function as fiction at all. To them, his book represents not one more myth of race and sex in America, destined to be replaced by the next, as it replaced the one before it, but the replacement of all "racist" and "sexist" myths by the unchangeable, irrefutable non-mythological truth. If only, they are convinced, everyone would come to understand such matters as they and Haley do, black and white would be able to live at peace in our land, sharing a single valid view of the past and a single viable hope for the future. But, of course, there is no such "truth" about slavery or Reconstruction or the Civil War, at least none we can recover from our vantage point in the present. Even scholarly, "objective" historians disagree about what really happened in those irrecoverable times, much less what it means.

It is scarcely surprising, then, that writers of fiction differ even among themselves and with the historians. Not only are they, like the latter, time-bound, class-bound and gender-bound, but, unlike them, they owe their primary allegiance to fantasy rather than fact, to what we know we dream rather than what we dream we know. Fortunately or unfortunately, however, even authors read by millions cannot change history for better or worse. Harriet Beecher Stowe, whatever Lincoln may have said, did not cause the War Between the States, and Alex Haley, despite the hopes of his fans, did not usher in an era of better race relations.

Popular literature does nonetheless influence a little how we perceive, in prospect as well as retrospect, what we cannot otherwise alter. More important, it permits us to imagine dark catastrophes and utopian solutions we were not even aware that we feared or wished and which, in full consciousness, we are likely to believe neither probable nor desirable. I myself, for instance, find dubious much that Haley (or for that matter Dixon, Mitchell or Stowe) asserts as fact or accepts as articles of faith. I believe as little in the absolute purity (or malevolence) of all native Africans as I do in the unmitigated malevolence (or purity) of all Southern white Americans. Moreover, I, who as a Jew am convinced—or so at least the erotic-ethnic myths of my own people assure me—that there are alien rapists among my male ancestors, have little difficulty in acknowledging what of them survives in me. I consider them no more nor less mythological than the high priests of Israel from whom an even more ancient legend tells me I am descended. I have, therefore, not been a bit moved to search for my identity in oral or written pedigrees.

Nonetheless, *Roots* moves me deeply, even as *Uncle Tom's Cabin* and *Gone With the Wind* move me, because, like them, it takes me into a world of primordial images where "truth" and "falsity" seem as irrelevant as "good" and "evil." Haley possesses, though perhaps only by fits and starts, that mythopoeic power which neither ineptness of language nor banality of ideas can impugn. Let me be quite clear. I am not *proud* of liking *Roots;* nor do I *approve* of what I feel obliged to acknowledge: all in myself which responds to all that is sentimental and sado-masochistic in it. I am, I must confess, still enough of a vestigial elitist to be ashamed of my vulnerability (and yours, *hypocrite lecteur*) to so gross an appeal.

Nonetheless, I suspect that what chastens pride (rather than feeds it, like the ability to respond to refined sensibility or hermetic allusions) cannot be all bad. As I finish rereading the last page of the last work of our inadvertent epic, I am left with a sense of at-oneness not just with the majority audience I was long taught to despise, but with much in myself I was long afraid to confront—and feeling therefore somehow happy. Not that such books reassure us with easy eucatastrophes. On the contrary, the Good Bad Books of our tradition, which, though excluded from the canon, refuse to die, have not lasted into our time by providing improbable happy endings to their fables or suggesting that such endings lie just ahead for Americans, black and white.

A FTERWORD: "A BACKWARD GLANCE O'ER TRAVELLED ROADS"

It is not the deaths which occur en route to the happy endings of books in the domestic tradition which cast a pall of gloom over their final pages. Though such deaths, particularly of old men and young girls, are essential to their appeal, this makes them more rather than less pleasurable to their faithful readers, who (like all of us, if the truth be told) enjoy a "good cry," the therapeutic release of tears. What I find dismaying is the fact that those characters who, like Mrs. Stowe's Eliza or Miss Mitchell's Scarlett, survive are granted as their final reward a homecoming to segregated households: in the former case, one which is all black, and in the latter, one in which the blacks are confined to the servants' quarters.

It is as if the makers of our inadvertent epic are incapable of evoking even in wish-fulfillment fantasy an American future in which blacks and whites live together in equality and peace. Consequently, the politics implicit in their myth, whether they be abolitionists or apologists for the Klan, starts from the bleak assumption that interethnic hostility will never cease in the United States until history can be persuaded to run backward, so that the confrontation of white ex-Europeans and black ex-Africans which has helped make us uniquely American is undone—not by assimilation or integration, but by separation.

Mrs. Stowe, for instance, urged that black Americans be freed and raised to full literacy, then baptized and shipped back to Africa (after more than two centuries of acculturation elsewhere) to educate and Christianize the descendants of those left behind by the slavers. Clearly, her millennial black "Zionism" is based on the quite un-utopian conviction that there is no future for Africans in America: a defeatist view shared not just by eighteenth- and nineteenth-century white statesmen like Thomas Jefferson and Abraham Lincoln, but by twentieth-century black nationalists like Marcus Garvey and Malcolm X. Moreover, though in practice the dream of repatriation has produced nothing but the abortive experiment of Liberia, it has persisted as a political slogan, along with a somewhat less drastic alternative, called by Communists in the 1930s "Self-Determination for the Black Belt," which envisages establishing in the United States itself a ghetto enclave "For Blacks Only."

Whatever the ostensible ideological arguments of the anti-integrationists, white or black, it seems evident to me that at the deepest psychic levels they are moved by an irrational fear of miscegenation, a desire to avoid "racial pollution," which they assume would be inevitable once Afro-Americans were granted social and economic equality. Dixon and Mitchell both confess this, as does Haley in his own way; and even Mrs. Stowe does not entirely deny it. She, however, suggests that miscegenation is not the inevitable result of the mingling of races, but a specific byproduct of the slave system; thus it would cease once white masters no longer had absolute power over the bodies of black women. The possibility that black males might lust for white females (or vice versa) she did not acknowledge; nor did it apparently occur to her that, given the opportunity, blacks might seek revenge for the indignities visited upon their mothers and sisters by "rape from above." For her, as we have already noted, "Africans" were "feminine" by nature, and feminine meant "passive."

To be sure, such rape had given their sons a sufficient admixture of "Anglo-Saxon" blood to make some of them, in her racist view, "masculinely" aggressive. But when she imagined them rising in wrath, it was with murder in their hearts rather than sexual violation, and against their masters rather than their mistresses. It is scarcely surprising that the menace of black rebellion is felt everywhere in *Uncle Tom's Cabin*, since by the time Mrs. Stowe sat down to write it, not only had there been slave revolts in Haiti but, after 1848, the specter of revolution was haunting the ruling classes of the whole Western world. Her novel was influenced by those forces which were moving Marx and Engels at the same historical moment to write *The Communist Manifesto*. Moreover, Mrs. Stowe was quite aware that if the oppressed revolted in America, the ensuing conflict would be between races as well as classes, since in her country most of the oppressed were blacks.

These insights she expressed through Augustine St. Clare, a doomed Southern dandy, utterly alien yet somehow profoundly sympathetic to her dowdy New England self. Arguing with his brother at one point, Augustine says prophetically, "If there is anything that is revealed with the strength of a divine law in our times, it is that the masses are to rise, and the under classes become the upper one." When his brother scorns his arguments, calling them "red republican humbugs" and contemptuously dismissing the "greasy masses," Augustine answers, "Greasy or not greasy, they will govern *you*, when their time comes . . . and they will be just such rulers as you make them." Then he goes on to prophesy, "If ever the San Domingo hour comes . . . some of white fathers, with all our haughty feelings burning in their veins . . . will rise, and raise with them their mothers' race."

What Mrs. Stowe did not foresee was the liberation of the blacks by victorious Union forces, who, far from repatriating them, placed them in positions of power over their former masters at the very heart of the defeated Confederacy. If Thomas Dixon, Jr., and D. W. Griffith are to be believed, as millions did in fact believe them, this meant the fulfillment of the nightmare of black-white rape which Mrs. Stowe had sought to deny; threatening not only the "sanctity" of the American home but the "purity" of the Anglo-Saxon stock pledged to protect it. Their revised version of the domestic myth proved especially attractive at a time when most white Americans were experiencing a "pacifist" revulsion from the martial passions of the Civil War and the punitive excesses of Reconstruction.

It appealed also both to the Southern poor whites' resentment of the free Negro as an economic competitor and the growing hostility of immigrant European workers in the cities of the Northeast toward the flood of black peasants migrating from the South. Even in liberal intellectual cir-

cles, there was a reaction against the sentimental racism
which had prompted Mrs. Stowe to declare through George
Harris: "I think that the African race has peculiarities, yet
to be unfolded in the light of civilization and Christianity,
which, if not the same with those of the Anglo-Saxon, may
prove to be morally of even a higher type." What did persist, growing more and more exacerbated as it became clear
that the experiment in Liberia had failed and that black and
white were destined to live together in America for as long
as that country lasted, was the miscegenation horror shared
by Mrs. Stowe and Dixon, and for that matter, to be shared
also by Margaret Mitchell and Alex Haley.

Though not always overtly expressed, that horror, we
must not forget, is also present in the "classics" we have
been taught to consider the supreme achievement of our
literature. Though they envision a wilderness union of
white and nonwhite, first red, then brown, eventually
black, the passion which cues it is not merely homoerotic
but totally sublimated. It is, therefore, in the phrase of
Henry David Thoreau, "fruitless and blossomless," i.e.,
without issue and without a future. Outside of home and
family, society and history, space and time, the idyll of male
bonding in the woods has the evanescent quality of certain
comforting dreams we have toward morning, in which we
are aware all along that we are doomed to awaken soon,
soon—that they are too good to be true.

Perhaps this is why, unlike Mrs. Stowe's myth of racial
separation, that of a love between black and white transcending the hostilities of race, class and gender proved
almost impossible to translate into political slogans, much
less social action. For one flickering moment during the
cultural revolution of the 1960s, black and white male comrades, particularly members of SNCC, stood shoulder to
shoulder against racial intolerance, like so many Hucks and
Jims. But the mythic eros which joined them was threatened as soon as white females appeared on the scene; and
even more perhaps when, under pressure from black females, some black longtime comrades began to talk from
their side about keeping ethnic bloodlines "pure." In any
case, it all ended with the murder in darkness of two white
boys and a black by Mississippi white Yahoos still trapped
in the old nightmare of miscegenation, rape and lynch law.

But there is a prescience of all this from the start in the

myth of an interethnic love "passing the love of woman." Even in the most idyllic of the classic fictions in which it is embodied, one partner is portrayed as dying before the other; or else they are prophetically described as inevitably drifting apart. So at the end of *Huckleberry Finn,* we are aware of how hollow is Huck's promise that somewhere outside of "civilization," where women have not yet come, he and Jim will be reunited—if not forever, at least for a few weeks or months. Certainly, Mark Twain could never quite manage to keep that promise in fiction, though he kept trying. The best he could produce were trivial stories without mythic resonance, like *Tom Sawyer Abroad* and *Tom Sawyer, Detective,* whose very titles indicate that they are really Tom's books, not Huck's and Jim's. And he finally bogged down in an unfinished and unconvincing account of the adventures of Huck and Jim among the Indians.

It was impossible, Twain discovered, to alter the shape of the myth he had inherited, which insists that the wilderness companion of the white refugee *disappear* before his story is done. Since it was invented to deal with relations between white men and red, which is to say, ex-Europeans and native Americans, that myth cannot, like Mrs. Stowe's, envisage a solution to interethnic conflict by repatriation of the "lesser breed." But no more than hers does it foresee their permanent fusion into a single multi-ethnic American community. Instead (as I first argued some years ago in *The Return of the Vanishing American*), it predicts the eventual eradication of the unassimilable Other—not, to be sure, as a result of brutal genocide but in a kind of subintended race suicide in face of a "superior" civilization.

The Indians, however, have *not* conveniently vanished, though for a brief historical moment they seemed on the verge of doing so; nor have the blacks, whose situation the myth of extinction never fit at all. Rather, both were rendered temporarily "invisible" by being confined to reservations and ghettos, from which they have recently re-emerged to renew hostilities in an urbanized society, in which the idyll of wilderness companionship has become harder and harder even to dream, much less to live.

In this sense, the ending of *Huckleberry Finn* has proved truly prophetic, since the white refugee from white civilization now finds himself, like Huck, alone in his further flight. Forever alone. Some apologists for anti-civilization and male bonding, especially city boys like Walt Whitman and Jack Kerouac, have pretended that being thus in perpetual transit—"on the road," as they prefer to say, "the open road"—is a fate to be celebrated rather than deplored. But a note of sadness resonates beneath the euphoria of their theoretically Happy Never-Endings, in which their surrogates, incapable of returning to their old homes or founding new ones, move eternally to the next place and the next and the next . . .

Moreover, Kerouac, like Whitman before him, has given up the dream of the nonwhite companion. Black music may ring in the head of his protagonist, but he moves to it in an all-white company of Hucks and Toms trying to make it without any Jims in a pseudo-Territory long since crisscrossed with the white man's concrete highways. This seems fair enough, however, in light of the fact that long before Twain had finished his book, the true Nigger Jim had already died from his imagination. Twain, that is to say, loses Jim forever even before Huck does. And with him he loses his vision of black and white America coming to love each other in the real world of the riverbank, as Jim and Huck have in the play world of the raft, by learning to experience each other as fully (or is it merely?) human.

Exactly where and when Jim vanishes for good is a matter of debate. Ernest Hemingway insisted it was at the moment when a steamboat plows into the raft and he and Huck disappear from each other on the fog-shrouded river. But later critics tend to agree that he remains a valid mythic character up to the point where the Duke and the Dauphin turn him over to the Phelpses for a reward. In any event, when he does reappear for a second time at their farm, where Huck finds a temporary home, the only place for him is the slave quarters. To be sure, Huck and Tom make a pointless, burlesque attempt at rescuing him, in which they strip him of his last shreds of human dignity. Ironically, he is already "free," has been in fact ever since the death of the Widow Douglas; but when Tom so oddly and belatedly tells him this, it turns out that he is "free" only to "go home," to a black family in which Huck has, of course, no place.

No more does he have a place in white Hannibal, to which Tom will return but from which Huck has been driven by his only living blood relative, Pap. Yet when Jim, compounding the novel's ironies, tells Huck, even more oddly and belatedly, that his drunken, murderous father is dead, he still has to confront Aunt Sally: that surrogate white mother, who offers him the shelter of a rural home based on black slavery. He has, however, as he notoriously observes, "been there before"—and lights out alone. It is an ambiguous ending to an ambiguous book, which though no one seems ever to have quite understood (perhaps least of all Twain), almost everyone has begun by considering dangerous and ended by finding innocuous.

First the Miss Watsons of the world, the official guardians of bourgeois morality, banned it from children's libraries, until familiarity had persuaded them it was an innocent boys' book. Then the critics, latter-day Tom Sawyers with their heads full of other, more pretentious books, excluded it from "serious" literature, until, for reasons I have never quite understood, they decided to smuggle it into the canon of okay "art" novels. Last of all, militant late twentieth-century blacks, descendants of such manumitted slaves as Jim, have proved as incapable of coming to terms with Twain's novel as with Mrs. Stowe's, finding both of them travesties on their race, even though (or just because) these two books created the enduring myths through which almost everyone, including Afro-Americans, has perceived them ever since.

That they have not yet made their peace with *Huckleberry Finn* (aware only that Jim is called "Nigger, nigger, nigger"), I was reminded when I read recently that protesting black parents in suburban Chicago, doubtless backed by guilt-ridden "liberal" white ones, had succeeded in getting that novel banned from classroom use. Ironically enough, this serves only to confirm Twain's perception (embodied in the book they will not let their children read) of the inevitable failure of even the purest love to transcend the division between blacks and whites in a civilization long based on slavery. But there is pathos as well as irony in that continuing failure of us all, even as there is in Twain's personal failure to flee "civilization," as Huck finally resolves to do.

Though he subscribed in print to the notion that the American home is an artificial paradise camouflaging a real Hell, Twain lived as if he believed that bourgeois domesticity was the only true Eden. And how could it have been otherwise? Like Whitman before and Kerouac after him, he was an unreconstructed "mama's boy," his father's dying words ringing forever in his ear, "Sam, don't break your mother's heart." It is hard, indeed, to think of any laureates of male bonding who were wholly immune to the view of Home as Heaven which possessed the imaginations of the mothers and wives whom they travestied savagely in their fiction, but tended to honor exaggeratedly in fact.

Nor were the women they loved entirely without ambivalence in such matters, smiling tolerantly when their scribbling sons wrote books about running away from home, and murmuring, "Boys will be boys." They knew that it was Good Bad Boys they were dealing with, wicked enough to be interesting, virtuous enough to break no female hearts —since the Good Good ones became bankers and judges rather than authors, and the Bad Bad ones outlaws or Western sheriffs, like the real-life prototype of Huckleberry Finn. Yet the values implicit in the books which they rather condescendingly tolerated, even when they did not actually read, gradually, almost imperceptibly, influenced their own; just as theirs had influenced those of their unruly but dutiful sons.

Huckleberry Finn, in particular, from the moment the guardians of morality made it a required rather than a banned book, has troubled its female readers, especially those who were entering the college classrooms of America even as it did. Few American women encountering it, in school or out, have been able to resist identifying with its anti-hero in his flight from a "civilization" imposed on him by members of their own sex. Moreover, some of them, long past the point at which (according to their own mothers as well as Mark Twain) they should have assumed the roles of Aunt Sally or the Widow Douglas, are either still fantasizing themselves in Huck's role or resenting the "sexist" society which tries to deny them that option. In light of all this, it would appear that the myths of Home as Heaven and Home as Hell do not divide, as certain male critics (including me) have been tempted to believe, women from men and popular fiction from art novels. We are all divided against ourselves, irremediably ambivalent on this score, as both best sellers and the canonical "great books" of our tradition reveal.

What we are likely to remember from *Huckleberry Finn* are moments on the river and under the open sky, yet it contains, too, almost as many detailed descriptions of domestic interiors as *Uncle Tom's Cabin.* Similarly, we tend to forget that Mrs. Stowe's characters travel the Mississippi and its tributaries, not merely in quest of a home but in flight from enemies rather like those who beset Huck and Jim. Nonetheless, whatever some may argue to the contrary, the natural world remains theoretical and inert in her domestic romance: a painted backdrop, less real than those who move through it or the places to which they move. Not so the households in Twain's novel, however. Two are rendered with special vividness and convincingness: the Grangerfords' patriarchal domain, and the farmhouse of the Phelpses, presided over not by the kindly, essentially impotent Uncle Si but maternal Aunt Sally.

Fathers do not fare well in Twain; so it is no surprise that the Grangerford home, at first glance so attractive, proves a delusory haven—a place not of nurture but death. Despite its clutter of sentimental female kitsch, it serves only to foster the stark macho code of the feud: kill or be killed, until there are none but women left. Except, of course, for wily Huck, who gets out while the getting is good, pausing just long enough after the final shoot-out to cover the face of his dead friend Buck and weep. Yet initially he fell in love with the "elegance" of the establishment to which the Grangerfords retreat between battles; impressed by every pretentious adornment, right down to the plaster-of-paris parrots on the mantelpiece, the artificial fruit in the bowl on the oilcloth-covered table and the pictures on the walls of Washington, Lafayette and Highland Mary.

"There was an old piano, too," Huck admiringly reports, "that had tin pans in it, I reckon, and nothing was so lovely as to hear the young ladies sing 'The Last Link is Broken' and play 'The Battle of Prague' on it." Then he concludes, "Nothing couldn't be better. And warn't the cooking good and just bushels of it too!" But when in *Life on the Mississippi,* Twain had described in his own voice such an ostentatious monument to chivalry and domestic bad taste as "The House Beautiful," he was openly scornful of all that had dazzled Huck. Indeed, even in the later book, he cannot resist making Huck finally confess, after the chivalric code of the Grangerfords has driven them to death and him back to the river, "I was powerful glad to get away . . . there warn't no home like a raft, after all. Other places seem so cramped up and smothery."

The maternal homestead of the Phelpses, however, not merely seems but is utterly different: the real thing at last —unpretentious, genuinely nurturing, as close to a true domestic refuge from loneliness and terror as Twain could conceive. He has Huck describe it in the longest single sentence he ever permits him to write. And this time we feel no distancing irony between author and persona, as the hypnotic cadences translate us, too, back into the Eden of childhood, the idyll of coming home:

Phelps's was one of these little one-horse cotton plantations, and they all look alike. A rail fence round a two-acre yard; a stile made out of logs sawed off and up-ended in steps, like barrels of a different length, to climb over the fence with, and for the women to stand on when they are going to jump onto a horse; some sickly grass-patches in the big yard, but mostly it was bare and smooth, like an old hat with the nap rubbed off; big double log house for the white folks—hewed logs, with the chinks stopped up with mud or mortar, and these mud-stripes been whitewashed some time or another; round-log kitchen, with a big broad, open but roofed passage joining it to the house; log smokehouse back of the kitchen; three little log nigger cabins in a row t'other side of the smokehouse; one little hut all by itself away down against the back fence, and some outbuildings down a piece the other side; ash-hopper and big kettle to bile soap in by the little hut; bench by the kitchen door, with bucket of water and a gourd; hound asleep there in the sun; more hounds asleep round about; about three shade trees away off in a corner; some currant bushes and gooseberry bushes in one place by the fence; outside of the fence a garden and a watermelon patch; then the cottonfields begin, and after the fields the woods.

That it was his own childhood memories Twain was evoking we learn from a passage in his *Autobiography,* in which he reveals that his model was the farm of his uncle, John A. Quarles, where he had spent summers from "the fourth year after we removed to Hannibal until I was eleven or twelve years old," and telling us "it was a heavenly place for a boy." He returned to that scene once again in *Tom Sawyer, Detective,* as if unable to exorcise it. But this last time, his nostalgic evocation of the past is entangled in a fable of guilt and death—making us aware that from the start there had been an undertone of melancholy in his renderings of that presumably "heavenly" place. "When I got there," he writes in *Huckleberry Finn,* "it was all still and Sunday-like . . . there was a kind of faint droning of bugs and flies in the air that makes it seem . . . like everybody's dead and gone." And after his long descriptive sentence, Huck continues, "When I got a little ways, I heard the dim hum of a spinning wheel . . . and then I knowed for certain I wished I was dead—for that *is* the lonesomest sound in the world."

Furthermore, Twain reminds us almost immediately that the prosperity and peace of the Phelps household is based on slavery, so we are scarcely surprised that it is precisely here that Jim ends up in "durance vile," and Huck decides not to stay. In Huck's final flight ("The End. Yours truly"), Twain has in effect symbolized his own abandonment of the last best hope of home, all possibility of domestic accommodation. But of course he did not himself "light out for the Territory." Instead, after a brief foray into the mining camps of the West, he retreated to a series of more and more magnificent homes in the urban and suburban Northeast, with occasional tours to foreign lands and vacations on the sunny beaches of Florida.

One of these homes, aptly enough, was next door to that of Harriet Beecher Stowe in Nook Farm, a posh suburb of Hartford, Connecticut, where both could afford to live, since ambivalent America had made them equally rich and famous—her for celebrating Home and Mother, him for fantasizing escapes from both. But what they made of each other is a little unclear. It seems certain that she never read *Huckleberry Finn,* though she lived long enough to have done so, and improbable that Twain ever read *Uncle Tom's Cabin,* about whose literary merits he never commented for the record. It is highly unlikely, in any case, that he would have liked her pop masterpiece very much, any more than she would have liked his.

The only one of her books that he displayed prominently on his bookshelves was her last work of fiction, *A Dog's Mission,* which was uncharacteristically a boys' book. And she in turn preferred to all else his equally uncharacteristic sentimental romance, *The Prince and the Pauper*, of which he reports her saying, "I know it is the best book for young folks that was ever written"—"bringing," he adds, surely not without irony, "tears to my eyes." It is fascinating, I think, that they preferred to think of each other as authors of juveniles rather than as "great novelists," but inevitable, perhaps, in light of their disparate tastes. For Mrs. Stowe, Sir Walter Scott's *Ivanhoe*, which she had read as a child, remained a lifelong inspiration, and her favorite contemporary novel was *Daniel Deronda* by George Eliot, whom in their long correspondence she insisted on styling respectably "Mrs. Lewes." Twain, however, detested Scott, and the novel published in his own time that he seems to have loved best was Rudyard Kipling's *Kim*, of which he says in his *Autobiography*, "I read the book every year."

Yet *Uncle Tom's Cabin* was a work whose marketplace success obsessed him; when his *Innocents Abroad* first appeared and began to sell well, he wrote to Livy, not yet his wife, "Nothing like it since *Uncle Tom's Cabin*, I guess." But his prediction proved overoptimistic; though *Tom Sawyer* and *Huckleberry Finn* came close, the total sales of none of his books ever matched those of Mrs. Stowe's all-time best seller. In the last decades of the nineteenth century, however, his name had become as well known worldwide as hers, and he began to outstrip her in critical acclaim. Nonetheless, he seems to have remained jealous of her to the last, flying into a rage when his children came home from school one day and reported that he had barely beat her out in a classroom poll on who was America's greatest writer. Once, when I still believed like Ernest Hemingway that all modern American literature worth taking seriously came out of a single book, *Huckleberry Finn*, I would have agreed that ranking her so high was a vulgar error, which, fortunately, we had since outgrown. But it seems to me now that if Sam Clemens is a literary father to us all, Hattie Stowe is our mother—however long some of us may in our macho pride have denigrated and denied her.

Clearly Twain was in no position to have confessed this to himself, though he seems to have been scrupulously, if a little condescendingly, polite to the aging woman next door (she was twenty-five years his senior and beginning to fail by the time he met her): stopping by frequently to assure her that she was still remembered and loved; sending her specially bound copies of his books, embossed in gilt with her name; even inviting her to address meetings of the Saturday Morning Club, which met weekly in his house "as a cultural and social aid to the young women of Hartford." The last involved something of a risk, since Mrs. Stowe had grown more than a little dotty with advancing age, and one could never be sure whether or not she would be coherent. In fact, privately Twain sometimes referred to her as a "maniac," expressing horror at what he called "her hideous gabblings."

But she was apparently harmless enough even at her worst, escaping from her Irish nurse to embrace strangers on the street, whom she took for her lost drunkard of a son, or sneaking up behind passersby to scare them with sudden war whoops. It was incidents like the latter which Twain remembered most vividly. But the scene which continues to haunt me is of him being awakened very early in the morning by the sound of this great demented lady playing the organ and singing hymns in his parlor, into which she had wandered uninvited and unnoticed. It is a symbolic moment in our culture, it seems to me, the true American equivalent of the British Madwoman in the Attic. On this side of the Atlantic, however, the Madwoman is not the doomed, disreputable, disavowed wife of Charlotte Brontë's *Jane Eyre* (which Mrs. Stowe considered a vulgar, melodramatic tale), but the spoiled darling of the civilized world, the most famous of all American writers, with the possible exception of the man whose sleep she was troubling.

Even without such invasions of his privacy, it was an uneasy sleep that Mark Twain slept; and it seems to have grown even uneasier after the death of his young daughter, Susie, had driven him beyond the range of Mrs. Stowe's music. It was his wife, he claimed, who insisted on their moving from the Hartford house of death to a new home in New York. But he yielded to her in this, as he did in every major decision of their life together—including the initial one of letting himself be domesticated. He even wrote to please her and his daughters (but surely also in response to something in his most secret self) books ending in triumphant homecomings and integration into the family—most notably, perhaps, *The Prince and the Pauper,* which for this reason they, like Mrs. Stowe, considered his best. And surely he must have thought, hearing their cries of admiration and delight as he read aloud by the fireside its final installment, that he had attained precisely the kind of Happy Ending he described, merely by having described it.

This turned out, however, to be only one more delusion, since he did not live happily ever after, ending indeed in something close to total despair. At the close of his life, Twain found himself separated from all of the women he loved not just by disease and death, but by mutual misunderstanding and his own sense of guilt at having betrayed something, someone. Himself? Them? His mother? He seems never to have been quite sure. He had, at any rate, alienated the single child who was to survive him and—though he never quite confessed this—his wife as well. In her last months of neurotic interior flight, she had shut herself away from him, making her room in the grand house he had built as a monument to conjugal bliss a world for women only. Finally, he could communicate with her only —as he had learned to communicate with the world of strangers—in *writing,* slipping notes under her door.

And when she was dead, he drifted in silence through his grand house inhabited now only by servants, as lonely in its elegantly furnished rooms as Huck in the Territory. Hair white, mustache white, clothes white, he must have seemed not, as he liked to boast, the "only clean man in a dirty world," but a ghost reenacting the macho ritual of the mining camp and the saloon, with no woman left to say him nay. All alone, he would smoke, we are told, forty cigars a day, drink God knows how many shots of bourbon, and end playing pool with himself, until he passed out on the billiard table and was carried off to bed by a servant. There doubtless, in intervals between the nightmares of diminution and dissolution recorded in his last unfinished sketches, he must surely have had good dreams, too. But it is hard to say whether he dreamed himself in them as impostor, warmly embraced by Aunt Sally as her own dear sister's son, or a kinless boy forever in flight with an eternally fugitive slave.

INDEX

Abbott and Costello, 134
Adams, Robert, 106
Aeneid, The, 110, 111, 138
Aeschylus, 40
Agee, James, 192–93
"Alas, Poor Richard"
    (Baldwin), 220
Alcott, Louisa May, 148, 155
Algren, Nelson, 202
"Alexander's Ragtime Band"
    (Berlin), 85
Alger, Horatio, 31
Allen, Hervey, 210
Ambassadors, The (James), 78
American Federation of
    Television and Radio
    Artists (AFTRA), 20
American Medical Association
    (AMA), 48
American Renaissance, 88
American Renaissance, The
    (Matthiessen), 27, 146
American Woman's Home
    (Stowe and Beecher), 157
Anatomy of Melancholy
    (Burton), 34–35
Andersen, Hans Christian, 45,
    47
"Annabel Lee" (Poe), 88
Anna Karenina (Tolstoi), 117
Anthony Adverse (Allen), 210

"Archetype and Signature"
    (Fiedler), 14, 36
Archie, 45
Aristophanes, 134
Aristotle, 38, 39, 42, 50–51, 128,
    136, 138
Arnold, Matthew, 78, 104, 128,
    129
"Art of Fiction, The" (James),
    76
Art of Poetry (Horace), 51
Ashbery, John, 90
Asimov, Isaac, 132
Association of American
    Publishers, 80–81
Association of Medical
    Schools, 35
Auden, W. H., 90, 91
Aunt Phillis's Cabin, 178
Austen, Jane, 68
Autobiography (Twain), 241,
    243
*Autobiography of Malcolm X,
    The* (Haley), 223, 224, 226–
    227

Bach, Richard, 78
Back to China (Fiedler), 17
Baldwin, James, 69, 148, 174,
    197, 220, 221